The New York Times

CROSSWORDS

FOR A

LAZY DAY

130 Fun, Easy Puzzles

Edited by Will Shortz

St. Martin's Paperbacks

THE NEW YORK TIMES CROSSWORDS FOR A LAZY DAY

Copyright © 2006 by The New York Times Company.

Puzzles originally appeared in *The New York Times* daily editions from March 31, 2003, to June 22, 2004. Copyright © 2003, 2004 by The New York Times Company. Reprinted by permission.

Cover photo © Gib Martinez/Veer.

ISBN: 0-312-93943-4
EAN: 80312-93943-4

Printed in the United States of America

St. Martin's Paperbacks edition / April 2006

St. Martin's Paperbacks are published by St. Martin's Press, 175 Fifth Avenue, New York, NY 10010.

10 9 8 7 6 5 4 3 2 1

The New York Times

CROSSWORDS

FOR A

LAZY DAY

ACROSS

1 Part of Miss America's attire
5 Syrian president Bashar al-—
10 When tripled, et cetera
14 4:00 socials
15 Hobbits' home, with "the"
16 Gutter locale
17 "That — hay!"
18 34-Down for a politician?
20 "Spare the —, spoil . . ."
21 Fabricate, as a signature
22 Visionaries
23 34-Down for a bookkeeper?
26 Put on board
27 "As my final point . . ."
31 Japanese beer named for a city
33 Farm-related: Prefix
36 — de Janeiro
37 34-Down for a stenographer?
41 Bank acct. amt.
42 10 million of them equal a joule
43 Speechify
44 Dale Earnhardt org.
47 When shadows are short
48 34-Down for a dentist?
54 San Diego baseballer
57 Together
58 Prefix with sex
59 34-Down for a florist?
61 Cutlass or Delta 88
62 Additions
63 Shoelace end
64 Suspenseful
65 VCR insert
66 Wanting
67 Card above a deuce

DOWN

1 Lennon bandmate
2 "Wheel of Fortune" buys
3 Removes paint, in a way
4 D.D.E.'s predecessor
5 On land
6 Knifelike
7 Burn slightly
8 Shakespeare's Forest of —
9 Girl at a ball
10 Watch rims
11 Loll
12 Claim
13 His's partner
19 Govt. cultural org.
21 Angry, and not going to take it anymore
24 Theda of the silents
25 Roman 152

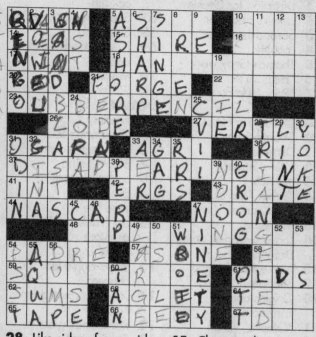

28 Like sides of pyramids
29 Jacket buildup
30 Oxen holder
31 Chief Norse god
32 — Louise of "Gilligan's Island"
33 — Lingus
34 Pre-April 1 purchase
35 Monopoly quartet: Abbr.
38 Cop's collar
39 Who preceded Adam and Eve on earth
40 Sailor's rum drink

45 Cherry red
46 Downsizer
47 Nonagenarian's age
49 Not quite jumbo
50 "— Mio"
51 Gave, as an Rx
52 Excessive
53 Moist, as the air
54 "Hey there!"
55 Color of water
56 Hauler's destination
60 Color of sand
61 Baseball's Mel

ACROSS
1 Direction for Greeley
5 Helen's abductor
10 Spreadsheet filler
14 Locality
15 Thomas Gray work
16 "Help — the way!"
17 "Poor Little Fool" singer
19 Quickly, in the I.C.U.
20 Shooting star
21 Dissertation
23 Use a Singer
25 No-nos
26 "What Kind of Fool Am I" singer
33 Met song
34 Lane co-worker at the Daily Planet
35 Norse thunder god
39 Short skirt
40 Orioles and cardinals
41 "Othello" villain
42 Genesis paradise
43 Annul
44 French airport
45 "The Fool on the Hill" bandleader
49 Dundee residents
52 "Norma —"
53 Where bowlers may go
57 Wall Street employee
62 Tooth trouble
63 "She's a Fool" songstress
65 Perlman of "Cheers"
66 Prefix with face or faith
67 Supreme Norse deity
68 Salon job
69 Puts on the bulletin board
70 Missing

DOWN
1 Friendly
2 Cleveland's lake
3 Religious group
4 Bit of filming
5 Looked intently
6 Everybody
7 Take five
8 Dr. Frankenstein's assistant
9 "Auld Lang —"
10 Wide-angle lens concern
11 John of "The Addams Family"
12 Raise one's glass to
13 Starts a pot
18 Like a yenta
22 Word modifier: Abbr.
24 Regaining consciousness
26 Identical
27 Like the Gobi
28 Coal hole
29 Not the fringes
30 "Rigoletto" composer
31 Kind of plumbing
32 Thoroughfares: Abbr.
36 Knotty

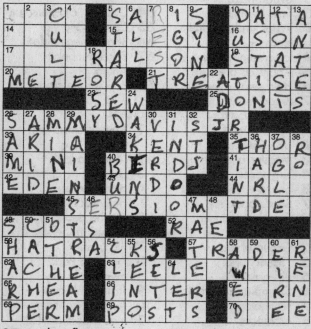

37	Look at flirtatiously	
38	Rogers and Clark	
40	Prickly husk	
46	Spaniard's "that"	
47	Alma __ (grads' schools)	
48	Mysterious: Var.	
49	Quick-witted	
50	Hiding place	
51	Different	
54	Fast pace	
55	Lotto relative	
56	Some arrivals at 44-Across	

58 Wide-eyed
59 Knucklehead
60 Ireland, in poesy
61 Philosopher Descartes
64 Allow

ACROSS

1 Urban haze
5 Tests by lifting
10 What kindergartners learn
14 Ice cream holder
15 Apply, as pressure
16 Hold sway over
17 Bread maker
18 San __, Calif.
19 "__ my way"
20 UPS alternative
23 Mediterranean fruit
24 Tiny toiler
25 Sheen
27 Boat's back
29 French composer Erik
32 Group of eras
33 "Silent" prez
35 Big galoot
36 Olympian sovereign
37 Technologically advanced
41 "__ on first?"
42 Long distance letters
43 Perfect gymnastics score
44 Unidentified John
45 Ballot caster
47 Pine sap
51 Takes effect
53 "Bali __"
55 Carry on, as a trade
56 Cheap chat
60 Be worthy of
61 "Merrily We Roll __"
62 Estimator's phrase

63 Supply-and-demand subj.
64 Garden "crashers"
65 Campus bigwig
66 Borscht vegetable
67 Peace Nobelist Anwar
68 Popular ice cream

DOWN

1 Treats dismissively, with "at"
2 "Shake a leg!"
3 Uptight
4 Hackman of Hollywood
5 Macho dude
6 Praises to the sky
7 Big bash
8 "Jurassic Park" menace, briefly
9 Traffic halter
10 Astrological ram
11 Inadvisable advice
12 Liquidation sale
13 V.I.P. in D.C.
21 Attacked, in a way
22 Feel regret over
26 T.L.C. givers
28 Some TV's
30 1966 Michael Caine role
31 Boy king of Egypt
34 Car buyers' protection
36 Western writer Grey
37 Common place for a knot

Puzzle 3 by H. Estes and N. Salomon

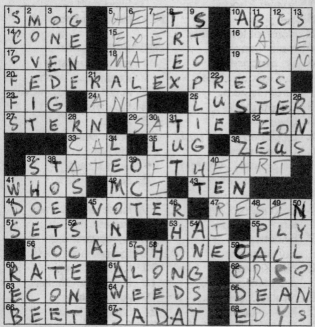

38 Direct, as a confrontation
39 Halloween's mo.
40 Like Halloween sounds
41 Dict. entries
45 By way of
46 Girl in a Beach Boys song
48 Dealt leniently with
49 "And how!"
50 Sheer stockings
52 Bloodhound's trail
54 Uneasy feeling

57 "Not guilty," e.g.
58 Got rid of 64-Across
59 The "C" in U.P.C.
60 Yank's foe

ACROSS

1 Painter Chagall
5 Suit
10 Home of Iowa State
14 Muffin topper
15 Do penance
16 "I, Claudius" role
17 Virgin Is., e.g.
18 Cheap shot?
20 Overwhelm
22 Block and tackle part
23 Use an épée
24 14 pounds, in Britain
26 Kimono accessories
29 Germ-free
33 Sosa vs. McGwire, e.g.?
37 Evidence of drunkenness
38 Necessities for pregnancies
39 Insulted, lovingly
42 Kay follower
43 Cuzco's country
45 Commotion in the commuters' terminal?
47 Watergate, e.g.
50 Israel's Abba
51 Rent again
53 Puts ice on, maybe
57 "One ___ Jump"
60 "The Natural" game
63 Feature of a girls-only gathering?
65 Scottish hillside
66 Mark time
67 Sri ___
68 The auld sod
69 ___ off (angered)
70 Sling mud at
71 Hard to fathom

DOWN

1 Recurring theme
2 Coeur d'___, Idaho
3 Any "Seinfeld," now
4 Pipe type
5 Ali ___
6 South Dakota, to Pierre
7 Links shouts
8 Bach's Mass ___ Minor
9 Place to put some leaves
10 Fly-casters, e.g.
11 It may be prix fixe
12 Canal of song
13 PlayStation maker
19 Ancient letter
21 Shut out
25 Feared fly
27 Skater Midori
28 Dobbin's home
30 "___ a song go . . ."
31 Put to sleep
32 ___ Stanley Gardner
33 Conks on the head
34 "___ plaisir"
35 Ancient Irish kings' home
36 Baton Rouge sch.
40 Go back
41 Musician Eddy or Allman
44 Got naked

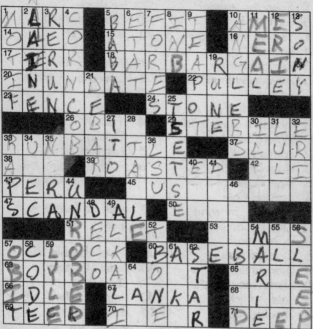

46 Gave the cold shoulder
48 Art __
49 Ethyl and propyl, for two
52 Steak selection
54 An Osmond
55 Traffic jam noise
56 Sack out
57 News item often written in advance
58 Programmers' writing
59 Singer Lovett

61 One of the Aleutians
62 Magi guide
64 Video maker, for short

ACROSS

1 Enjoy the taste of
6 Log home
11 Yeshiva student
14 Baloney
15 Refrigerator brand
16 Air-quality monitoring org.
17 Looks at lustfully
18 Incursion at a sorority
20 Where San Juan is
22 Formerly
23 Hospital fluids
24 Pipe player of myth
25 — King Cole
27 6-4, e.g., in tennis
29 Classic Cadillac
33 — Na Na
36 Qaddafi's country
39 Diarist Nin
40 Media consultant's field
43 Shoelace tip
44 Boxing venue
45 Michigan's — Canals
46 Wobbles on the edge
48 Canine warning
50 Mao —-tung
51 Pedal digit
53 Dashing style
57 "Garfield" dog
60 Colonial silversmith
63 Substantial entrees
65 Cut into tiny pieces
66 Ripen
67 Likewise
68 Like the walls at Wrigley Field
69 Moon vehicle, for short
70 Center of a sink
71 Tears apart

DOWN

1 Comes to an end
2 Bicker
3 Nastier
4 "Falstaff" and "Fidelio"
5 Take five
6 Frank who directed "Mr. Deeds Goes to Town"
7 With full force
8 Judges' seat
9 Chant
10 "Aye" canceler
11 Artist Millet or Corot
12 Homer's "Iliad," e.g.
13 Ford a shallow stream, say
19 Spiral pasta
21 Of the eye
26 Personification
28 Groups with influence
29 Valley
30 Neighbor of Vietnam
31 Prefix with type
32 Old "Happy motoring!" sloganeer
33 Petty quarrel
34 Bigger than big
35 Competent
37 Maidenform products

Puzzle 5 by Janet R. Bender

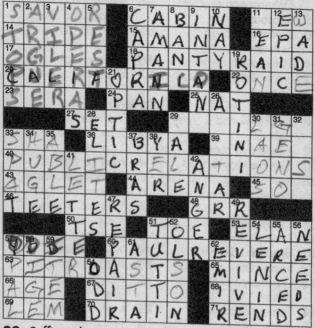

38 Suffix with saw or law
41 Envelope's contents
42 Make blood boil
47 Fix
49 Bring back
51 —-frutti
52 Game show announcer Johnny who cried "Come on down!"
54 Stalin's predecessor
55 Curve-shaped
56 Requires

57 Silica gem
58 Former Venetian magistrate
59 Couple in a gossip column
61 "The Thin Man" pooch
62 Ruler of Qatar
64 Unmatched, as socks

ACROSS

1 TV reception problem
5 Scissors sounds
10 Breezed through, as a test
14 Make over
15 Prefix with -pathic
16 Appoint
17 Appear
18 Old-fashioned dances
19 Indigo dye source
20 Like most toy models
23 Lawyers' org.
26 Homes on wheels, for short
27 Complained bitterly
28 Fountain treat
30 Hitter of 755 home runs
32 Common meeting place
34 Sammy Sosa, e.g.
37 Storm centers
38 Average guy?
39 Say "aye," say
40 Draft org.
41 Stopped by
44 Herb used in pesto
46 Cisco Kid's horse
47 Aussie lassie
50 Bacillus shape
51 Japanese moolah
52 Theme of this puzzle
56 "Picnic" playwright
57 Hang loosely
58 Disney dog
62 In the vicinity
63 Persian Gulf state
64 Solo appropriate for this puzzle
65 Lith. and Ukr., formerly
66 Mushers' vehicles
67 Abound

DOWN

1 Promgoers: Abbr.
2 Born, in bios
3 "__ to Joy"
4 Baby carrier?
5 Get dry and wrinkly
6 Christmas songs
7 "Since __ You Baby" (1956 hit)
8 Trapper's prize
9 "My apologies"
10 Motrin alternative
11 Word with ear or Erie
12 Author Zola
13 Struck out
21 River to the Caspian
22 __ Paulo, Brazil
23 Fire residue
24 Keeps afloat
25 Chips in
29 __ Moines
30 Bubbling over
31 In the sack
33 Resort town near Santa Barbara
34 "I Spy" star Bill
35 Of value
36 "Don't __ it!"
39 By way of

Puzzle 6 by Adam G. Perl

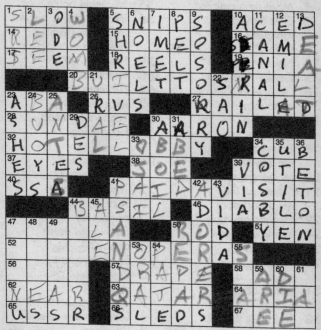

41 Manners
42 Worshipers
43 "Livin' la — Loca"
44 Those who wait
45 Pub order
47 They may get splints
48 Jazz's Earl "Fatha" —
49 Mystery writers' award
50 Give more cushioning
53 Exam sans pencils
54 It's chopped liver
55 Blind segment
59 "All the Things You —"
60 Run out of steam
61 Candied vegetable

ACROSS

1 More meanspirited
6 Elvis moved his, famously
10 Cole —
14 Now, in Spain
15 Gaelic
16 George W. Bush's alma mater
17 Big name in weight loss
19 Sound preceding crackle and pop
20 Mornings, for short
21 "There — the neighborhood!"
22 Genetic anomaly
24 Inning divisions
25 Withered
26 "Take my wife . . . please!" comedian
31 Lumps of Clay?
32 Quote
33 "I do," at the altar
35 Chancellor von Bismarck
36 "Hyperion" poet
38 Baseball's Ruth
39 Poe's "The Murders in the — Morgue"
40 Unload, as stock
41 Took a stab at
42 "Big" director, 1988
46 Sounds of pleasure
47 Singer Redding
48 Color of Duke Ellington's "Mood"
51 Its slogan is "Where America's Day Begins"

52 Little lie
55 Medicine bottle
56 Real-life comic played in film by Dustin Hoffman
59 Feed the kitty
60 "Heavens to Betsy!"
61 Furniture polish scent
62 Requirement
63 Scatters, as seed
64 Happening

DOWN

1 — California
2 Throat clearing
3 Princes, but not princesses
4 Suffix with north or south
5 Sci-fi weapons
6 Rejection of church dogma
7 Levin and Gershwin
8 Letter before omega
9 Divisions
10 Network
11 Glamorous actress Turner
12 Broadway's — Jay Lerner
13 Cried
18 1950's French president René
23 Press on
24 Cognizant of
25 Business attire
26 Try to get money from, slangily
27 Cosmetician Lauder

Puzzle 7 by Randall J. Hartman

B	A	S	E	R		H	I	P	S		S	L	A	W
A	H	O	R	A			E	R	S	E		Y	A	L	E
J	E	N	N	Y	C	R	A	I	G			S	N	A	P
A	M	S			G	O	E	S			M	U	T	A	N	T
			O	U	T	S			S	E	E				
	B	E	N	N	E	Y			T	U	N		M	A	N
	E	S	T	S			A	I	T				V	O	W
O	T	T	O			E	M	T	S			B	A	B	E
	O	E		D	U	M	P			T	R	I	E	D
	N	E	V		M	A	R	S	H	A	L	L
			H	S		O	T	I	S
I	N	D	I	G	O		G	U	A	M			F	I	B
V	I	A	L		L	E	N	N	Y	B	R	U	C	E
A	N	T	E		E	G	A	D		L	E	M	O	N
N	E	E	D		S	O	W	S		E	V	E	N	T

28 Florida citrus city
29 Be of use to
30 Prestigious prize
31 Supporting
34 Join in holy matrimony
36 Peepers' places
37 Shade trees
38 Playtex products
40 Glitch
41 Sewing aid
43 Caught in the act
44 Doctors make them in hospitals

45 Not leave
48 — the Terrible
49 Number dialed before two ones
50 July 4, 1776, e.g.
51 Chew (on)
52 Show anger
53 Bit of Windows dressing?
54 Not straight
57 Freudian topic
58 Gun, as an engine

ACROSS
1 Very dry, as wine
5 Future blooms
9 Witch trials site
14 Minstrel's instrument
15 Put __ writing
16 Wear away
17 Went __ smoke
18 Foolishly enthusiastic
19 Spooky
20 Hundreds in New York, perhaps
23 Kitchen pest
24 __ Baby
25 Russian empresses
27 Pesky e-mails
29 School of Buddhism
30 Workout site
33 Back problem
39 Ark builder
41 Floral necklace
42 Time past
43 Polynesian restaurant offering
48 Holiday drink
49 1989 General Motors debut
50 First of all
52 Inspects again
57 Lack of vigor
61 J.F.K. posting
62 House exterior choice
64 Prefix with millionaire
66 Algerian seaport
67 Forearm bone
68 Runs with minimal power
69 Whistler's whistle
70 Barely read
71 Impart knowledge
72 Sailboat feature
73 Headed for foreign ports

DOWN
1 Brief ad
2 Indian coin
3 Ancient city NW of Carthage
4 Mortise insertions
5 "So what?!"
6 Where the first transcontinental railroad was completed
7 Finger, say
8 Hitches
9 Is plenty angry
10 See 31-Down
11 System for pilots
12 City near Minneapolis
13 Runs into
21 Places for patches
22 Part of many a summer forecast
26 __ 500
28 "__ 18" (Uris novel)
30 Econ. measure
31 With 10-Down, 1983 Lionel Richie hit
32 Traveler's guide
34 Most preferred
35 Kind of sandwich
36 Saturn model
37 Sellout indicator

Puzzle 8 by Nancy Kavanaugh

38 Center of a blowout, maybe
40 Actor Grant
44 Easily irritated
45 Places
46 Lou Grant portrayer
47 Hindu princess
51 Snaky-locked woman of myth
52 "Please ___" (invoice stamp)
53 Practice piece
54 Arum lily
55 Stomachs may be in them
56 Pancake topper
58 Exploits
59 Bellybutton type
60 Brightly-colored lizard
63 Actress Wood of "Peyton Place"
65 Investigator, slangily

ACROSS

1 Skillful
6 French friends
10 It precedes "Over here!"
14 Check recipient
15 Actress Spelling
16 Sailor's hello
17 When "S.N.L." ends in N.Y.C.
18 Beach promenade
20 Bench surrounded by pigeons?
22 1973 Rolling Stones #1 hit
23 Thin wood strip
24 WSW's opposite
25 Aesop's stories
29 Most sarcastic, as remarks
33 Writer __ Stanley Gardner
34 Overturn, as a government
37 __ Beta Kappa
38 Noted 19th- and 20th-century coal hauler
41 "You da __!"
42 Places to get manicures
43 Pinnacle
44 Annoying
46 Gives 10%
48 Lincoln or Vigoda
49 British submachine gun
51 Milan's La __

54 Pleasant sight at a supermarket checkout
59 Tariff on valuables
61 Indy competitor
62 Life sentences?
63 "__ want for Christmas . . ."
64 Gas company bought by BP
65 Alleviate
66 City on the Rhine, to locals
67 Ballplayers in pinstripes

DOWN

1 Each, in pricing
2 Comedian Carvey
3 Looker
4 Pinnacle
5 Place to observe Saturday Sabbath
6 Up, in baseball
7 Be a sponge
8 "Dies __" (hymn)
9 Madam's mate
10 Hocked
11 Dance popularized in the 1930's
12 Songs for one
13 Young 'un
19 Book before Hosea
21 Part alphabetized in a telephone directory
24 Army volunteer
25 Physicist Enrico
26 Toward the back
27 Entry form
28 Was in front

Puzzle 9 by Jim Hyres

Note: The eight circled letters can be rearranged to spell an appropriate
bonus word.

29 The Golden Gate's
is 4,200 feet
30 Notable period
31 Embarrassment
32 Ebb and others
35 Look at flirtatiously
36 No amateur
39 Weather line
40 Snitch
45 Gesture to a general
47 Where papers
accumulate on a desk

49 "I — return"
50 Poison
51 — gin fizz
52 Havana's home
53 Line of rotation
54 D-Day invasion town
55 Dalai —
56 Screen pic
57 Part of a bottle
58 God of love
60 Chatter on and on

ACROSS

1 1930's movie dog
5 To boot
9 Couric of "Today"
14 Bleats
15 Per — (daily)
16 Icon
17 "Diana" crooner Paul
18 Mrs. Copperfield
19 Stocking stuff
20 American composer working at a bakery?
23 Bowler or boater
24 "To Autumn," e.g.
25 Alias initials
26 English playwright working at a press?
33 Inspiration for the Frisbee
35 Levy collector, for short
36 Koufax stat.
37 Petite desserts
38 At all
39 Blue eyes or baldness, e.g.
41 Titled Turk
42 Opposite of post-
43 Pan-fries
44 Vaudeville star working at a van company?
48 From S.F. to Las Vegas
49 "The Gold-Bug" writer
50 Scepter accompanier
53 Comedian working at an oil field?
58 Nice jacket material
59 Tide type
60 Sheltered, at sea
61 Be generous, at a bar
62 M. Hulot's creator
63 Actress Campbell
64 Diarist Samuel
65 Nabisco cookie
66 Turned blue, say

DOWN

1 Put to shame
2 Nick name?
3 Be a fall guy
4 "Quick!"
5 Like a postscript
6 Big name in small trains
7 Lowly worker
8 Gen. Bradley
9 Filmdom's Nastassja
10 "The Bonesetter's Daughter" writer
11 It may be spun around a campfire
12 Composer Stravinsky
13 Bard's nightfall
21 Bar mitzvah dances
22 Dinghy pair
27 Well put
28 Place for hash browns
29 Be nosy
30 Refreshment server on wheels
31 Cleveland's lake
32 Squealers
33 School grps.
34 Othello's betrayer

Puzzle 10 by Norma Johnson

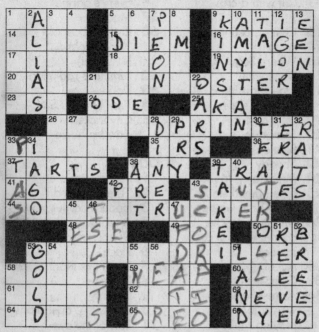

38 Piece by Matisse
39 Sulu portrayer on "Star Trek"
40 Boulevard crosser
42 Strip
43 Many a November birth
45 Best of times
46 Specks in the sea
47 Latest news
51 Superman player
52 Kennel Club classification
53 24-karat

54 Dickens's Uriah
55 Making a hobby of
56 Affix a brand to
57 Touch the tarmac
58 Inits. at a gas station

ACROSS

1 Cut with a crosscut
5 /
10 Castro's country
14 As to
15 Where Seoul is
16 Done with
17 One choosing a sweater, e.g.?
19 Let it all out
20 Sombrero, e.g.
21 Blame
22 Shoddy
24 Mrs. Harry Truman
25 One-named singer and Oscar winner
26 Item that may be connected to a car's ignition
29 Act of philanthropy
33 Opposite of out
34 Actress Tammy who won a Tony for playing Molly Brown
36 Genetic inits.
37 Recognize terrific fountain treats?
40 — de Cologne
41 Theater passages
42 Not straight
43 Hard-to-decide predicaments
45 Pal
46 "If — be so bold . . ."
47 Get together
49 Penny-pinching
52 The "shrew" in "The Taming of the Shrew"
53 Honey maker
56 Every's partner
57 Mace?
60 Riverbed deposit
61 "Goodnight —" (1950 hit)
62 Luminous radiation
63 Do in
64 The "N" of U.S.N.A.
65 City tricked with a wooden horse

DOWN

1 Punjabi believer
2 "The King and I" tutor
3 Habeas corpus, e.g.
4 After expenses
5 Drums, in jazz lingo
6 Place
7 Boats like Noah's
8 Envision
9 Severity
10 Like C.I.A. operations
11 Part of the eye containing the iris
12 Mercedes-—
13 Painterlike
18 Robert Frost piece
23 Fido restrainer
24 Beer, say
25 Dumas's Monte Cristo, e.g.: Fr.
26 Named, as a price
27 Hawaiian island
28 Run — of (violate)
29 Places a call on an old phone
30 Irritated

Puzzle 11 by Mel Taub

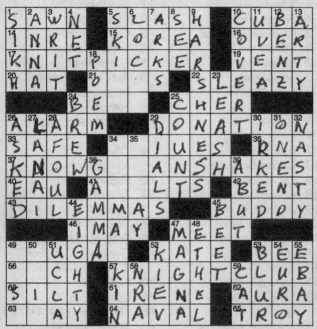

S	A	W	N		S	L	A	S	H		C	U	B	A
I	N	R	E		K	O	R	E	A		O	V	E	R
K	N	I	T	P	I	C	K	E	R		V	E	N	T
H	A	T		D		S		S	L	E	A	Z	Y	
		B	E			C	H	E	R					
A	L	A	R	M		D	O	N	A	T	I	O	N	
S	A	F	E		I	U	E	S			R	N	A	
K	N	O	W	G		A	N	S	H	A	K	E	S	
E	A	U		A		L	T	S		B	E	N	T	
D	I	L	E	M	M	A	S		B	U	D	D	Y	
		I	M	A	Y		M	E	E	T				
U	G	A		K	A	T	E		B	E	E			
S	C	H		K	N	I	G	H	T	C	L	U	B	
S	I	L	T		I	R	E	N	E		A	U	R	A
A	Y		N	A	V	A	L		T	R	O	Y		

31 Upright, as a box
32 Very unpleasant
34 Old female tabby
35 State again
38 Letter before delta
39 Border on
44 Fourscore
45 Symbol of redness
47 __ cum laude
48 Lucy's landlady
49 Own (up to)
50 Commuting option
51 Bruins' sch.
52 Chicken __ (dish)

53 Become hazy
54 Continental currency
55 Auctioneerless auction site
58 Gunners' org.
59 Tabby

ACROSS

1 Athens rival
7 Power glitch
12 One-dimensional
13 Best of the best
17 Basements' opposites
18 Surpasses in slyness
19 "Wow!"
21 Corp. bigwig
22 Loudness units
23 Decorative jugs
25 On vacation
28 Its cap. is Sydney
29 Alpine call
31 Strike back, say
33 Wheel's center
34 "M*A*S*H" star
37 "Wow!"
41 Env. abbreviation
42 Send via phone line
43 Salami choice
44 Chico's "ciao"
46 From _ Z
48 Explosive inits.
49 Pine exudation
51 Magnet for a moth
53 Cereal grain
54 "Wow!"
60 War crimes trier
62 Win the heart of
63 Completely surround
64 It may be vinyl or aluminum
65 Little laugh
66 Takes a nibble of

DOWN

1 Blind strip
2 Central part
3 Opposed to
4 Jockey's straps
5 Supplement, as a bill
6 Acts investigated by insurance companies
7 Highlanders, e.g.
8 "Nah!"
9 "The Godfather" composer Nino _
10 Supertalented
11 Environmental prefix
14 "Wow!"
15 Palm reader, e.g.
16 General _ chicken (Chinese dish)
20 Not a lot
24 Use a loom
25 Killer whale
26 Accomplishment
27 "Wow!"
29 Bald Brynner
30 Kimono tie
32 Singer Lauper
33 Witch's work
35 Singer Celine
36 Rat-___
38 ET carrier
39 Some undergrad degs.
40 "I" problem?
45 Do harm to
46 Actress MacGraw
47 Least wild

Puzzle 12 by Karen M. Tracey

49 Superficial teaching method
50 Bring in
51 N.J. city near the George Washington Br.
52 "Zounds!"
55 Not up or down, as a stock price: Abbr.
56 Shopper's lure
57 Not genuine: Abbr.
58 Zero
59 Work units
61 Took the bait

ACROSS
1 Bygone airline
4 Mass confusion
9 Demean
14 Roll of bills
15 Greeting
16 Rodeo participant
17 Subject of the biography "Float Like a Butterfly"
18 Home of the Blue Grotto
20 — of March
22 Braxton or Tennille
23 — Maria
24 Feed
27 Guarantees
30 Unfounded, as gossip
31 Lariat in the Southwest
32 Sheep's plaint
35 Work to get, as someone's trust
37 Outfit
40 Regular's request
44 Station
45 15-Across, in Spain
46 Full house sign: Abbr.
47 List components
50 Give a hoot
52 Ate at home
54 Smarts
58 Exiled Amin
59 Neighbor of Cambodia
61 Apiece
62 Theater guides

67 Maiden name preceder
68 Observant one
69 Hotelier Helmsley
70 Cereal grain
71 On the briny
72 Ninth mos.
73 — and outs

DOWN
1 "Tom Sawyer" author
2 Elusive children's book character
3 Farewell
4 "The Sweetheart of Sigma —"
5 "For — a jolly . . ."
6 Sane
7 Table spread
8 Later's alternative
9 L'— de Triomphe
10 Feathery wrap
11 Equipment
12 Deliver, as a summons
13 Great Lakes Indians
19 Speeder's penalty
21 — Lanka
25 Thought creatively
26 Cyrillic alphabet user
28 Large cactus
29 Sport — (off-road vehicles)
32 Bridge declaration
33 Beverage that's bitterer than beer
34 Mountain climbers
36 To the — degree

Puzzle 13 by Sarah Keller

38 Egypt and Syria, once: Abbr.
39 Arafat's org.
41 Table d'___ (restaurant offering)
42 Pawning place
43 Verve
48 Pepper grinder
49 Slow movers
51 Ram's mate
52 Ross of the Supremes
53 Dunderhead
55 Vietnam's capital
56 Where the waves are

57 Sharpens
60 S-shaped molding
63 Actress Michele
64 Time in history
65 Explosive
66 KLM competitor

ACROSS

1 An article may be written on it
5 Purse part, often
10 Cake with a kick
14 Baccarat alternative
15 Brownish gray
16 Bass products
17 Yellowstone figure
19 — out (barely gets)
20 "Yertle the Turtle" author
21 Rake with fire
23 "Quiet!"
24 Where cubs are raised
26 Permit
27 "I know the answer!"
30 Contract bridge tactics
33 Bother
35 Like modern clocks and recordings
36 Home on the range
38 Divine path, in Asian religions
39 Firm belief
43 Wash
46 Heat to 212°, as water
47 Where weapons are forbidden
51 Need for a keg
52 Takes too many tranqs, say
53 Peak SE of Olympus
54 "La-la" lead-in
56 Color, as a hippie's shirt
58 Breakaway country from Ethiopia
62 Other, in Oaxaca
63 Send around the bend
66 Astronaut Armstrong
67 Nonstudio film
68 Plowing unit
69 Swirl
70 Achieves perfectly
71 They're split for soup

DOWN

1 Bay Area patrollers: Abbr.
2 Carson predecessor
3 Miscalculates
4 Soda fountain choices
5 Hid
6 Catches some rays
7 Toupee, slangily
8 Copy
9 Keep going
10 1930's heavyweight champ Max
11 Acid-neutralizing compound
12 Complained
13 Selling points
18 German industrial valley
22 "Don't — on me"
24 Daewoo model
25 Operatic passage
27 Toward the rear
28 Tint
29 Egyptian viper

Puzzle 14 by Todd McClary

31 Blood pressure, body temperature, etc.
32 Campy 1958 sci-fi film, with "The"
34 Split-off group
37 Jetsons' lad
40 Came down with
41 Unaccounted-for G.I.
42 Saint-Moritz sight
44 Entered gradually
45 Main courses
47 Zero
48 Reworked, as text
49 Log-on name

50 Rocker Clapton
55 Fall into — (get caught)
57 Carson — of MTV
58 Malevolence
59 Marathon
60 Pound of literature
61 Yeoman's yeses
64 Genetic info carrier
65 Uganda's Amin

ACROSS

1 Mr. Fix-It's job
7 Diamond officials
11 Internet pop-ups, e.g.
14 Blake of "Gunsmoke"
15 "Chicago" star Richard
16 Note after fa
17 Marksmanship contest
19 It may be stubbed
20 World-weary
21 Med. plan
22 Lamb's mother
23 Ice sheets
25 Slightly sour candy
28 San — Obispo, Calif.
29 Contradict
30 Game of observation
31 Everything
32 A.M.A. members
33 "My dog — fleas"
35 Roar with mirth
41 Disreputable paper
42 Apropos of
43 — & Perrins (sauce brand)
44 "Dancing Queen" quartet
47 Rent-A-Wreck competitor
48 Aggressively publicize
49 Like a basset hound
52 Stop, Yield and No Passing
53 Dowsing need
54 Future C.E.O.'s deg.
55 Cosmetician Lauder
57 Bowl over
58 Survivalist's structure
62 Make funny faces
63 Singer Brickell
64 Rainbow color
65 Pesticide-monitoring grp.
66 Everything else
67 "Newhart" actor Tom

DOWN

1 Long-tailed pest
2 Relative of an ostrich
3 Precooks, in a way
4 Joints that may be twisted
5 Bright thoughts
6 Sunbathers catch them
7 "Eww, gross!"
8 Quaint exclamation
9 Movie trailer, e.g.
10 Attack
11 Autumn blooms
12 1950's music style
13 Not wide-awake
18 Pick
23 Opposite of muscle
24 Humdinger
26 Put into servitude
27 Piece of china
29 Magician Henning
32 — double-take
33 Humble homes
34 In the past
36 1-Down catcher
37 Comments to the audience
38 Phone answerer's cry

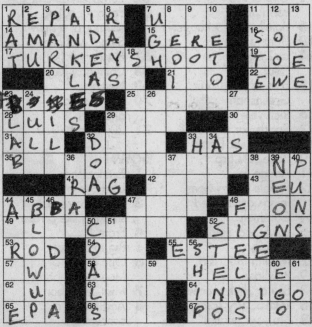

39 Element #10
40 Jokes that may be "running"
44 Steep-roofed house
45 Explode
46 Spanish grocery
47 One of the Three Musketeers
48 Pastures
50 Fire remnant
51 Place to live
52 Shorthand expert
56 Nina, Pinta or Santa Maria

59 "Wanna __?"
60 Self-image
61 Harry Potter's best friend

ACROSS

1 One of Franklin's two certainties
6 Spielberg blockbuster
10 Library item
14 ___ Detoo of "Star Wars"
15 Former Fed Chair Greenspan
16 Rich vein
17 Sports car at a deli?
19 Sportswear brand
20 Bake sale grp.
21 Amigo
22 People after whom things are named
24 Extremely
26 Lowly foot soldier, slangily
27 Muslim in Russia
29 Bewilder
33 Bell or shell preceder
36 Take ___ (try some)
38 "To your health!"
39 Elvis's middle name
40 Unseen title character in a Beckett play
42 "Gladiator" setting
43 Get through to
45 Arctic ice
46 Tabloid tidbit
47 Feeling of pity
49 Midway alternative
51 Building add-on
53 Pirate's supporter
57 Something to turn over on January 1
60 Alley ___

61 Buckeyes' sch.
62 European automaker
63 Pancake-eating senator at a deli?
66 Singer McEntire
67 Hand over (to)
68 Cathedral features
69 Netting
70 Co. medical offerings
71 2001 and 2010

DOWN

1 Extinguishes
2 Lord Byron's Muse
3 It may come out smelling like a rose
4 From A ___
5 Big to-do
6 One corner of a Monopoly board
7 Miss. neighbor
8 Addition to a concentrate
9 Grab quickly
10 Onslaught of crepe orders at a deli?
11 Leaking
12 1960's baseball All-Star Blue Moon ___
13 Some sneakers
18 Company with a "lonely repairman"
23 Burden
25 What an English student wore to a deli?

Puzzle 16 by Peter Abide

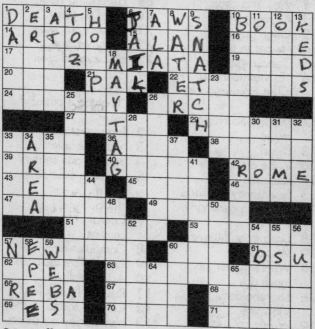

26 Traffic problems at a deli?
28 Beginning on
30 — suiter
31 Liberace fabric
32 K-6, as a sch.
33 Canvas cover
34 Length × width, for a rectangle
35 Part of a suit
37 Literary bear
41 Place to put bags?
44 Sharpen
48 Grab quickly

50 Slo-mo footage, perhaps
52 Violinist Zimbalist
54 "— luck!"
55 Glacial ridge
56 Conjecture
57 Bell curve peak
58 Fencing blade
59 Spiders' work
60 Bills not stocked in A.T.M.'s
64 Tokyo of old
65 Mimic

ACROSS

1 Was in a choir
5 All-night bash
9 Tough guys
14 Award in the ad biz
15 Genesis garden
16 "To the moon, —!" ("The Honeymooners" phrase)
17 Much modern popular music
18 Direct
20 In the offing
22 Requisite
23 Emergency message
24 Wedding ceremony, e.g.
28 Drop from the eye
29 Wandered
33 Where fighter jets touch down
38 Shareholder's substitute
39 Wrath
40 Animal hides
42 Mincemeat dessert
43 Touches down
46 Targets of football kicks
49 Stuffed shirts
51 Derrière
52 Flier at Kitty Hawk
58 Row a boat
61 Nut
62 Unearthly
63 Be a secret author
67 "Ain't Misbehavin'" star Carter
68 Musical show
69 List-ending abbr.
70 Any Poe story
71 Improve, as text
72 Lowly worker
73 Underworld river

DOWN

1 "Hightail it out of here!"
2 Island welcome
3 More friendly
4 Speedy one-seaters
5 Gridiron official, for short
6 Hubbub
7 Captain Nemo's creator
8 Computer key
9 Convertible look-alike
10 Actor Wallach
11 Russian fighter jets
12 Canyon sound
13 New Jersey hoopsters
19 Legacy receiver
21 Regimen
25 Org. for people 50 and over
26 "Peer Gynt" composer
27 Spot for a headphone
30 Swabs
31 Escape route
32 Brunette-to-redhead jobs
33 Is under the weather
34 Tehran's locale
35 Ashcroft's predecessor
36 Negotiator with Isr.

Puzzle 17 by Lynn Lempel

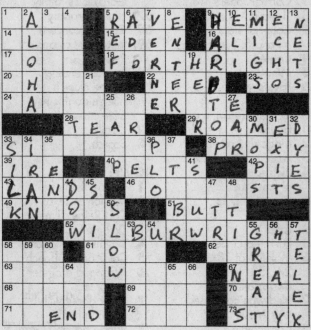

37 One of the Fab Four
41 Whole lot
44 Wall Street index, with "the"
45 Unnatural-sounding
47 Reduce, as expenses
48 Adjusts to the surroundings
50 Glacial
53 Yawn inducers
54 Merge
55 "Super!"
56 Not flat

57 Pre-Internet communication
58 Brute
59 Pause filler
60 Wander
64 Natural tanner
65 Road cover
66 Santa's helper

ACROSS

1 Cartographers' works
5 "I did it!"
9 Count of stars on a U.S. flag
14 Canted
15 Minute bit
16 Lavatory sign
17 Gawk
18 Catskills resort, e.g.
20 Hint at
22 Magazine number
23 Azer. or Ukr., once
24 Rich source of fossil fuel
26 Utmost degree
28 Dejected
29 Land
33 Part of a circle
36 Makeup of 18-, 24-, 53- and 64-Across
39 Ned who composed "Air Music"
42 Commotion
43 Candidate of 1992 and '96
44 Component length of 36-Across
47 Inspire respect
48 Withdraws
49 Coach Parseghian
52 Mortarboard, e.g.
53 Large real estate purchase
58 Computer key
61 Flowering shrub
63 Pago Pago's locale
64 Members of Elián González's family, e.g.
67 Highly graphic
68 Camera concern
69 Inhabitant of ancient Persia
70 Launder ending
71 All the clues in this puzzle do this with 36-Across
72 Gaelic
73 Scorch

DOWN

1 Copperfield's field
2 Mission in Texas
3 Carl Reiner film "Where's __?"
4 Witches' recitations
5 Color on the beach
6 Arranged a dinner at home
7 Walk about with a divining rod
8 Vanderbilt and Grant
9 Risky building to be in
10 India __
11 Complain
12 Medicinal amts.
13 Calendar's span
19 Scale unit at the post office
21 Warbler Sumac
25 Passports and drivers' licenses, for short
27 Nectar-pouring goddess
29 Origin suffix
30 Incantation beginning

Puzzle 18 by Patrick Merrell

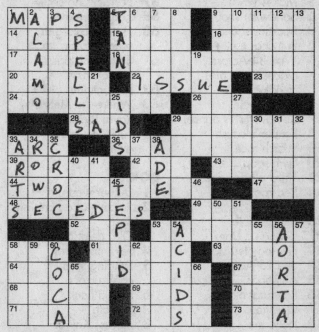

31 Develop
32 Medieval Italian fortress city
33 Sciences' partner
34 Investment firm T. __ Price
35 Gator's relative
37 Makes lace
38 Orange or lemon drink
40 Major util.
41 Decorated Olympian
45 Warmish
46 Okinawa honorific
50 Interstate syst.

51 Maxims
53 Cager at the Staples Center
54 Corrosive liquids
55 Milk a scene for all it's worth
56 Arterial trunk
57 Coating
58 Flunking marks
59 Schedule position
60 Cola's beginning
62 Flimsy, as an excuse
65 Capek play
66 Married name modifier

ACROSS

1 Makes yawn
6 Sandwich shop
10 Backfire sound
14 Bullying, e.g.
15 With 34-Across, places to set pies to bake
16 Killer whale
17 — nova (60's dance)
18 Fender blemish
19 Watch face
20 "Is it soup —?"
21 Third-place prize
24 Red roots in the garden
26 Maid's cloth
27 Grand — Dam
29 Five-pointed star
34 See 15-Across
35 Auditions, with "out"
36 Rowboat blade
37 Questions
38 Holy one
39 Animal caretakers, for short
40 Father's Day gift
41 Piano piece
42 On the — (close to defeat)
43 Pre-repair job figure
45 "Unto the Sons" author Gay —
46 Band booking
47 Exterior
48 Southeastern Conference mascot
53 Towel stitching
56 "Hold on a moment!"
57 Barracks no-show
58 F.B.I. operative
60 Former Georgia senator Sam
61 Something passed in music class?
62 Discontinue
63 Where the Mets play
64 Royal Russian
65 Fund, as one's alma mater

DOWN

1 Diaper wearer
2 Relative of an English horn
3 Old, deteriorated ship
4 Feminine suffix
5 Landing strip constructors
6 Extinct flock
7 Smooth
8 Actress Kay of "Breezy," 1973
9 E-mail deliverer, with "the"
10 Store with taco shells
11 Like a dust bowl
12 March Madness org.
13 Effrontery
22 I-95, e.g.: Abbr.
23 Shoes are wiped on them
25 The "E" in B.P.O.E.
27 Orange container
28 Caravan's stopping point

Puzzle 19 by Gregory E. Paul

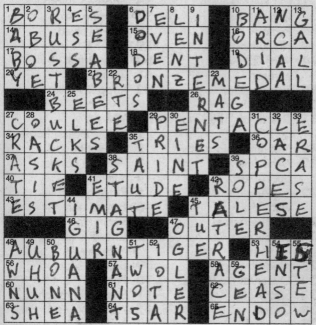

B	O	R	E	S		D	E	L	I		B	A	N	G
A	B	U	S	E			O	V	E	N		O	R	C	A
B	O	S	S	A		D	E	N	T		D	I	A	L
Y	E	T		B	R	O	N	Z	E	M	E	D	A	L
		B	E	E	T	S				R	A	G		
C	O	U	L	E	E		P	E	N	T	A	C	L	E
R	A	C	K	S		T	R	I	E	S		O	A	R
A	S	K	S		S	A	I	N	T		S	P	C	A
T	I	E		E	T	U	D	E		R	O	P	E	S
E	S	T	I	M	A	T	E		T	A	L	E	S	E
			G	I	G			O	U	T	E	R		
A	U	B	U	R	N	T	I	G	E	R		H	E	S
W	H	O	A		A	W	O	L		A	G	E	N	T
N	U	N	N		N	O	T	E		C	E	A	S	E
S	H	E	A		T	S	A	R		E	N	D	O	W

29 Group of lions
30 German "a"
31 Venomous viper
32 Shoestrings
33 Shake, as an Etch A Sketch
35 Pulled tight
38 Like backwater
39 Shoe part that's wiped on 23-Down
41 Royal Arabian
42 Workaday world
44 Large lizard
45 Wed. preceder

47 Person likely to say "Hubba hubba!"
48 Barley beards
49 "Nope!"
50 Rib or ulna
51 Deuces
52 Bit
54 — many words
55 Goulash
59 Tommy Franks, for one: Abbr.

ACROSS

1 O'Neill's "Desire Under the —"
5 Peak
9 Hayloft stack
14 With 23-Across, crimson
15 Horse's pace
16 Speedy train
17 The "I" of "The King and I"
18 Not limited to roads
20 "Absolutely, guaranteed"
22 Big Apple subway, with "the"
23 See 14-Across
24 Barbecuers' equipment
28 Kind of weight
30 Queen of the fairies
33 Spooky
34 Oracle
35 Directed
36 "Definitely worth getting"
39 Beats the backside of
40 "— Yankees"
41 Like it —
42 Award bestowed by a queen: Abbr.
43 Paper mates
44 Comfort
45 Tide alternative
46 Peter, Paul and Mary: Abbr.
47 "As a matter of fact . . ."

55 "Star Wars" weapon
56 Sporting sword
57 Wading bird
58 Self-involved
59 007
60 A bit drunk
61 Refuges
62 Raggedy fellow

DOWN

1 Cyberauction house
2 Late-night host
3 Waiter's handout
4 Attempt
5 Playing marbles
6 Flower part
7 Venus de —
8 Caesar's words to Brutus
9 Beef — soup
10 Pungent
11 Browse (through)
12 Author Wiesel
13 — Diego
19 Goofs
21 "Oklahoma!" aunt
24 Really irk
25 Place to kick a habit
26 Singer Cara
27 They're kissable
28 Swarms
29 Check
30 — Carta
31 Kind of committee
32 Davis of "All About Eve"
34 Computerized photo
35 Engage in logrolling

37 Paradigms
38 Perch
43 Comely
44 Isaac and Howard
45 Early anesthetic
46 Arab chief
47 Buster Brown's four-legged friend
48 Shrek, e.g.
49 Hot rock
50 Ski lift
51 Country artist McEntire
52 Atop
53 Take care of
54 Actress Lamarr
55 Isr. neighbor

ACROSS

1 Vineyard fruit
6 Goes on and on
11 Pale
14 Rand McNally product
15 Cosmetician Lauder
16 Pres. Lincoln
17 Enjoy summer air-conditioning, say
19 Dieters' units: Abbr.
20 Sigma's follower
21 Right on a map
22 Frontiersman Carson
23 1970 Beatles chart-topper
27 Strikes out
29 Santa __, Calif.
30 Cenozoic and Paleozoic
32 Brother of Cain and Abel
33 Squid's squirt
34 "Alas" and "alack"
36 Thorns' places
39 Felt bad about
41 Party list
43 The Beehive State
44 Exercise for the abs
46 African antelope
48 Southern constellation
49 __ d'oeuvre
51 Green shade
52 Can topper
53 Washing machine cycle
56 Surgeon who pioneered the artificial human heart implant
58 Driver's need: Abbr.
59 Gymnast's feat
61 Film locale
62 "Put __ Happy Face"
63 Be entirely satisfactory
68 "For shame!"
69 Former Chinese premier Zhou __
70 Walkie-talkie
71 Actress Caldwell
72 Breathers
73 Guinness, e.g.

DOWN

1 Go on and on
2 Hwy.
3 Pie __ mode
4 Page who sang "How much is that doggie in the window?"
5 Fancy homes
6 Director Spike
7 Queens's __ Stadium
8 It precedes fast and follows farm
9 Coquettes
10 Takes up residence (in)
11 Live up to one's word
12 Hoffman who wrote "Steal This Book"
13 Hatching posts?
18 Arrogance
23 Lions' dens

Puzzle 21 by Randall J. Hartman

Grid letters as filled in:

G	R	A	P	E		L	A		S				
A	T	L	A	S		E	S	T	E	E		A	B	E
B	E	A	T	T	H	E	H	E	A	T				
			T	A	U		E	A	S	T		K	I	T
L	E	T	I	T	B	E				L	E			
A	N	A		E	R	A	S		S	E	T	H		
I	N	K		S	I		H			S	T	E	M	S
R	U	E	D		S		A				U	T	A	H
S	I	T	U	P			L			D			R	
		H	O	R	S		L			E		L	I	D
S		E		O	A					B		E		
W		P	L						S	E	T			
O	N	A		O	I			T	H	E	B	I	L	L
		K		S	N			I		R	A	D	I	O
N		E	E					S			S	T	O	U	T

Across / Down clues

24 The blahs
25 Top everything else
26 Birdie beater
28 "—, Brute?"
31 "I — return"
35 Not flighty
37 One of the Osmonds
38 Disreputable
40 Chad & Jeremy and others
42 Catch, as in a net
45 Suggest, as a deal
47 Big name in diamonds
50 Like ocean water
53 Fall over in a faint
54 Classic laundry detergent
55 Spikes, in volleyball
57 Up, in baseball
60 Surveyor's map
64 "— the season . . ."
65 Altar vow
66 Lucy of "Charlie's Angels," 2000
67 Auction grouping

ACROSS

1 Cone maker
4 "Don't you recognize the voice?!"
9 Give up, as a habit
13 Part of a Latin conjugation
15 Boarded
16 Prince William's school
17 Making trouble
19 Shiny gold fabric
20 Gabs and gabs
21 "Mercy!"
22 Permit
23 Cent
25 Glimpse
26 Away from the bow
29 Semi-colon?
30 One who walks a beat
33 Going to the dogs, e.g.
35 It's fit for a queen
37 "I feel great!"
41 Flash point?
42 "What's in —?"
43 Sophs. two years later
44 Shade tree
46 Prefix with meter
47 That lady
50 Indian state
52 Birth-related
54 Ink spots
57 Making no sound
60 Ladies' man
61 Fancy duds
62 Neutral color
63 Like some cereals
64 Folk singer Guthrie
65 Delicate lock of hair
66 Unpromising
67 D.C. bigwig

DOWN

1 Regional groups of animal life
2 Stick on a stick
3 Nursery noisemaker
4 Composer Stravinsky
5 Duds
6 Not stand erect
7 Butted out?
8 Put the kibosh on
9 Green shade
10 Emphatic type: Abbr.
11 Hair straightener
12 Lower joint
14 Dog in Oz
18 Forwarding info on a letter
21 Rich, now
24 "Pretty nice!"
27 Big exams
28 Young 'un
30 Foldout bed
31 Lunch hour
32 Each
33 —-de-France
34 Entrepreneur's deg.
36 Way to go: Abbr.
37 Syringe measures, for short
38 Paddle
39 Sounds of hesitation

Puzzle 22 by Elizabeth C. Gorski

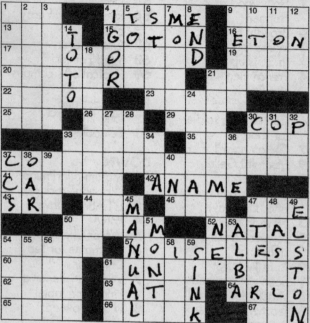

40 Record producer Brian
45 Car owner's reference
47 Has the wheel
48 Fuss
49 — Howard, 1963 A.L. M.V.P.
50 Consumed with gusto
51 Three-card —
53 Jessica of "Dark Angel"
54 Beer, informally
55 Venues
56 Yours and mine
58 Bean product?
59 Completed, as a putt
61 Weep

ACROSS

1 Hollywood snooper Hopper
6 Brought to bay
11 Winter hrs. in St. Louis
14 French cinema star Delon
15 Therefore
16 Confederate soldier, for short
17 Get on board
19 Mentalist Geller
20 Pub perch
21 Early __ (one up at 6 a.m., say)
23 Nevada town
25 "Sweet Caroline" singer
29 "__ Like It Hot"
31 Soup eater's need
32 Vegetables that roll
33 Teacher's charges
35 Designer __ de la Renta
37 Game show originally hosted by Monty Hall
42 Opposite of fronts
43 From east of the Urals
45 Pet protectors' org.
48 Bloodhound's clue
51 Spanish girl: Abbr.
52 1990 road film starring Nicolas Cage and Laura Dern
55 With it, 50's-style
56 N.B.A.'s Shaq
57 Bullwinkle, for one
59 Genetic info dispenser
60 Planter's tool
66 Room with an easy chair
67 Online letter
68 West Pointer
69 Radical 60's campus grp.
70 Slender and long-limbed
71 Befuddled

DOWN

1 Muslim pilgrimage
2 "Xanadu" rock grp.
3 Li'l Abner's love
4 Force
5 Writer Chekhov
6 Nickname for Leo Durocher
7 __ room (site for a Ping-Pong table)
8 Photo blow-up: Abbr.
9 Antique French coin
10 Actress Winger
11 Literary castaway
12 Venus's sister on the courts
13 Sporty Fords, informally
18 Weed whackers
22 Awe
23 Computer key: Abbr.
24 Laze
26 Peek
27 Amount of medicine
28 Peruvian Indian

Puzzle 23 by Norma Johnson

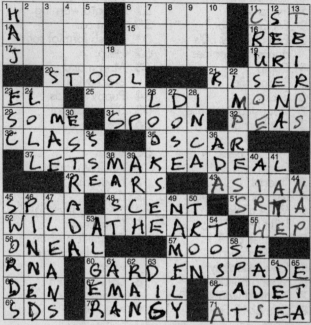

30 Erik who played Ponch on TV
34 NNW's opposite
36 Nabokov novel
38 A crow's-nest is atop it
39 Keystone site
40 Bubblebrains
41 Missing a deadline
44 Quick shuteye
45 Musketeers' weapons
46 Fastened (down)
47 Gets rid of dust bunnies

49 To wit
50 1982 Jeff Bridges film
53 Author Horatio
54 Raven-haired Puccini heroine
58 Lover's quarrel
61 Doctors' org.
62 Did a marathon
63 Unkind remark
64 Fiddle-de-___
65 Airport posting: Abbr.

ACROSS

1 Pequod captain
5 Immense
9 Footnote abbr.
13 End of many 60's dance club names
14 Cupid
15 Bridge site
16 Sticky
17 Disgusted response
18 Did horribly on, as a test
19 "You __ here"
20 French yeses
22 "Nerts!"
24 Lazy one, slangily
26 Make unclear
27 Trifle (with)
28 Chinese drink
32 1948 also-ran
35 Talks raucously
36 Mound builder
37 Plaintive woodwind
38 One of 18 French kings
39 Good name for a Dalmatian
40 Place for a plug
41 Courted
42 Like saltwater taffy
43 Orchestral performance
45 Any ship
46 Frenchman Descartes
47 Hamilton and Burr did it
51 Cuckoo
54 Seethe
55 Eggs

56 1997 title role for Peter Fonda
57 Hazard warning
59 Farm call
61 Welsh form of John
62 Hero
63 Moran and Brockovich
64 Puppy sounds
65 Slangy denial
66 "Not on __!"

DOWN

1 Ancient market
2 Nonsense
3 ID info
4 "Hot-diggity-dog!"
5 Flavorless
6 Quantities: Abbr.
7 Exemplar of little worth
8 Delivery room surprise?
9 Natural
10 __ tie
11 "Ah, yes"
12 Like a lawn at dawn
13 1946 hit "__ in Calico"
21 180° turn, slangily
23 Tints
25 To __ (exactly)
26 Pigtail, e.g.
28 Causing to stick
29 Item for a D.J.
30 Sufficient, once
31 Lawyer: Abbr.
32 Executes
33 Web auction site

Puzzle 24 by Susan Harrington Smith

Note: Sixteen answers in this puzzle have something unusual in common. What is it?

34 Bird's find
35 Pat or Daniel
38 Place of wildness, informally
39 Author Silverstein
41 "Thank heaven that's over!"
42 Onetime White House daughter
44 Primps
45 — generis

47 Last name in mysteries
48 Sarge's superior
49 Happening
50 During working hours
51 Chop —
52 Ovid's 156
53 Bring in the sheaves
54 Betty —
58 Japanese vegetable
60 Sphere

ACROSS

1 Islamic holy war
6 Channel showing Cong. hearings
11 Transatlantic flier, for short
14 Pac-Man maker
15 Native whale-hunter
16 Toddler's age
17 Where horses drink
19 Tire filler
20 Tempest
21 Mount in Sicily
22 Show on which the Blues Brothers debuted: Abbr.
25 Sufficient
29 Make fun of
32 Elevates
33 The __ Brothers of 1960's–70's R & B
34 Treaty
35 Flipping pages
42 Ostrichlike bird
43 Magazine
44 Delicacy with champagne
47 Certain whimsical Dutch lithographs
49 It's kneaded
51 Moscow's land: Abbr.
52 It may be due on a duplex
53 Stonehenge worshiper
56 Top flier
57 Mythical pass to the underworld
63 "The Sweetheart of Sigma __"
64 Sign before Taurus
65 Prefix with mural
66 Baseball legend Williams
67 Looks closely (at)
68 Prophets

DOWN

1 Target of a punch, maybe
2 "Give __ rest!"
3 Derby or bowler
4 Greek war god
5 Gossip
6 Rabbit's treat
7 Replay feature
8 Little, in Lille
9 Mo. before Labor Day
10 Ultimate ordinal
11 Display on a pedestal
12 Equipment near teeter-totters
13 Synagogue scroll
18 Roman Senate wear
21 Dawn goddess
22 Skirt opening
23 "Candy / Is dandy / But liquor / Is quicker" poet
24 Lollapalooza
26 "Phooey!"
27 Individually
28 Kind of acid
30 Opal or onyx
31 Gas-electric car, e.g.
34 Org. for Tiger Woods

Puzzle 25 by Raymond Hamel

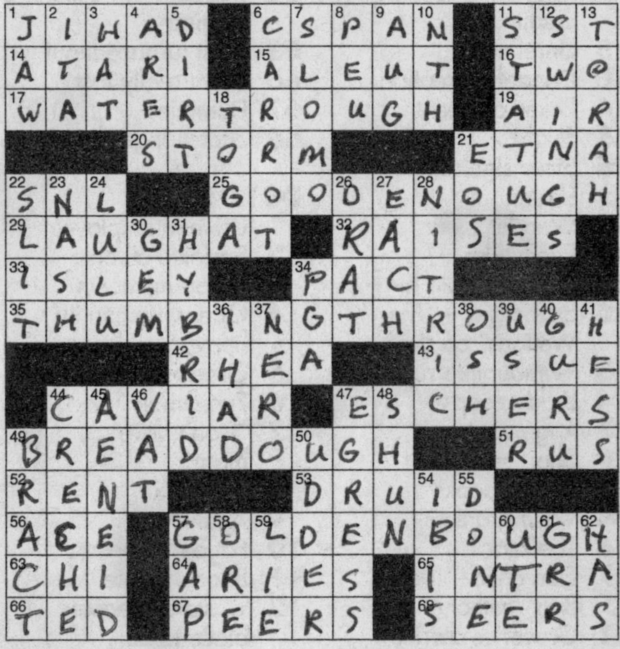

36 "If — a Hammer"
37 Poisoner of Britannicus
38 —Kosh B'Gosh
39 Not an abstainer
40 Knowledgeable one
41 Dame Myra
44 Christmas display
45 Poem with the story of the Trojan horse
46 Big wine holder
47 Exit
48 Avoid
49 Leaflike appendage
50 Milk giver
54 Everglades wader
55 Ready to be removed from the oven
57 Interruption
58 Prospector's prize
59 Fib
60 Western Indian
61 Dog's warning
62 Owns

ACROSS

1 Alternative to check or credit
5 Unrefined
10 Daedalus creation
14 Poker payment
15 "Ugh!"
16 Store sign after 9 a.m.
17 Wander
18 Really like
19 Hawaii's state bird
20 Sexologist + "The Waltons" co-star
23 Without interruption
24 Kiddy coop
28 Mtge. units
29 Short sprint
33 Picture books
34 Wish granters
36 The East
37 Film critic + "Native Son" author
41 Groceries carrier
42 Deep dislikes
43 Gap
46 "A Death in the Family" writer
47 Easter decoration
50 Third-place finisher, e.g.
52 Legend maker
54 College basketball coach + "L.A. Law" co-star
58 Pizazz
61 Scottish landowner
62 Classroom drills

63 Cockeyed
64 Refrain from children's singing?
65 Blast furnace input
66 Went really fast
67 Dummies
68 Scotch ingredient

DOWN

1 Drive-in employee
2 Sprinkle oil on
3 Union members
4 Ones who can lift heavy weights
5 Greenish blue
6 Funnyman Foxx
7 "Don't have —, man!"
8 Deep-six
9 Aussie gal
10 Fat cat
11 Boorish brute
12 — state (pleasant place to be)
13 From K.C. to Detroit
21 Threw in
22 1960 chess champion Mikhail
25 Midwife's instruction
26 Broadcast
27 Code-breaking org.
30 Alicia of "Falcon Crest"
31 —-Japanese War
32 Ibsen's Gabler
34 Become familiar with
35 Great gulp
37 Racetrack fence

Puzzle 26 by N. Johnson and N. Salomon

Crossword grid (partially filled in by hand):

Row 1: C A S H _ A R A _ _ _ A _ _
Row 2: A N T E _ Q E C _ _ O P E N
Row 3: R O A M _ U D O _ _ E _ _
Row 4: H I _ _ A D W _ _ _
Row 5: P N _ _ _ _ P L A Y P E N
Row 6: P T S _ _ _ S _ _ _ U _ S
Row 7: G E N I E S _ S _ A S I A
Row 8: E E _ N _ _ _ H
Row 9: C A R T _ _ C _ _
Row 10: _ A T _ _ _ _ _ E G G
Row 11: _ S O _ _ _ _ _
Row 12: _ K _ _ _ _
Row 13: E L A N _ _ _ _
Row 14: L O C O _ _ _
Row 15: F L E W _ _ _

Clues:

38 Historic periods
39 Wish undone
40 "That is to say . . ."
41 Chinese tea
44 Samovar
45 Took a cruise
47 Writer Welty
48 Grimm girl
49 Most mirthful
51 Marsh of mystery
53 Data holder
55 Went very fast
56 The Stooges, for instance

57 Hullabaloos
58 Keebler cookiemaker
59 Chat room chuckle
60 Biggest diamond

ACROSS

1 Fashionable
5 Where bats "hang out"
9 Triangular traffic sign
14 Sweep under the rug
15 Like droughty land
16 Typo
17 Neck and neck
18 Lion's locks
19 Popular dip for 48-Down
20 Gain wealth opportunely, in a way
23 "Two Mules for Sister —" (1970 film)
24 Three, on a sundial
25 "That feels good!"
28 Snake that may warn before it strikes
31 Harper Valley grp., in song
34 Lock of hair
36 "— was saying . . ."
37 Any day now
38 Nickname in James Fenimore Cooper tales
42 Artist Warhol
43 Vintner's tank
44 Cruise ship
45 Put into words
46 Hot pepper
49 Give it a whirl
50 Little League field surface, probably
51 Stethoscope holders
53 She played TV's Amanda Woodward
61 Shake hands (on)
62 Per person
63 — Major
64 More vigorous
65 Suffix with buck
66 Appearance
67 Be head over heels about
68 Prospectors' receptacles
69 Tiptop

DOWN

1 Bake-off figure
2 Honey factory
3 "The very —!"
4 Piggy bank filler
5 Tourist's take-along
6 Where Noah landed
7 Chianti or Soave
8 Place of bliss
9 Boot camp affirmative
10 Tehran resident
11 Writer — Stanley Gardner
12 Profit's opposite
13 "Darn!"
21 Severe
22 "Old MacDonald" refrain
25 World Almanac section
26 Madison Square Garden, e.g.
27 Exciting

Puzzle 27 by Gregory E. Paul

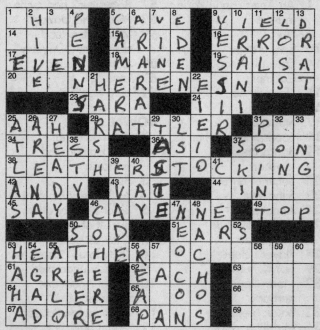

H	I	P		C	A	V	E		Y	I	E	L	D
I		E		A	R	I	D		E	R	R	O	R
E	V	E	N		M	A	N	E		S	A	L	S	A
	E		N	H	E	R	E	N	E	S	N	S	T
		S	A	R	A				I	I	I		
A	A	H		R	A	T	T	L	E	R		P		
T	R	E	S	S			A	S	I		S	O	O	N
L	E	A	T	H	E	R	S	T	O	C	K	I	N	G
A	N	D	Y		V	A	T			I	N		
S	A	Y		C	A	Y	E	N	N	E		T	O	P
		S	O	D		E	A	R	S				
H	E	A	T	H	E	R		O	C				
A	G	R	E	E		E	A	C	H				
H	A	L	E	R		A	O	O				
A	D	O	R	E		P	A	N	S				

29 One of the senses
30 "Saving Private Ryan" craft: Abbr.
31 Score unit
32 Laser printer powder
33 Hopping mad
35 Hog's home
37 Go downhill fast?
39 Dodge
40 Element of hope?
41 Pencil pusher
46 Stick together
47 Converted liberal, informally

48 Mexican snacks
50 Beef animal
52 Losing streak
53 "That is so funny"
54 "Goodness gracious!"
55 Guthrie who sang at Woodstock
56 Harvest
57 Zhivago's love
58 New York's ___ Canal
59 Toward the big waves
60 Captain, e.g.

ACROSS

1 An American in Paris, maybe
6 "By __!"
10 Sch. groups
14 Edwin in Reagan's Cabinet
15 "Excuse me . . ."
16 Pathetic
17 Stupefied
18 Superman's mother
19 Board member, for short
20 Summer retreat
23 Silhouette
24 Annoyance
25 With deliberate hamminess
28 Player's club?
29 N.Y.C. subway
32 More slippery, perhaps
33 Break bread
34 Middling
35 Summer retreat
39 Author Dinesen
40 "I want my __!" (1980's slogan)
41 Sword handles
42 __ Paul guitars
43 Gossip
44 Mocks
46 Shoveled
47 Initial venture
48 Summer retreat
54 Promotable piece
55 Fictional detective Wolfe
56 Dangerous gas
57 Babysitter's headache
58 Perón and Gabor
59 Work often read before the "Odyssey"
60 Compos mentis
61 Lone
62 Euro fractions

DOWN

1 Actor Jannings
2 TV's leather-clad princess
3 Busiest
4 At this very moment
5 Bit of summer attire
6 Bucket of bolts
7 Midway alternative
8 "Billy Budd" captain
9 Grossly underfeed
10 Naval Academy freshman
11 Travel before takeoff
12 "Right on!"
13 Very short wait, in short
21 Film producer Roach
22 Workmanship
25 Polite
26 Build __ against (work to prosecute)
27 Layered minerals
28 Bit of luggage
29 Cries one's eyes out
30 Sporty Mazda
31 Romantic rendezvous
33 Letter container: Abbr.

Puzzle 28 by Karen M. Tracey

34 Story that might include a dragon
36 Conceives of
37 Gambling site, briefly
38 Flamboyantly overdone
43 Astronaut Grissom
44 Humorous
45 Suffix with ranch
46 "Inferno" poet
47 Not domesticated
48 Poet Teasdale
49 McGregor of "Down With Love"
50 "Whip It" band
51 Tennis score after deuce
52 Bearded animal
53 Leaves off
54 "Nova" network

ACROSS

1 Karate blow
5 Microscope part
9 Separates, as flour
14 Super-duper
15 Baseball's Moises or Felipe
16 Dunderhead
17 Poker holding lower than three-of-a-kind
18 Oscar winner Patricia
19 Big
20 Punish action star Norris?
23 Superlative suffix
24 "Anchors Aweigh" grp.
25 CPR expert
26 "Moby Dick" whaler
28 Lipton competitor
30 Hurrying
33 Parts of gowns that go over the shoulders
36 Detroit baseballer
37 Titled lady
40 Massage
42 Fast jets, briefly
43 Alex Haley saga
45 River in a Strauss waltz
47 Spills clumsily
49 Big name in small planes
53 Close by
54 Letters before an alias
55 Balloon filler
56 High-jumper's hurdle
58 Rely on comic Keaton?
62 In the sky
64 Delhi dress
65 "Well done!"
66 Roast host
67 The dark force
68 Miners' finds
69 Worker with autumn leaves
70 Dicker
71 Toward the sunset

DOWN

1 Kid's pistol
2 Like laryngitis sufferers
3 Whopper toppers
4 Lima's locale
5 Acquire slugger McGwire?
6 Put into office
7 Biblical ark builder
8 "Star Trek" navigator
9 Formal headgear
10 Actress Lupino
11 Dismiss gangster Moran?
12 Clothing
13 Proofreader's "leave it"
21 Hair removal brand
22 Jail, slangily
27 Crops up
29 Fearsome fly
30 "No man — island . . ."
31 Ready

Puzzle 29 by N. Salomon and H. Estes

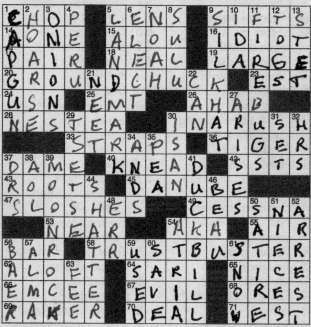

32 "48 —" (Nick Nolte film)
34 "No ifs, — or buts!"
35 Sweet — (flower)
37 E.R. workers
38 "You've got mail" co.
39 Drop drawers on actor Hudson?
41 Avoid President Clinton?
44 Break into bits
46 Boyfriend
48 Goof up
50 Lampoon

51 Sisters' daughters
52 Collar
54 Skylit lobbies
56 30's boxing champ Max
57 — mater
59 Like Goodwill goods
60 Prepare for a rainy day
61 Falling flakes
63 Membership charge

ACROSS

1 Civil rights org.
6 Madame Bovary
10 Choice on "Let's Make a Deal"
14 Come to pass
15 Castle defense
16 Henry VIII's second or fourth
17 1954 movie starring 25- and 44-Across
20 Storm center
21 Kelly's possum
22 "I swear!"
23 Worth a C
24 Half of a sawbuck
25 Half of a famous comic duo
29 Tibetan priest
33 Jennifer Garner spy series
34 Bachelor's last words?
35 Rah-rah
36 Some auction bids
37 Arsonist, e.g.
39 Grin from ear to ear
40 Blunted blade
41 William Halsey, e.g.: Abbr.
42 Marilyn Monroe's real first name
43 Virgin Is., e.g.
44 Half of a famous comic duo
47 Sheepcote
48 Beanery sign
49 Source of mohair
53 Diner handout

54 ___ alai
57 1956 movie starring 25- and 44-Across
60 Kind of page
61 Skin soother
62 It comes from the heart
63 Desires
64 A bit less than a meter
65 Steadfast

DOWN

1 Musical mark
2 "___ Breaky Heart" (1992 hit)
3 Farm measure
4 Pool tool
5 Takes care of charges ahead of time
6 Political refugee
7 Like early LP's
8 Periodical, for short
9 Kansas town famous in railroad history
10 Mend, in a way
11 Story starter
12 Burden of proof
13 Musical mark
18 Muddy up
19 Charged particle
23 "George of the Jungle" star Brendan
24 Generic pooch
25 A singing Jackson
26 Run off to wed
27 Bill tack-on
28 One of the Flintstones

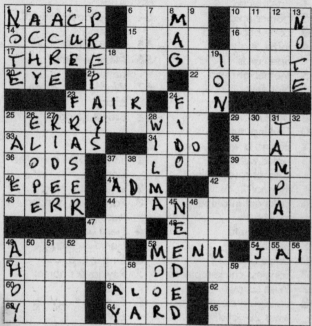

29 Hercules had 12
30 Turn away
31 Orange Bowl city
32 Jingle writer
37 Backward-moving basketball shot
38 Delightful place
42 Musical mark
45 Had to have
46 __-war bird
47 Act the snoop
49 "Hey, sailor!"
50 "Uh-uh"
51 Campbell of country
52 GM line, once
53 Othello was one
54 Trial group
55 "The Thin Man" dog
56 Emphatic type: Abbr.
58 Plug or pay ender
59 Ghost's cry

ACROSS

1 Spellbound
5 Homer epic
10 Early baby word
14 Ibiza, e.g., to Spaniards
15 Mother-of-pearl
16 Not new
17 Extended family
18 Unique
20 Chilling out
22 Behind a wrecker, say
23 Actor with the catchphrase "I pity the fool!"
24 Picks out in a lineup, for short
27 In-flight info
28 Eight: Prefix
32 Uncle of old TV
34 Boneless chicken pieces
37 Wise — owl
38 Satisfying close . . . or what 20- and 55-Across have in common?
41 Gazillions
42 Port of southern Italy
43 Some French Impressionist paintings
46 Nothin'
47 Life story
50 "Indeed!"
51 Notes after dos
53 Moves like a dragonfly
55 Not going anywhere
59 1950's–60's adolescent
62 Same, in Somme
63 Augury
64 "Breakdown ahead" warning
65 "Good shot!"
66 Metal in some batteries
67 Wards (off), as an attack
68 Brown quickly

DOWN

1 1980's–90's hitmaker Lionel
2 Leaning
3 Farms with banana trees
4 Fiery ballroom dance
5 Home — (near)
6 Singer k. d. —
7 Reykjavik's home: Abbr.
8 Forster's "— With a View"
9 Bend out of shape
10 John Wayne nickname
11 "Just — suspected!"
12 TV room
13 Do sums
19 Spumante region
21 "Forget it!"
24 "Nothing to worry about . . ."
25 Corner-to-corner: Abbr.
26 Capitol V.I.P.: Abbr.
29 401, to Nero
30 Change for a twenty

Puzzle 31 by Elizabeth C. Gorski

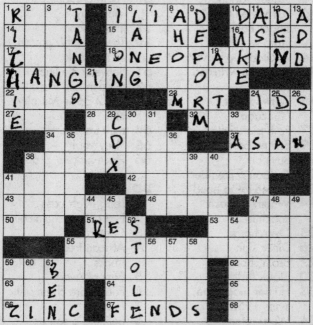

31 Radio City Music Hall fixture
33 Reclined
35 Suffix with Rock
36 Actress Ward
38 Polar bear's transport?
39 Actor Beatty
40 Alternative to a volunteer army
41 "Little Women" woman
44 Chicago paper, for short, with "the"
45 Trigger

48 Cornell's home
49 Horse farm hand
52 "Lifted"
54 They may be placed on a house
55 In __ (coordinated)
56 Classic supermodel
57 Dweeb
58 Some coll. tests
59 Dickens's pen name
60 French friend
61 London's Big __

ACROSS

1 Lettuce variety
5 "La Vie en Rose" singer Edith
9 From way back
14 Available to serve
15 Fruit with wrinkled skin
16 Zellweger of "Chicago"
17 Fruit plate item
19 Saltine brand
20 Buys off
21 Jackson 5 member
23 Coffee-to-go need
24 Whom a coach coaches
25 Overcharge
26 Diner sign
27 Broth shortcut
30 States further
33 Humor magazine since 1952
34 Word reference pioneer
35 —-Magnon
36 Spike Lee's "Summer of __"
37 Mom-and-pop grp.
39 Medical plan, for short
40 Transcribers' goofs
42 Battery size
43 British gun
44 Ben & Jerry's offering
48 Blow off steam
49 Fitzgerald forte
50 Snigglers' prey
53 Roth __
54 Saxophonist Stan
55 Fix in a cobbler's shop, say
57 Impression
59 Theme of this puzzle, so to speak
61 Between the lines
62 Golden rule word
63 2002 Eddie Murphy film
64 Inuit transports
65 "Hey you!"
66 Place-kickers' props

DOWN

1 Long, high pass
2 Not active, chemically
3 Contradict
4 African trees with thick trunks
5 Bars of Avon
6 Food store chain inits.
7 In sum
8 Befitting a son or daughter
9 Petite pasta
10 Contingency —
11 Blitz
12 1960 Everly Brothers hit
13 Determined to have
18 Verne's reclusive captain
22 Ali vs. Liston outcome, 1964
25 Thailand, once
26 Prefix with management

Puzzle 32 by Harvey Estes

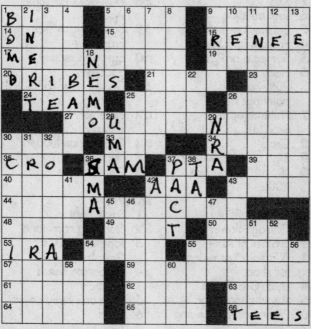

28 Thurman of "Pulp Fiction"
29 Gun rights org.
30 They've got issues
31 Corn flakes or raisin bran
32 Atone
36 Ukr. or Lith., once
37 Treaty
38 Lao-tzu's "__ Te Ching"
41 Columbus Day mo.
42 Hippolyta's warriors

43 Deems it appropriate (to)
45 Language suffix
46 Goes haywire
47 Cry out for
51 Freewheeling
52 Ski run
54 Comes down with
55 Urban disturbance
56 Häagen-Dazs alternative
58 Half brother of Tom Sawyer
60 Capt.'s inferiors

ACROSS

1 Kiss
6 Tool building
10 Butcher's or bakery
14 Process in a blender
15 Sampras or Rose
16 Place to see 20th-century paintings in N.Y.
17 Philanthropist Brooke —
18 Grad
19 Sign on a store door
20 "Royal" action film, 2002
23 "— Haw"
24 Yo-yo or Slinky
25 Corsage flower
29 Brother of Abel
31 "Camelot" president, for short
34 U. S. Grant's foe
35 Angel's headgear
36 Prefix with commuting
37 "Royal" Bogart/Hepburn film, 1951
40 Knife handle
41 Grades 1–12, for short
42 Let loose, as pigs
43 No longer used: Abbr.
44 Over hill and —
45 Like bread dough
46 Brief instant
47 Hurry
48 "Royal" film based on a classic children's story, 1974

57 Maui dance
58 Nest eggs for seniors: Abbr.
59 Bottled water from France
60 Egyptian fertility goddess
61 On-the-hour radio offering
62 Extremely successful, slangily
63 Old Iranian leader
64 Heredity carrier
65 Deuce takers

DOWN

1 Small fight
2 Sled dog command
3 Johnson of TV's "Laugh-In"
4 Corporate heads, for short
5 Woman's head cover
6 Extra
7 Aid
8 Needle case
9 Drop from major to captain, say
10 Great — Mountains National Park
11 Pueblo Indian
12 Augury
13 Sharp pain, as from hunger
21 Multivolume ref.
22 Oui's opposite
25 Right: Prefix
26 Addict's program, in short

Puzzle 33 by Andrea Carla Michaels

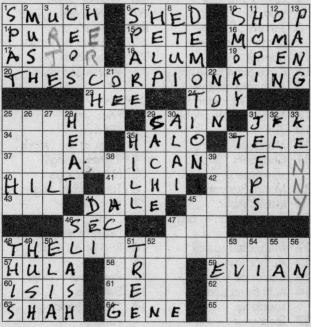

S	M	U	C	H		S	H	E	D		S	H	O	P
P	U	R	E	E		P	E	T	E		M	O	M	A
A	S	T	O	R		A	L	U	M		O	P	E	N
T	H	E	S	C	O	R	P	I	O	N	K	I	N	G
			H	E	E			T	O	Y				
			H		G	A	I	N			J	F	K	
			E		H	A	L	O		T	E	L	E	
			A		I	C	A	N		E			N	
H	I	L	T		L	H	I			P			N	
			D	A	L	E			S				Y	
		S	E	C										
T	H	E	L	I		T	R	E						
H	U	L	A			R		E	V	I	A	N		
I	S	I	S		E									
S	H	A	H		G	E	N	E						

27 Heads of staffs?
28 Furnace output
29 Hidden stash
30 Jai __
31 Army vehicles
32 Navy unit
33 Singer Rogers
35 San Francisco's Nob __
36 Sandwich fish
38 Responding (to)
39 Most odd
44 Agnus __
45 Puppy sound
46 /
47 "Steppenwolf" author
48 1950's TV's "__ Is Your Life"
49 Silence
50 Director Kazan
51 Elm or oak
52 Place for an Easter egg hunt
53 Songwriter Novello
54 Kindly
55 Like dry mud
56 Genesis grandson

ACROSS

1 Letters that lack stamps
6 Johnny —, "Key Largo" gangster
11 Bar bill
14 Circulation mainstay
15 Acquired relative
16 Yale Bowl rooter
17 Mistreated vegetable?
19 Zip
20 Make well
21 Choppers, so to speak
22 Mount Rushmore locale: Abbr.
23 Summer Games org.
25 Cupcake brand
27 Mistreated spice?
32 Author Rand
33 Castor or Pollux
34 A to E, musically speaking
37 Start over
39 Three, in a saying
42 Writer Ephron
43 Intimidate, with "out"
45 "Cold one"
47 Arles assent
48 Mistreated spread?
52 Wrinkly-skinned dog
54 In the past
55 Leprechaun's land
56 Select group
59 Words of woe
63 Speed limit abbr.
64 Mistreated meat?
66 Wall St. debut
67 Have a feeling
68 Jeweler's unit
69 Impresario Hurok
70 Coin words
71 Worshiped ones

DOWN

1 Price word
2 "Encore!"
3 Neck of the woods
4 Right-leaning?
5 Hasty escape
6 Tilt-A-Whirl, e.g.
7 Story starter
8 Dress
9 Drive-in server
10 Part of B.Y.O.B.
11 Greenhorn
12 Rap sheet handle
13 Swindles
18 "Yada, yada, yada . . ."
22 45-Across holder
24 Gives the go-ahead
26 Tanning lotion letters
27 Be a kvetch
28 Some whiskeys
29 Pop art icon
30 Patriotic women's org.
31 Space explorer
35 In alignment
36 Salon sweepings
38 Earthy pigment
40 Tie the knot

Puzzle 34 by Steven Kahn

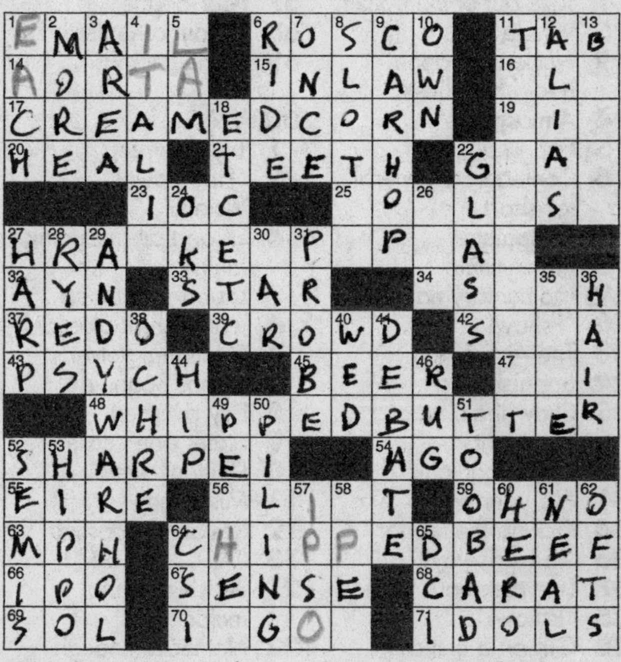

41 Discuss pros and cons
44 In fashion
46 Toupee, slangily
49 Bird with a showy mate
50 Pier's support
51 "What a shame"
52 They're weighed at weigh stations
53 Zoo heavyweight
57 — facto
58 Made tracks
60 Sizable sandwich
61 "Square" thing
62 New newts
64 Popular CBS drama
65 601, in old Rome

ACROSS

1 Take out of the freezer
5 Whole lot
9 Nuclear weapon, in old headlines
14 Atmosphere
15 Fish in a salad
16 Confederate general, for short
17 Customer
18 Battery fluid
19 Momentary flash
20 "Pshaw!"
23 The Amish, e.g.
24 Spanish king
25 Show the effects of weight
28 Coffee container
31 "__ your age!"
34 Pick up the tab for
36 "In what way?"
37 Like rush hour traffic
38 "Pshaw!"
42 Gift on a first date, maybe
43 Can metal
44 Pilot light
45 She sheep
46 Kitchen set
49 End a fast
50 Cul-de-__
51 Warlike god
53 "Pshaw!"
61 Knock for __
62 Sen. Bayh of Indiana
63 Lumber source
64 Wait on
65 Blend

66 Composer Stravinsky
67 Four-bagger
68 Whom a hunter hunts
69 Verne captain

DOWN

1 Tightly strung
2 "Pipe down!"
3 Vicinity
4 __ and all (including faults)
5 Laundry stiffener
6 Transparent plastic
7 "National Velvet" author Bagnold
8 Dry riverbed
9 States one's case
10 "Button" site
11 Miscellany
12 Restaurant posting
13 "All __ are off!"
21 Bench-clearing incident
22 Not leave enough room
25 Blank look
26 Cupid's projectile
27 Silly ones
29 German wine valley
30 Fashionable, in the 60's
31 Pond buildup
32 Pause indicator
33 Sound from a nest
35 Favorable vote
37 Weekend TV show, for short
39 City east of Syracuse

Puzzle 35 by Gregory E. Paul

40 Family
41 #1 Beatles hit "— Fine"
46 Certain piano pedal
47 Tex-Mex treat
48 Hip
50 Hotpoint appliance
52 Fine blouse material
53 Salt amount
54 Butter alternative
55 Typical amount
56 Dole's running mate, 1996
57 At any time
58 Press upon
59 Subj. with circles and such
60 Person with a medal, maybe

ACROSS

1 Window base
5 One-tenth: Prefix
9 Within reach
14 Operatic solo
15 Dash
16 Children's song refrain
17 Al Capp parody of Dick Tracy
20 Octad plus one
21 Princely initials
22 On the sheltered side
23 Examines a passage
24 A prospector may stake one
26 Midwest hub
28 B westerns
33 Repair tears
36 MasterCard rival
38 Salman Rushdie's birthplace
39 User of air abrasion to clean teeth
43 Bewildered
44 Exam taken in H.S.
45 Pipe joint
46 African bloodsucker
48 It's given to a waiter
51 Breathing room
53 Reggae fan, often
57 Play divisions
61 Actor Wallach
62 Shoe part
63 Muscleman's garment
66 "Careless Hands" singer Mel
67 List-ending abbr.
68 Otherwise
69 Fess up
70 Wall St. trading center
71 Prognosticator

DOWN

1 Equipped with air bags, say
2 Castle of dance
3 Tropical vine
4 "The Streets of —" (cowboy song)
5 Exploit
6 Golfer Ernie
7 What credit cards may bring about, eventually
8 Prefix with structure
9 "For — a jolly . . ."
10 Verdi opera
11 Filmmaker Jordan
12 They show their faces in casinos
13 Oxen's harness
18 Whip
19 The Buckeye State
24 Like new dollar bills
25 Common street name
27 — Maria
29 Big blast maker
30 Make changes to
31 Soufflés do it
32 Glut
33 Squabble
34 Food, slangily
35 Sage

Puzzle 36 by Ed Early

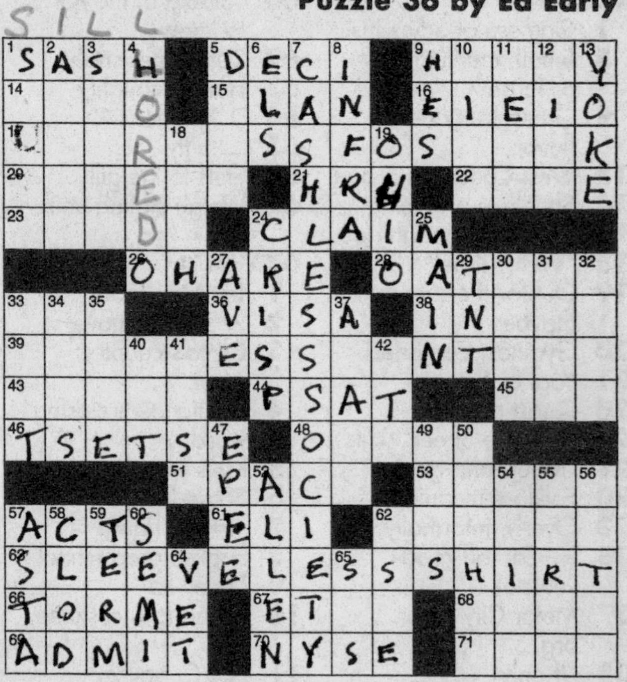

37 How a prank may be done, after "on"
40 Mosquito protection
41 Edinburgh girl
42 J.F.K. approximation
47 Sporting blade
49 Shore birds
50 Diaper wearers' woes
52 __ wrench
54 Subway station device
55 To the point
56 More inclined
57 "The Thin Man" dog
58 Lump of dirt
59 Contract stipulation
60 Big rig
62 Castaway's home
64 One who looks Rover over
65 Swedish carrier

ACROSS

1 Games nobody wins
5 Small, medium or large
9 Green fruit drink flavor
13 West Coast gas brand
14 Shoelace problem
15 Get — a good thing
16 "Well, I'll be!"
19 Out for the evening, maybe
20 Gymnast Comaneci
21 Yogi or Smokey
23 Quart divs.
24 "Sesame Street" skills
28 Get-up-and-go
30 Folklore meanie
33 Overly, informally
35 —-Cat (off-road vehicle)
37 Motor City labor org.
38 "If only . . ."
41 Late columnist Landers
42 Broadway hit letters
43 Cat that catches rodents
44 No longer on active duty: Abbr.
46 "Dumb" girl of old comics
48 Fourposters, e.g.
49 Got together
51 007
53 Photo tint
55 Port in "The Marines' Hymn"
60 "Stupid of me not to know"
62 Defeat decisively
63 Handle roughly
64 — gin fizz
65 —-bitty
66 Stuff to the gills
67 Weigh station units

DOWN

1 Tex-Mex snack
2 Wrinkle remover
3 Quito's country: Abbr.
4 Auctioneer's closing word
5 Kid's wheels
6 Scared (of)
7 Animal house
8 English prep school
9 Deceived
10 Wearing a costume, say
11 N.Y.C. gallery
12 U-turn from WSW
17 Apply gently
18 Napkin's place
22 Greet the day
24 Battling
25 Daniel with a coonskin cap
26 "I don't want any part of it"
27 Cardinals' team letters
29 Dictatorship
31 Thumped fast, as the heart
32 Decorative jugs

Puzzle 37 by N. Salomon and H. Estes

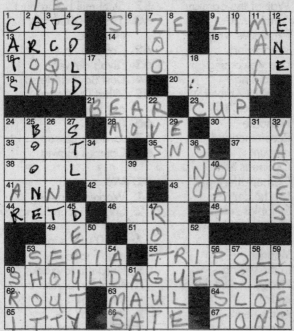

34 Takes too much, briefly
36 Lennon's lady
39 Doofus
40 Kernel
45 Sheriff's sidekick
47 Cheap booze
50 Up to, informally
52 Fizzle out
53 Flu season protection
54 U.S.N. bigwigs
56 "Check this out!"
57 Norway's capital
58 "Exodus" author Uris
59 Fateful March day
60 — Lanka
61 Battery size

ACROSS

1 Was of the opinion
5 "Shake —!"
9 Expensive wraps
13 Woodwind
14 Less welcoming
15 Straddling
16 Novelist Ambler
17 1970's–80's TV twosome
19 Recommended amount
20 Overseas Mrs.
21 Gerber offerings
22 Log holder
24 Syllables sung in place of unknown words
25 Winner
27 In the wrong
32 Pledge of Allegiance ender
33 Actor Bean
35 Androcles, e.g.
36 Fill the chambers, say
38 Arab League member
40 Put in storage
41 Company in 2002 headlines
43 Countrified
45 Barely maintain, with "out"
46 Mimics' work
48 Frequent ferry rider
50 "Kidnapped" author's inits.
51 Composer Boulanger
52 Black mark
56 Signal at Sotheby's
57 Steel mill by-product
60 1990's–2000's TV twosome
62 Coveted prize
63 Diva's delivery
64 Dust Bowl drifters
65 What Dubliners call home
66 Poverty
67 Jordan's Queen —
68 Campus bigwig

DOWN

1 Worked in rows
2 Spain's second-longest river
3 1990's TV twosome
4 Iago's specialty
5 Hard nut to crack?
6 Money replaced by the euro
7 Rat alert?
8 Dads of dads
9 Evenhanded
10 Magazine of reprints
11 Took a cab
12 1974 Sutherland/Gould film
14 #1 hit for Brenda Lee
18 Imperatives
23 Outback hopper
24 — notes
25 Jacket holder
26 Massey of old movies
27 Personification of mockery

Puzzle 38 by D. J. DeChristopher

28 Oerter and Unser
29 1980's TV twosome
30 Elicit
31 Having a higher model number, say
34 Feudal laborers
37 John —
39 Water nymphs
42 Silent film star Mabel
44 It was dropped in the 60's
47 Wine holder
49 Didn't speak clearly
51 More polite

52 E. B. White's "The Trumpet of the —"
53 Goodyear product
54 Tennis great Nastase
55 Delighted
56 Scott of "Happy Days"
58 A celebrity may have one
59 Feds
61 "King Kong" studio

ACROSS

1 Gladiators' locale
6 Eskimo's vehicle
10 Office message
14 Snouted animal
15 "— Get a Witness" (Marvin Gaye hit)
16 Sandler of "Big Daddy"
17 In reserve
18 Dashiell Hammett dog
19 Andes capital
20 Best available
23 —-mo
24 Campaign (for)
25 Philosopher —-tzu
28 Music, ballet, sculpture, etc.
31 Liquid part of blood
36 Shade trees
38 Trot or canter
40 Not for the first time
41 Quick, easy motion
44 Old silo missile
45 Pond duck
46 Countertenor's counterpart
47 Lackey
49 Men-only affair
51 Thesaurus listing: Abbr.
52 Whisper sweet nothings
54 Toy with a string
56 Where punches are hardest
65 Opera set in ancient Egypt
66 Greek promenade
67 Word before circle or tube
68 "Roger, — and out"
69 Hosp. printouts
70 Gawk (at)
71 County center
72 Attention-getting sound
73 More than dislikes

DOWN

1 Above
2 Punjabi princess
3 "Ben-Hur," for one
4 Shaving mishaps
5 Space on a leaf
6 "Begone!"
7 Eyelid attachment
8 Computer key
9 Telephone
10 Drink with a foamy head
11 Work for Hearst, e.g.
12 Hit musical with the song "Bosom Buddies"
13 Gen. Bradley
21 Do without
22 Acquired relative
25 Southpaw
26 "Kate & —"
27 Leaves out
29 Roly-poly president
30 Locations
32 Home of the Taj Mahal

33 Explores the seven seas

34 Like some eyes at a wedding

35 Playwright Chekhov

37 Pyramid scheme, e.g.

39 "— does it!"

42 Special skill

43 Tickle pink

48 Hangmen's ropes

50 Cry in a kids' card game

53 A lot

55 Ship of Columbus

56 New Mexico town on the Santa Fe Trail

57 Busy place

58 Brainstorm

59 Golfing vehicle

60 Robe for Caesar

61 Trunk fastener

62 Picnic pest

63 "From — to Eternity"

64 Uno y dos

ACROSS

1 Use a swizzle stick
5 Sarcophagus
9 Skater Henie
14 Humanitarian org.
15 Track shape
16 Goodbye to José
17 Birthstone for many Libras
18 Personal staff member
19 Massaged places
20 Super
23 Ally
24 Versailles habitant
25 Married madrileña: Abbr.
28 Natural hairstyle
31 Disney's dwarfs, e.g.
33 Thick slice
37 Score of 100-0, say
39 Letter from a teacher
40 Treat with chips
43 Five-note refrain
44 Start of Caesar's last gasp
45 "Witness" director Peter
46 Doesn't contain one's anger
48 "Note to ___ . . ."
50 Stroke
51 Part of WWW
53 West of Nashville
58 Condition of utmost perfection
61 Capital near Casablanca
64 Cupid's Greek counterpart
65 Qatari leader
66 Dumbfound
67 Big name in auto parts
68 Sport in which players wear masks
69 "Unsafe at Any Speed" author
70 No short story
71 Orderly

DOWN

1 Jeer
2 Piglike animal
3 Farsi speaker
4 Confederate signature
5 How pendulums swing
6 "Metamorphoses" author
7 Volunteer org. launched in 1980
8 Cloudiness
9 Lindbergh Field site
10 Jazz singer Anita
11 Small bite
12 Friday on TV
13 Simpleton
21 Santa ___, Calif.
22 Classical Japanese drama
25 Investment
26 Diameter halves
27 "Doe, ___ . . ."
29 Lecher
30 Removes from power

Puzzle 40 by Adam Cohen

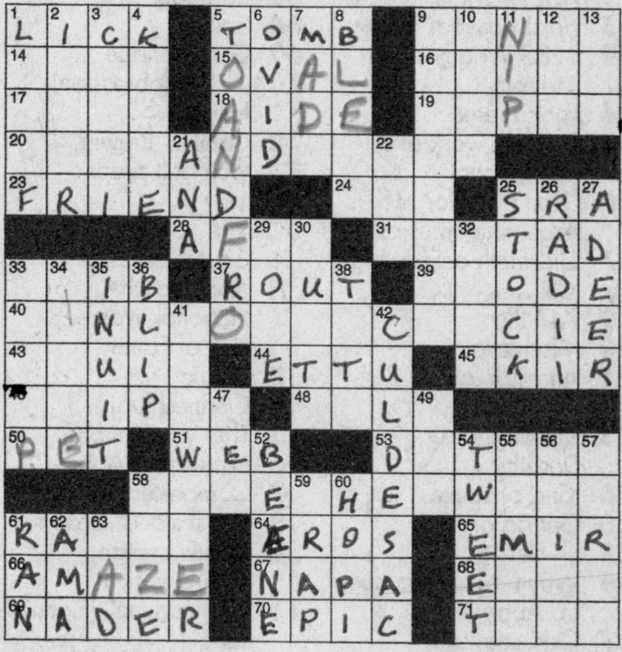

32 Ship's front
33 Exorbitant
34 Longest river in France
35 Alaskan native
36 Spot on the radar
38 Head in a guillotine?
41 Big trouble
42 Dead-end street
47 Sun. delivery
49 Combatant
52 Geoffrey of fashion
54 Birdcage sound
55 Adagio and allegro
56 "But you promised!" retort
57 Tito Puente's nickname
58 Discomfit
59 Duffer's obstacle
60 Arizona tribe
61 Oversaw
62 Famous jour. publisher
63 One-star

ACROSS

1 Help in crime
5 Hard baseball throws
9 1983 Woody Allen title role
14 Foot: Prefix
15 Do desk work at a newspaper
16 "Don't Cry for Me, Argentina" musical
17 Old math calculating tool
19 747 flier
20 Mischievous
21 Attention-getter in an ad
23 Mystery writer Dorothy
25 Kind of sauce
26 Get rid of
29 __ clef
34 When a plane is due in: Abbr.
37 Odd souvenir
39 Defect
40 Baseball . . . with a hint to this puzzle's theme
44 Mishmash
45 African-American
46 Duffer's goal
47 Blind dates, e.g.
50 Hibernation
52 Locale for Switz. or the U.K.
54 Creek
58 Top 40 song list
64 Welsh dog
65 Early computer
66 Barn tool
68 Sassy
69 Get __ shape
70 __ fixe (obsession)
71 Irritable
72 Campus bigwig
73 Golf ball props

DOWN

1 Church recesses
2 Abzug of the National Women's Hall of Fame
3 Instruct
4 Cleaned (up)
5 The "p" in m.p.g.
6 Instruction: Abbr.
7 __ monster
8 "Let it stand" orders
9 Gentle breeze
10 Devil's work
11 "__ Marlene" (classic song)
12 "Try __ for size"
13 Garden entrance
18 Physicist Fermi
22 Place for a nap
24 Shock
27 Ill-tempered one
28 Rome has seven
30 Eastern newt
31 Radar image
32 Buddhist monk
33 Pitcher, but not the diamond kind
34 1940's–50's All-Star __ Slaughter

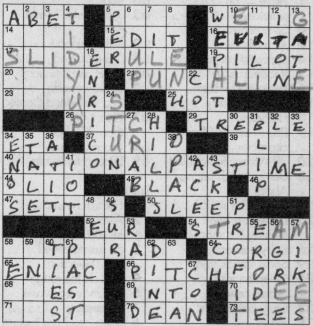

35 Narrative
36 Going — tooth and nail
38 Milky gem
41 Paper in lieu of payment
42 They're worth 1 or 11 in blackjack
43 Outline
48 "Splendid!"
49 Big —, Calif.
51 Business motive
53 Swift
55 Eat away at
56 Be in accord
57 Studio sound equipment
58 Weight
59 Concerning, to a memo writer
60 Neckwear
61 History, with "the"
62 Eat fancily
63 Kett of old comics
67 Jailbird

ACROSS

1 Have __ on one's shoulder
6 Sumptuous
10 At a distance
14 Sprocket projections
15 Ready to eat
16 Dear, to Donizetti
17 Muse of poetry
18 Hipbones
19 Red "Sesame Street" character
20 39-Across component
23 Denver clock setting: Abbr.
24 Suffix with social
25 Drive-thru bank feature, for short
26 Baby carrier?
29 Some beach toys
31 Question for a brown cow?
33 Early baby word
36 Place
38 Two-time U.S. Open winner Fraser
39 Way to fitness
42 Reluctant
43 Shorebird
44 Radiation measures
45 In the unique case that
47 Common mistakes, say
49 Concorde
50 Form of ID: Abbr.
52 Wish undone
53 Flapper accessory
56 39-Across component
60 Iota
62 1997 Peter Fonda role
63 Milk: Prefix
64 "And __ bed"
65 Baseballers Guidry and Swoboda
66 Old-fashioned theater
67 Name of more than 20 popes
68 Scared sounds
69 Diaper, in Britain

DOWN

1 Special Forces unit
2 Asteroid first sighted in 1801
3 It's strengthened by 20-Across
4 "Tell __ the judge"
5 You may have one for spiders
6 Sales brochure feature
7 Perfume ingredients
8 Star in Virgo
9 It can be improved by 39-Across
10 Air force heroes
11 Alias
12 Offshoot
13 Milne marsupial
21 Formal reply to "Who's there?"
22 Surrounded by
27 Automaton
28 Actress Verdon and others

Puzzle 42 by Karen M. Tracey

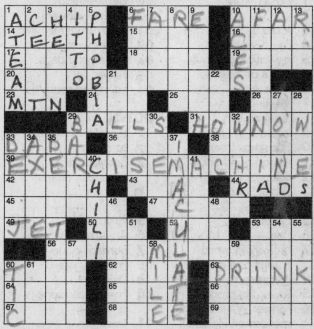

29 Socialists, e.g.
30 Knight's need
32 River dams
33 Site of an oracle of Apollo
34 Certain transmitters
35 Took care of
37 Perfect
40 Texas cook-off dish
41 Boredom
46 It can be improved by 39-Across
48 Pan films?

51 Ravel's "Daphnis et —"
53 It's strengthened by 56-Across
54 Leading
55 Intense suffering
57 Harrow rival
58 Lengthy footrace
59 "And here it is!"
60 Dow Jones paper, for short
61 —-ha

ACROSS

1 Plaster work
7 Icy
11 Jacuzzi
14 Pay a visit to
15 Hawaiian cookout
16 What an assessor assesses
17 Meeting all requirements
19 Inventor Whitney
20 Christmas trees
21 Ahead of schedule
22 Backs of the thighs
23 Subject of an S.E.C. inquiry
25 Go out with
26 Heel
27 Unlikely Planned Parenthood member
32 Precedes
35 Lower the grade of
36 Former White House spokesman Fleischer
37 "__ only me"
38 Pay-__-view
39 Mrs., in Madrid
40 Babe
42 Monastery or convent
44 Not planned
46 Aussie hopper
47 Bit of sunshine
48 Expensive fur
52 Computer in-box annoyance
54 Prison-related
56 Café au __

57 Santa's subordinate
58 Unpretentious
60 Whistle-blower?
61 Away from the wind
62 Cantankerous
63 Undergrad degs.
64 Holler
65 Far-flying seabird

DOWN

1 Leave a mark on, as shoes
2 Snouted Latin American animal
3 Ne plus __
4 Finality
5 Firms: Abbr.
6 A while back
7 Bordeaux and others
8 Factory store
9 Delicate
10 Forehead-slapper's cry
11 Loyal
12 Body part that's sometimes "greased"
13 Line of symmetry
18 Spates
22 Barber's focus
24 Investigate
26 White-collar workers?
28 Annoyed, eventually
29 Cinema house name
30 Raison d'__
31 Derrière
32 Go bankrupt

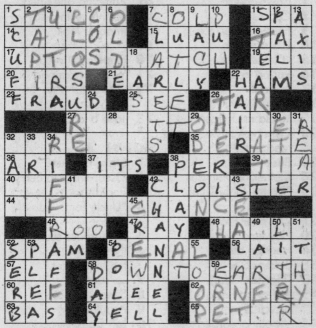

33 19th-century writer Sarah — Jewett
34 Disreputable groups
38 Dabble in
41 Speck
42 TV selection
43 Leak stopper
45 Embroidery yarn
49 Less decorated
50 Petrol measure
51 Antiknock compound
52 Belgrade native
53 Not guilty by reason of insanity, e.g.

54 Vaulter's tool
55 Orbit
58 Calendar unit
59 Prior to, to Prior

ACROSS

1 Cows and sows
5 Coarse file
9 Four-alarmer, e.g.
14 Lt.'s superior
15 "Dies —"
16 Raring to go
17 To boot
18 Muses count
19 Wield, as influence
20 Get angry, as a mechanic?
23 Buck's mate
24 Mother of Dionysus
25 "Do the Right Thing" pizzeria
27 City near Provo
30 Play time
34 Houston athlete
38 Bakery buy
40 "Garfield" dog
41 Get angry, as a bicyclist?
44 Wholly absorbed
45 Like hen's teeth
46 Jennifer of "Flashdance"
47 "The Lion in Winter" star
49 Actress Lanchester
51 Make over
53 When mastodons disappeared
58 Grp. with students' interests at heart
61 Get angry, as a missile designer?
64 Arrival at a refinery
66 Estrada of "CHiPs"
67 Bumping one's head on the ceiling, say
68 Impolite look
69 A few
70 First name in scat
71 Yankees manager Joe
72 50's British P.M. Anthony
73 Take a load off

DOWN

1 Strike breakers
2 Oscar-winning Berry
3 English racing town
4 "Uncle Tom's Cabin" author
5 Horseshoes score
6 It might hit the high notes
7 — souci
8 Sneaks a look
9 Popular VW
10 Left Coast airport letters
11 Old
12 Round number?
13 Old Harper's Bazaar artist
21 Distant
22 You're on it
26 Serving with tea
28 Suffix with oper-
29 Olympic skier Phil
31 Early Icelandic literature
32 Place to dust
33 Matches, as a wager

Puzzle 44 by Richard Hughes

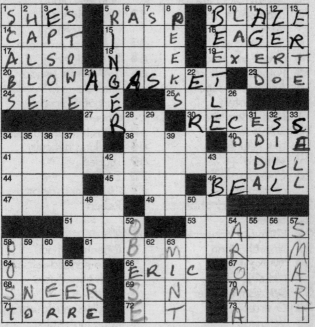

34	Big do
35	Bed support
36	Keyboard slip
37	Turbine part
39	Walk like a sot
42	A Corleone son
43	Old adders
48	4-Down's Simon
50	Smooth and soft
52	Beyond pudgy
54	Fragrant substance
55	Dickens title opener
56	Breathers?
57	Brilliance

58	Drop in the mail
59	Former Yugoslav leader
60	Winged
62	Noted A.L. third baseman, for short
63	Drink garnish
65	Blow it

ACROSS

1 "Moby-Dick" captain
5 Excellent, in modern slang
9 Speedy
14 Greek sandwich
15 Poland's Walesa
16 Actress Verdugo
17 1998 Sarah McLachlan hit
18 Bullets, e.g.
19 Like lettuce or spinach
20 Considerable sum of money
23 Trigonometry abbr.
24 Soften
25 Barnyard honker
27 Apprehension
30 "Make it __!" ("Hurry!")
33 Dadaism founder
36 Overrun
38 Venus de __
39 Get schooling
41 "__ Fine Day" (1963 Chiffons hit)
42 Satisfy a debt
43 Just twiddling the thumbs
44 Recorded
46 Musician Brian
47 Red addition to a salad
49 Bring out
51 L'Enfant __, in Washington, D.C.
53 Knights' weapons

57 Gift offered with an "aloha"
59 Useful tip for puzzle-solving?
62 Variety of primrose
64 Struggle for air
65 1997 Peter Fonda title role
66 Part of a bicycle wheel
67 __ fruit (large tangelo)
68 Walking difficulty
69 Lugged
70 Espied
71 "Airplane!" actor Robert

DOWN

1 Open-mouthed
2 Nine-headed serpent
3 Sign after Pisces
4 Sailed
5 Toddlers' enclosure
6 Rope material
7 Pinnacle
8 Revealing beachwear
9 Use for support
10 Ginger __
11 Something smoked at an Indian ceremony
12 Data
13 Word with "Happy" and "Death Valley" in old TV titles
21 Shroud of __
22 Winning margin, sometimes
26 Identical

Puzzle 45 by Barry Silk

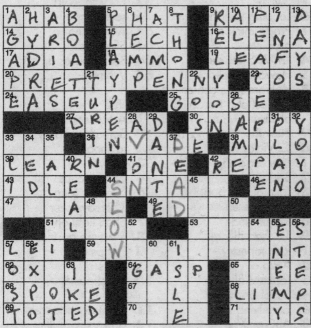

A¹	H²	A³	B⁴		P⁵	H⁶	A⁷	T⁸		R⁹	A¹⁰	P¹¹	I¹²	D¹³
G¹⁴	Y	R	O		L¹⁵	E	C	H		E¹⁶	L	E	N	A
A¹⁷	D	I	A		A¹⁸	M	M	O		L¹⁹	E	A	F	Y
P²⁰	R	E	T	T	Y²¹	P	E	N	N²²	Y		C²³	O	S
E²⁴	A	S	E	U	P			G²⁵	O	O	S²⁶	E		
			D²⁷	R	E	A²⁸	D²⁹		S³⁰	N	A	P	P³¹	Y³²
³³	³⁴	³⁵	I³⁶	N	V	A	D	E³⁷		M³⁸	I	L	O	
L³⁹	E	A	R⁴⁰	N		O⁴¹	N	E	R⁴²	E	P	A	Y	
I⁴³	D	L	E		S⁴⁴	N	T	A⁴⁵		E⁴⁶	N	O		
⁴⁷			A	⁴⁸	L		E⁴⁹	D	⁵⁰					
		⁵¹	L		O⁵²				⁵³			⁵⁴	E⁵⁵	S⁵⁶
L⁵⁷	E⁵⁸	I		⁵⁹	W		⁶⁰	I⁶¹					N	T
O⁶²	X	I⁶³				G⁶⁴	A	S	P	⁶⁵			E	E
S⁶⁶	P	O	K	E	⁶⁷			L		L⁶⁸	I	M	P	
T⁶⁹	O	T	E	D		⁷⁰		E		⁷¹			Y	S

28 English river
29 "Inferno" writer
31 Blueprint
32 Toy that does tricks
33 Touched down
34 Make over
35 Handheld computing device
37 Wanted-poster option
40 Honest-to-goodness
42 Summary
44 Move like molasses
45 Gun part
48 Bugged

50 "Stop right there!"
52 Cattle breed
54 Paramecium propellers
55 Foe
56 Dance components
57 Needing directions, say
58 Montreal ballplayer, once
60 Parrot's spot
61 __ of Man
63 1950's White House nickname

ACROSS

1 Swiftly
6 Leading the pack
11 Programming problem
14 "M*A*S*H" clerk
15 Hawaiian hello
16 William Tell's canton
17 Subject of a parable of Jesus
19 New IBM hire, maybe
20 __ Victor
21 Play for a sap
22 Bridge
23 Take off the books
26 Squandered
28 Major work
29 "__ had it!"
31 Rich tapestry
32 A sib
33 Tankard filler
34 Set of principles
36 Conniving sort
38 ABC or XYZ
41 Serving on a spit
42 Bar bill
43 Comedian Olsen
44 Greet the day
46 Run smoothly
47 Level on the evolutionary ladder
48 Produce, as heat
51 Villain's epithet
53 Nile cobras
54 Long-jawed fish
55 Black cuckoo
56 Two liters, e.g.: Abbr.
57 Lewis Carroll poem
62 Big time
63 Encyclopedia section
64 Actor Milo
65 Sloppy digs
66 Barn dances
67 Whinny

DOWN

1 Artist Jean
2 Something to try to shoot
3 Fuss
4 Core groups
5 Novelist Jong
6 J.F.K. overseer
7 Shed light on
8 Martini's partner
9 Pumps and clogs
10 Beachgoer's goal
11 Farm abundances
12 University of Illinois locale
13 Mel Ott's team
18 Telescope pioneer
22 Bit of mistletoe
23 Katharine of "The Graduate"
24 DeMille production, e.g.
25 "Boris Godunov," for one
27 Sir, in old India
30 "Make" or "break"
33 Honey-colored
34 Ides rebuke

Puzzle 46 by Ed Early

35 Mine transport
37 Lets up
39 Away from the wind
40 Leathernecks' lunch
44 Century plants
45 Vacation spot
46 Like some tea
47 Melodious
49 Playing marble
50 Put off, as a motion
52 Not achieved
57 Shake up
58 Pothook shape

59 Sorority letter
60 Fraternity party staple
61 Derisive cry

ACROSS

1 Dutch bloom
6 School session
10 Capital of Latvia
14 "I can take __!"
15 Mishmash
16 Grandson of Adam
17 His friends sat in the Peanut Gallery
20 Big Apple ballpark
21 Coup d'__
22 Caffè __
23 Calf's meat
25 Sunsweet item
26 His friends joined him under the Big Top
31 Scarlett of Tara
32 Soldier under Robt. E. Lee
33 Like molasses
37 Massachusetts' Cape __
38 Driver's need
42 Actress Gardner
43 North Pole "exports"
45 Rug rat
46 Xbox enthusiast
48 His friends visited his Neighborhood
52 Blue moon, e.g.
55 Simplicity
56 Revises, as text
57 The U.N.'s __ Annan
59 Religious offshoot
63 His friends came into his Treasure House
66 Tommie of the Miracle Mets
67 Black, as roulette numbers
68 Like a gymnast
69 One of the Ivies
70 Flower part
71 Popular skin cream

DOWN

1 Soda can features
2 "No way!"
3 Bygone picture weekly
4 On the side (of)
5 School org.
6 Flute sound
7 Isle where Napoleon was exiled
8 Unruly event
9 Group making an 8-Down
10 Stays behind
11 "Everything __ place"
12 John who was called the Dapper Don
13 Whitish
18 Wife of Jacob
19 Side dish with fried clams
24 List ender
25 Snatches a purse from, say
26 Ketch or yawl
27 "Yikes!"
28 Off-the-wall
29 Aegean vacation locale
30 Spy novelist Deighton
34 Like some excuses
35 Done with

Puzzle 47 by Leslie H. Nicoll

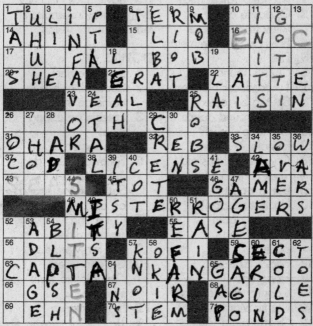

The completed crossword grid (best reading):

T	U	L	I	P		T	E	R	M		I	G		
A	H	I	N	T		L	I	O		E	N	O	C	
U		F	A	L	B	O	B		I	T				
S	H	E	A		E	R	A	T		L	A	T	T	E
		V	E	A	L			R	A	I	S	I	N	
O	T	H		C	Q									
O	H	A	R	A		R	E	B		S	L	O	W	
C	O	D		L	I	C	E	N	S	E		A	V	A
		S		T	O	T			G	A	M	E	R	
	M	I	S	T	E	R	R	O	G	E	R	S		
A	B	I	T	Y		E	A	S	E					
D	L	T	S		K	O	F	I		S	E	C	T	
C	A	P	T	A	I	N	K	A	N	G	A	R	O	O
G	S	E		N	O	I	R		A	G	I	L	E	
E	H	N		S	T	E	M		P	O	N	D	S	

36 "Star —"
39 —-bitsy
40 Camp bed
41 People with big heads have them
44 Struck by Cupid
47 Way back when
49 Midwife's words before boy or girl
50 Till again, as land
51 Shower
52 Make a long story short
53 Wise saying

54 Turn red, perhaps
57 Tight tie
58 Merle Haggard's "— From Muskogee"
60 Leprechaun land
61 Chilled
62 Little piggies
64 — and outs
65 Mountain pass

ACROSS

1 Archaeological find
5 Opposite of dry
10 View from Lucerne
14 Polygon measurement
15 Foe
16 Chick's sound
17 TV producer Norman
18 Split to be joined?
19 Jewish round dance
20 Old king's edict?
22 Female 29-Down
23 Cryptographer's aid
24 Rock concert venue
26 Like propellers
30 Hockey's Esposito
31 Take up again
32 Witty Orson's patter?
37 Facial flare-up
38 Hang back
39 Country star Jackson
40 Comic Martin's shirt?
42 "Symposium" author
43 It's banked in Bangkok
44 "You ready?"
45 Oblivious
49 Miss. neighbor
50 Silly mistake
51 Chess piece's move?
56 Administered with a spoon, say
57 Vegetation
59 Timber wolf
60 In the thick of
61 Duck that's not a duck

62 Genesis victim
63 Soviet news agency
64 Neural transmitters
65 Toy that "sleeps"

DOWN

1 Rash soother
2 Cookie that has its name on it
3 Freebie on a long flight
4 Unadorned
5 Followed, as a dog its master
6 Separate the strands of, as rope
7 Cat sound
8 Troublemaker
9 Just for Men, e.g.
10 Garden insect
11 "The Naked Truth" star Téa ___
12 Lost in France
13 Tic
21 Distort
22 "The Laughing Cavalier" artist
24 Like some cheddar
25 Minuscule
26 They have shoulder straps
27 Nobelist Walesa
28 ___ mundi
29 Animals with fawns
30 1992 also-ran
32 Wash
33 Built like Wilt

Puzzle 48 by Robert Zimmerman

34 "Unfortunately . . ."
35 Overdue
36 Shoelace problem
38 Romanov ruler
41 Skier's transport
42 Blueprint
44 Irving Berlin classic
45 The Lusitania's undoer
46 Bellini opera
47 Novelist Nin
48 Fuses by heat
49 Moses' brother
51 Somewhat, in music
52 Do in

53 Nonpaying train passenger
54 Word in old wedding vows
55 Game on horseback
57 Pharm. watchdog
58 N.Y.C. subway, with "the"

ACROSS

1. "So what — is new?"
5. Place for drawers
9. Fronts of ships
14. Ponce de —
15. Oscar winner Kazan
16. Send, as payment
17. Atlantic Coast states, with "the"
18. Coin grade higher than fine
19. African antelope
20. Hot movie of 1981?
23. Kitty starter
24. Minister: Abbr.
25. Get satisfaction for, as a wrong
28. Siren luring sailors to shipwreck
32. Mythical enchantress
33. Program
35. Bruin legend Bobby
36. Hot movie of 1974? (With "The")
40. — Lilly & Company
41. Cashews and such
42. — a million
43. Twisting, perhaps
46. 2000 Olympics city
47. Suffix with meth-
48. Draftable
49. Hot movie of 1966?
56. Permit
57. Artless one
58. Secluded valley

59. William and Harry's mother
60. Sign at the front of some bars
61. Biblical twin
62. "— Defeats Truman" (infamous 1948 headline)
63. Dame Myra
64. "Phooey!"

DOWN

1. Utility supply: Abbr.
2. Mrs. Rabin
3. Slugging Sammy
4. Beguile
5. Take down a notch
6. High society
7. Breaks a commandment
8. "The Green Hornet" role
9. Lean toward
10. Have déjà vu about
11. Bradley or Sharif
12. Champagne, e.g.
13. Basic version: Abbr.
21. Actress Stevens
22. Displeased look
25. Performed
26. String quartet member
27. Gen. Rommel
28. Lane in Metropolis
29. Actress Sophia
30. Tennessee — Ford
31. Literary device

Puzzle 49 by Sheldon Benardo

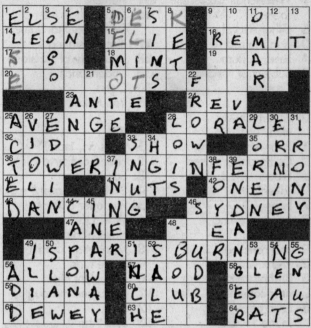

33 Tight, as a fit
34 Elev.
37 Around the center
38 Vestibule
39 Imperil
44 Gangster known as Big Al
45 Sort of
46 Stamps (out)
48 Theater awards
49 Tennis's Nastase
50 Cole —
51 Ruler unit
52 Store event
53 Rick's love in "Casablanca"
54 Orderly
55 Wildebeests
56 Do sums

ACROSS

1 Wheelchair-accessible routes
6 Either end of a gate
10 Is in the red
14 Love, in Roma
15 Subject of fission
16 Crooked
17 Homer
20 Become lively, with "up"
21 Poor movie rating
22 Calligrapher's need
25 Frost's "The __ Not Taken"
27 Ecru
28 Become extinct, with "out"
29 St. Francis of __
32 Prefix with natal
33 Birthplace of a hurricane
35 Ford popular in the 1970's
38 Homer
42 Bowl sites
43 Easy out
45 Beer buyers' needs, for short
47 Gas, to a Brit
50 Explosive initials
51 Yale students since 1969
54 Needing some kneading?
55 "For __ a jolly good fellow"
56 Got free

59 Gamma preceder
61 Homer
66 "A Death in the Family" author James
67 Biblical sibling
68 University of __ Island
69 Understands
70 Ogles
71 Iron Mike

DOWN

1 "Let's go, team!"
2 Friend of Pierre
3 Bon __
4 Skull in "Hamlet," e.g.
5 Pay after a layoff
6 Warm jackets
7 Hall-of-Famer Mel
8 Manhattan district
9 Some feds
10 Corpulent plus
11 Explained thoroughly
12 Pen
13 Less than quadraphonic
18 Son of Aphrodite
19 Presidents' Day mo.
22 Words President Buchanan never said
23 Pleasing
24 What a blabbermouth can't do
26 Quick reads
30 Witness
31 Drive up the wall
34 Subject of E.P.A. monitoring
36 Fruit pastry

Puzzle 50 by Michael Doran

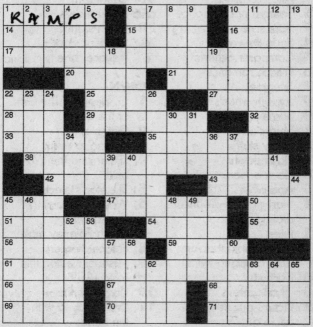

¹R	²A	³M	⁴P	⁵S		⁶	⁷	⁸	⁹		¹⁰	¹¹

37 Head of England?
39 Econ. statistic
40 "Norma —"
41 Adjust, as a radio
44 Goals, e.g.: Abbr.
45 Swelling reducer
46 Amount to be taken
48 Signs of spring
49 Subjects of assays
52 July 4, 1776,
   and others
53 Restful place
57 Suffix with persist
58 W.W. II turning point

60 Like fireplaces
62 Whopper
63 Pair of Mexicans
64 Hubbub
65 Hangout

ACROSS

1 Atlas contents
5 Sonny's partner, once
9 Jazz style
14 Spanish water
15 Composer Schifrin
16 French romance
17 Snuggles in
19 Jay Silverheels role
20 Some potatoes
21 Shirt part
23 Sticky stuff
24 Flops down
28 Have a look
30 And others: Abbr.
31 Start of long-distance dialing
32 Piles
34 What Santa's making (and checking twice)
36 Ho-hum
40 "If all — fails . . ."
41 Picture puzzle
42 5K, e.g.
43 Way off shore
44 Muslim holy man
45 Deluxe sheet fabric
46 Hit, as the knuckles
48 Shower alternative
50 Mag. staffers
51 Gets ready to sit
56 Prefix with metric
57 Health resort
58 Pacific weather phenomenon
61 Surgeon's assistant
63 Stays awhile
66 Fortuneteller's aid
67 Duet plus one
68 Count (on)
69 Snow sliders
70 Catch sight of
71 "Jurassic Park" menace, briefly

DOWN

1 O. Henry's "The Gift of the —"
2 Got gray
3 Helped to relax
4 "Peter and the Wolf" bird
5 Skeleton's place?
6 Western omelet ingredient
7 North Pole toy maker
8 Palace dweller
9 Michael Keaton title role, 1989
10 Comic Philips
11 Drum played with the hands
12 Words before sight and mind
13 Conclusive evidence
18 Fountain orders
22 Genealogy
25 Oregon's capital
26 Poor woodcutter of folklore
27 Actress Winger
28 Ballpark near Ashe Stadium
29 Snakelike fish
33 Oyster's prize
35 Shrub with red fruit

Puzzle 51 by Marjorie Berg

37 Early bird's opposite
38 — reflux
39 Egg layers
41 Shred
45 "— we dance?"
47 Desirable qualities
49 Comic 1982 Richard Pryor film
51 Pub orders
52 Typical
53 "Casablanca" actor Peter
54 Sticky stuff
55 Not moving
59 World's longest river
60 Cameo stone
62 Outfield surface
64 Hosp. areas
65 Start to fall

ACROSS

1 Sacrifices may be made with these
6 Social stratum
11 Supremely softly, in music
14 Run-of-the-mill
15 Gunning for
16 Hindu honorific
17 Celebrated legal event of 1925
19 Hither's partner
20 Tempting garden
21 Boot camp barbering job
23 Gusto
26 "__ Cadillac" (1989 hit)
28 "I see," facetiously
29 Lucy's landlady
31 Spots on dresses
34 Makes up (for)
36 Rouen's river
37 Perry Mason's field
38 Initially
40 Sugar Ray stats
43 Close, of yore
44 "That's that"
46 Baggie binders
50 Mrs. Doubtfire, for one
51 Final Four game
52 Onion's kin
54 Coupler
55 Patio grill
58 Certain plastic
60 Choler

61 It delivered in the Old West
66 Nutritional abbr.
67 "Ragged Dick" author
68 Uncanny
69 Young 'un
70 Methods: Abbr.
71 Hint to the start of 17-, 31-, 46- and 61-Across

DOWN

1 No-goodnik
2 G.I. morale booster
3 Mother Teresa, for one
4 "It's break time!"
5 Coaster
6 Feline fancy
7 Congo's continent: Abbr.
8 Perfectionist
9 Spree
10 __ Stanley Gardner
11 Hitchcock classic
12 French novelist Marcel
13 Painted ponies
18 "You betcha!"
22 Walk in water
23 Gusto
24 Blues singer James
25 Air
27 "Over my dead body!"
30 Tilted, once
32 Part of S.W.A.K.
33 Playwright Chekhov

Puzzle 52 by N. Salomon and G. Grabowski

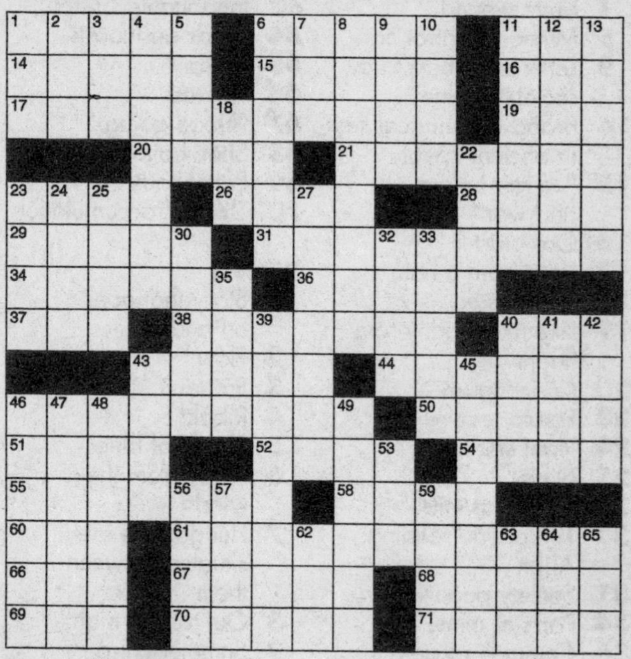

35 Galley notation
39 Personal faults
40 Gambling game
41 Sow's squeal
42 Eyelid infection
43 Laos's locale
45 San Francisco, Oakland, etc.
46 Casual top
47 Oddball
48 Pooped person's plaint
49 Cuts off
53 General Mills cereal
56 Number crunchers, for short
57 "O __ Night"
59 Hightailed it
62 "Are we there __?"
63 Suffix with west
64 [as printed]
65 Get the picture

ACROSS

1 Knife wound
5 Mission Control org.
9 Letter after Beta in a society's name
14 Broadway musical set in ancient Egypt
15 "__ fair in love and war"
16 Oak starter
17 Light from a halo
18 __ Marsala
19 Like many bathroom floors
20 Continuously
23 Potato feature
24 Plant starters
25 Ninny
27 Civil War inits.
30 Tire gauge reading: Abbr.
31 Society page word
34 Parts of mins.
36 Common place for a tattoo
38 Actor O'Brien
40 Continuously
43 Be almost out
44 Stamp's place: Abbr.
45 Tibetan monk
46 Choose
47 Letter before Beta in a society's name
49 Always, poetically
51 The "S" of CBS: Abbr.
52 Pool member
54 PC key
56 Continuously

62 It often follows a pun
63 Inhabitants: Suffix
64 Loads and loads
65 Vibrant
66 Harvest
67 "Good going!"
68 Shoe bottoms
69 Pretentious
70 Thieves' accumulation

DOWN

1 Story that goes on and on
2 Plow
3 Preadult
4 Ribald
5 Shade of blue
6 Away from the wind
7 Hungarians are situated between them
8 Out for the night
9 Summer chirpers
10 Citric and others
11 Silent film vamp Negri
12 The hunted
13 In addition
21 N.R.C. predecessor
22 Special portion of a vintner's output
25 Houston player
26 Clinch
28 Pourer's comment
29 Terrier's cry
31 Acadia, today
32 Group to attack

Puzzle 53 by Richard Chisholm

33 Authors Ferber and O'Brien
35 Inits. in TV comedy since 1975
37 One of the Three Stooges
39 Gibson of "Braveheart"
41 Hit parade contents
42 Le Monde article
48 Prime Minister Gandhi
50 Kind of room
52 Italian wine

53 Cousin of a mink
55 Not be perpendicular
56 Singer Guthrie
57 Disturb
58 Summer phenomenon
59 Catch sight of
60 Rooster
61 "Trick" body part
62 Stove option

ACROSS

1 "__ so fast!"
4 Georges who wrote "La Disparition"
9 Foundation
14 Pollution watchdog: Abbr.
15 Jobs in the computer biz
16 Girl with a looking-glass
17 Cardinal's insignia
18 Serve in the capacity of
19 With 59-Across, a 35-Down portrayer
20 35-Down portrayer
23 Baseballers Brock and Piniella
24 "Senior" in French names
25 Kind of bean
28 Come out for
31 __ de cologne
33 Marshy
34 Golfer Trevino
35 Crew needs
36 The Tin Man's prop
37 35-Down portrayer
40 "Whoo" caller
42 Biblical time of rest
43 Prior to, poetically
44 Alarming shout
45 Place to buy tickets: Abbr.
46 Parental adviser
50 Part of the Corn Belt
52 Seine tributary
54 "Man __ Mancha"
55 35-Down portrayer
59 See 19-Across
61 "Let __!" ("Go ahead!")
62 Surg. workplaces
63 Dweebish "Family Matters" boy
64 Long-legged bird
65 Midafternoon repast
66 Mystics
67 Decalogue recipient
68 Visitors from afar: Abbr.

DOWN

1 Snugly ensconce
2 Alternative
3 Rabbi's text
4 Exam for a jr.
5 Mark permanently
6 Confirm, as a password
7 Sidestep
8 Baby delivery method
9 Stagecoach robber Black __
10 Distant
11 Relinquish control of
12 Shelf material
13 Sun. speech
21 "__ Mio"
22 Trainee
26 Annoy
27 Partook of
29 Indicates, as a gauge
30 Clinton or Dole
32 Manual readers

Puzzle 54 by Kevan Choset

1	2	3		4	5	6	7	8		9	10	11	12	13
14				15						16				
17				18						19				
20			21					22						
23					24					25		26	27	
28				29	30		31		32		33			
		34				35					36			
	37				38					39				
40	41			42				43						
44				45			46				47	48	49	
50			51		52		53			54				
		55		56					57	58				
59	60				61						62			
63					64						65			
66					67						68			

35 Long-running film role
37 Snail, e.g.
38 Distrusting disposition
39 Bank takebacks
40 Samurai's sash
41 "Face/Off" director John
46 Wreckage
47 Distinguished
48 Popular table wine
49 Dorothy's home
51 Broadcaster
53 Brief brawl
56 Sushi fish

57 Tick off
58 Withdraws, with "out"
59 Juilliard subj.
60 Pay dirt

ACROSS

1 Jessica of "Dark Angel"
5 Calcutta's home
10 Partially open
14 Drug agent
15 Banks have them on property
16 Fury
17 Bit of whatnot
19 Gulf war missile
20 Vietnam's capital
21 Singer Adams
22 Squeezes (out)
23 Nap in Oaxaca
25 Ritzy
27 Again and then once again
30 Explosive devices
33 Places for experiments
36 Moo __ gai pan
37 Easily managed
38 "Days of __ Lives"
39 Certain ranch name . . . or this puzzle's theme
41 Blubber
42 Where the X-axis meets the Y-axis
44 One of Gen. Lee's men
45 Sitcom diner
46 Indiana basketballer
47 Soundness of mind
49 Prepared to be knighted
51 Knight, dame, etc.
55 __ fun at (ridicule)
57 Killer whale
60 Pulitzer Prize category
61 Final notice
62 Worker with a ledger
64 Pastrami purveyor
65 Almost any doo-wop song, e.g.
66 Between ports
67 In __ (together)
68 Like much hip-hop lingo
69 Relative of a sea gull

DOWN

1 Old Egyptian crosses
2 Hawaiian island
3 Pickling liquid
4 Confronts boldly
5 Variety
6 Almost perfect rating
7 Without juice, as an electrical wire
8 Cut into
9 Cockeyed
10 Poison in classic mysteries
11 Certain dive
12 Chills and fever
13 Commies
18 Friends and neighbors
24 Inert gas
26 Run __ (go wild)
28 Gambler's marker
29 Snake charmer's snake
31 Israeli airline

Puzzle 55 by Barry Silk

32 Complete collections
33 Chicago locale, with "the"
34 Surrounding glow
35 Oven for making building blocks
37 Subtraction from a bank account
39 In — straits
40 Novelist Deighton
43 Heredity-related
45 "It's on me!"
47 Leisurely walk
48 Neap, e.g.

50 University of New Mexico athletes
52 Expire
53 Mideast V.I.P.
54 Popular food wrap
55 Pea holders
56 Follow orders
58 Musical finale
59 Related
63 Beer barrel

ACROSS

1 Editor's overruling
5 Oddball
10 Antifur org.
14 "St. Elmo's Fire" singer John
15 Admit
16 North Carolina school
17 Pac-10 team
18 Played charades
19 Vessel that's poled
20 Is like a stumped puzzle solver?
23 Golf unit
24 Eyeshadow shade
25 Voluble
28 Morning cupful, slangily
30 Lennon's lady
33 Green beans
34 Disney's "___ & Stitch"
35 Cowboy boot attachment
36 Like a stumped puzzle solver?
39 Cologne scent
40 Parisian hangout
41 Old enough
42 Second letter addendum: Abbr.
43 Compassion
44 "Psycho" figure
45 Headmaster's title
46 Hatchling's sound
47 Where a stumped puzzle solver goes?
55 Feel sympathy (for)
56 Produce hurriedly, with "out"
57 Scott in a noted court case
58 Picnic dish
59 Halt
60 Piedmont province
61 Brewski
62 Less predictable
63 Leave behind

DOWN

1 Starchy veggie
2 Edible shell
3 ___ Stanley Gardner
4 Insults and such from athletes
5 Point-blank
6 Milk for un bebé
7 "___ boy!"
8 City on the Dnieper
9 Undertaking
10 Vantage point
11 Airline launched in 1948
12 Meat substitute
13 Kitty starter
21 "Wrong!"
22 Simile words
25 Jumper cable's end
26 Touch for funds
27 Build up
28 Instant
29 Burn remedy
30 Colleague of Dr. Phil
31 Prod gently
32 Canadian skater Brian

Puzzle 56 by Steve Jones

34 Future J.D.'s hurdle
35 Play down, as an issue
37 Volkswagen named for a desert wind
38 Gentleman caller, e.g.
43 Fruit center
44 Less kind
45 Depicts distortedly
46 Race winnings
47 McCartney's instrument
48 Bill of Rights defender: Abbr.
49 Neighbor of Niger
50 Outbuilding
51 Campus hangout
52 Roughly
53 Butterfly catchers' needs
54 Falco of "The Sopranos"

ACROSS

1 Sign of injury
5 Military sch.
9 Storied royal elephant
14 "Where the heart is"
15 The Bee Gees, e.g.
16 Like howls in a haunted house
17 [sigh]
18 Fruity pastry
19 Components of molecules
20 +, mathematically
23 Tangled up
24 Holds, as a hand
28 Baseball's Griffey
29 Suit accessory
30 Drivel
31 Wipe clean
35 Ruby or Sandra
36 Skater Thomas
37 The, grammatically
41 Hours-long film, perhaps
42 Oui's opposite
43 Put new ground cover on
44 Negative conjunction
45 Unreturnable serve
46 Grassland
48 Brando's wail in "A Streetcar Named Desire"
50 Tumbled like a waterfall
55 −459.67°F, scientifically
57 Inviting odor

60 __ avis
61 Aquatic bird
62 Sophia of "Two Women"
63 Author __ Easton Ellis
64 Suffix with switch
65 Many a parent/child bedtime ritual
66 All there
67 Irish native

DOWN

1 Circle or square
2 :
3 Collect
4 Sticky pine stuff
5 Outfit
6 Cowardly
7 Put on TV
8 You might connect them
9 Snoopy, for one
10 Prudential rival
11 Sis's sib
12 Order between "ready" and "fire"
13 Notes after dos
21 Not available, as a seat
22 More hazardous, as winter roads
25 Builder's plans, informally
26 Artist Picasso
27 Emulated 007
29 Mad Hatter's drink
31 Paradises
32 Move, as a plant

33 Burning
34 Order to attack, with "on"
35 Family room
36 Six-sided game piece
38 Early Peruvians
39 Sock part
40 Draw an outline of
45 The Empire State's capital
46 Fashion designer Ralph
47 Manor and its grounds

49 Not so good, as an excuse
50 Silent star Bow
51 Montezuma, for instance
52 Steel plow maker
53 Swashbuckling Flynn
54 Start of a prohibition
56 Spheres
57 Capp and Capone
58 Go to waste
59 Spanish gold

ACROSS

1 W.'s political affiliation
4 Take a paddle to
9 Barely beats
14 "Gotcha!"
15 Wore
16 Dickens's — Heep
17 Nothing at all
18 Eyes
19 Elephant gone amok
20 Mimic
23 Can't stomach
24 Got back into business
28 Resistance to change
32 Many a home purchase
33 Putin's land
36 "Treasure Island" inits.
37 Departure from reality
42 Designation for a sequel to a sequel
43 Lock, stock and barrel
44 Begs
48 Puget Sound city
52 Language of the Eddas
55 — Brockovich, Oscar role for Julia Roberts
56 "Dallas" spinoff
60 Aussie "bear"
63 Do penance
64 Wolfed down
65 Place to moor
66 Arrive at
67 Salon goop

68 Nick of "Cape Fear"
69 Krupp Works city
70 Windy City trains

DOWN

1 India's Mohandas
2 Buckeye Stater
3 Gourmet's sense
4 "Hold it, horse!"
5 Take an ax to
6 Together, on a score
7 Like practically all TV's, now
8 Bowie's weapon
9 Part of the Old World
10 Pilotless planes
11 Jazz job
12 — Claire, Wis.
13 Sow, ewe or mare
21 Gibbs of country music
22 Part of F.Y.I.
25 Bust maker
26 — May Clampett of 60's TV
27 — Plaines, Ill.
29 Harbor workhorse
30 Relative of -esque
31 Italian wine center
34 Cyclotron bit
35 Siesta times: Abbr.
37 "— 'er up!"
38 Told a whopper
39 Friend's opposite
40 — snail's pace
41 Jotted down
42 Nasdaq debut: Abbr.
45 Short sock

Puzzle 58 by Fred Piscop

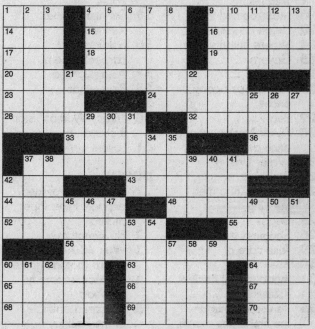

46 Visit a bloodmobile, e.g.

47 B'way hit sign

49 "M*A*S*H" procedure

50 Door frame part

51 Marx collaborator

53 Wild West vehicle

54 Kefauver who won fame investigating organized crime

57 Builders' sites

58 Stud fee?

59 Gas in signs

60 Family

61 Musical Yoko

62 The whole shebang

ACROSS

1 Treaties
6 Mushroomed
10 Union concerns
14 Where enfants learn
15 Govern
16 Aid and __
17 Al Capone's gang, once?
19 Pepsi-__
20 Boxer Norton who once defeated Ali
21 Writer Uris
22 Probable
24 Where Anna met the king
25 Brings in altogether
26 Shooting star
29 Take care of
30 Bee-related
31 Inhabitant of ancient Palestine
35 It's usually due on the first of the month
36 Budged
37 Prenoon period, in poetry
38 First person to fly a plane
40 Having prongs
41 Less strict
42 See 3-Down
43 Realms
46 Bugler's call
47 Tooted one's own horn
48 Watch's sound
49 Stun
52 Civil rights figure — Parks
53 Service for the Kennedys?
56 Soldiers and carpenters, e.g.
57 Asia's __ Sea
58 Pig sounds
59 Netting
60 "Pretty Woman" star Richard
61 Lovers' rendezvous

DOWN

1 Quantity of pickled peppers Peter Piper picked
2 Flu symptom
3 With 42-Across, starts of pro football games
4 Dr. Mom's remedy, for short
5 Flippered animal of the Pacific
6 Horse handler
7 Wreckage
8 Building wing
9 Up on literature
10 Young Eudora Welty?
11 Clarinet cousins
12 Girl who has a ball
13 Sticks around
18 Paraphernalia
23 Smidgen
24 Microsoft workers' laundry?
25 French playwright Jean

Puzzle 59 by Lynn Lempel

In the grid, at 19: **COLA**

26 Trading center
27 Sporting blade
28 Cookie containers
29 Relish
31 Nat and Natalie
32 Atoms that have gained or lost electrons
33 Ring bearer
34 Terminals
36 Diverse assortment
39 Reduce, as expenses
40 Tuft of hair on the head

42 Cinco de Mayo dish
43 Vamoose
44 Lying face downward
45 Party givers
46 Sir or madam
48 Russia's Nicholas I, e.g.
49 Madcap
50 Inquires
51 "Hey, you!"
54 Miner's load
55 Fallen space station

ACROSS

1 Tea, to Brits
5 Slow
10 Sound on cobblestone streets
14 Slender instrument
15 Like some numerals
16 Shot in the arm, maybe
17 Lawyers, to Brits
19 Eram, —, erat
20 Graham who wrote "The Quiet American"
21 Got a whiff of, old-style
22 Drug-yielding shrub
25 Guardian spirits
27 Bandage, to Brits
30 Hip roof
34 Like the farmer MacDonald
35 Composer Satie
37 Sofa
38 Richard —
39 Parting south of the border
41 Night watcher
42 Dodo has two
45 Those, to Robert Burns
47 Actress Peeples
48 Tougher, as a parent
50 Doctor's office, to Brits
52 Tree with catkins
54 Gift to a diva
55 Thin and light
58 Foul-up
61 Gardener's soil
62 Garters, to Brits

66 Pulitzer winner Quindlen
67 Slalomed
68 Author Kingsley
69 Bygone autocrat
70 Waits on
71 Subway, to Brits

DOWN

1 Firms: Abbr.
2 Home of "The Sopranos"
3 Earthlink competitor
4 Is a monarch
5 Mold-ripened cheese
6 Uncreative education method
7 — friends
8 N.B.A.'s Abdul-Jabbar
9 Lt.'s subordinate
10 Druggist, to Brits
11 Apollo's plaything?
12 Iridescent gem
13 Mail delivery, to Brits
18 Jalopy
21 Trig ratio
22 Fruits of victory
23 Mama Cass
24 Literature Nobelist Gordimer
26 Princeton's historic — Hall
28 Rubbed out
29 Free (of)
31 Makes up (for)
32 Update the alarm system

Puzzle 60 by John Underwood

33 Holds up
36 Uniform, to Brits
40 Surprised gasps
43 Elementary textbook, to Brits
44 Just
46 __ the side of caution
49 Chastise
51 Proficient in
53 Violin bow application
55 Apartment, to Brits
56 They're charged

57 Turner known as the Sweater Girl
59 Kind of page
60 Berths
62 It doesn't fly anymore
63 It doesn't fly
64 Tease
65 Indianapolis-to-Atlanta dir.

ACROSS

1 Self-satisfied
5 "Just as I thought!"
8 Without warning
14 South African archbishop Desmond
15 Famous London weather phenomenon
16 Macaroni topping
17 Conversation continuer #1
20 To the __ degree
21 Bird seed holder
22 Mouse catcher
23 Track star Lewis
24 Likely
26 Pollution control org.
27 Speed-chess accessories
30 Diva's solo
31 Juan Carlos, to his subjects
32 The golden calf was one
33 Having the same reach
35 Conversation continuer #2
41 Performance for Anna Pavlova
42 Pro __ (like some legal work)
43 Ticked off but good
46 Bearing
47 Respond to peevishly
49 "How was __ know?"
50 One of the Gabors
51 Crab grass, e.g.
52 Weaving machine
54 Avoid
56 Cry to a calf
59 Conversation continuer #3
62 At hand
63 "Chances __" (Johnny Mathis hit)
64 Mideast chief
65 Trial by fire
66 Take "for better or for worse"
67 Itsy-bitsy biter

DOWN

1 Musial of the Cards
2 Has to
3 2002 Winter Olympics locale
4 Doublemint, e.g.
5 Fore-and-__ (some ships)
6 Monopoly purchase
7 Sat in a cask
8 Zodiac creature
9 Like TV channels above 13: Abbr.
10 Skillful
11 More loved
12 Get away
13 Amount left after deductions
18 Miles off
19 Illuminated from behind
23 Us magazine cover subject
25 Aquarium

Puzzle 61 by Richard Miller

27 ___-tac-toe
28 Words before a kiss?
29 Second Sunday in May honoree
30 White-faced
33 If nothing else
34 Spoil
36 Barely risqué
37 Popeye's gal
38 Stylish dresser
39 Put ___ good word for
40 Youngster
43 Certain Italian-style cookie

44 Yom Kippur observer
45 Ornament
47 Be ticked off
48 Former House Speaker Gingrich
51 "Now ___ was I?"
53 Stallion's mate
55 Tobacco mouthful
56 "La Bohème" heroine
57 Taking action
58 Folklore fiend
60 Wizards' and Warriors' org.
61 Haw's partner

ACROSS

1 Jacks, in cards
7 Bikini part
10 Links org.
13 One of baseball's Alou brothers
14 Underage temptation, slangily
16 Mobile maker Alexander
17 He wants you
18 Some toy dogs, for short
19 Go kaput
20 French denials
21 Astronaut Grissom
22 Big bother
24 Reclined
26 Criticize harshly
27 Beatnik's "Gotcha!"
30 2003 war zone
31 — Baba
32 Glass splinter
34 Dessert —
35 "There, there"
37 Traffic marker
38 "Simone" star Al
40 Coquettish
41 Excursion
42 —-majesté
43 Challenge for a rat
44 Affirmatives
45 1831 Poe poem
47 PC screen
48 Calvary inscription
51 Sí, across the Pyrenees
52 Military medal, e.g.

54 Way to sway
56 Declarer
58 "Baby Baby" singer, 1991
59 Moon goddess
60 — Alamos
61 "Star Wars" extras, for short
62 Longtime Oreo competitor

DOWN

1 The Colonel's restaurant inits.
2 Kind of tide
3 Loyalty to the cause
4 Traitor of Norway
5 Blunted blades
6 Sun. talks
7 Send far, far away, maybe
8 Puts through a food press
9 —-nighter
10 El —, Tex.
11 Composer — Carlo Menotti
12 20's dispensers, briefly
14 Traitor of Jesus
15 Traitor of America
22 Sentry's cry
23 Small, in Dogpatch
24 Like a wet noodle
25 "He's — nowhere man" (Beatles lyric)
26 "Soap" actor Jimmy
28 Intellectual's retreat

Puzzle 62 by Brendan Emmett Quigley

29 Wish granter
32 ___ terrier
33 Sales team, informally
36 Flow like mud
39 Wedding column word
43 Shows grief
46 Like dietetic yogurt
47 Group of quails
48 Slanted type: Abbr.
49 Hurler Hideo
50 Beachgoers catch them

52 Beanery fare
53 Ashcroft's predecessor
55 Rap's Dr. ___
57 Stout of whodunits

ACROSS

1 Money hoarder
6 Frosts, as a cake
10 Notre —
14 Houston ballplayer
15 Former ruler of Iran
16 Fusses
17 Poker player's dream
19 Revivalists
20 Suspicious
21 Gown fabric
22 Faucet
26 Soup ingredient
28 K.F.C. founder, with "the"
30 King Kong, e.g.
31 Foray
32 Delete from a disk
35 Nutritional abbr.
38 Out of sorts feeling (and a hint to the starts of 17-, 26-, 49- and 59-Across)
42 Prof.'s degree
43 Opening bets
44 Coffee holders
45 Long-distance inits.
46 Run
49 Parachutist
54 Egg dish
55 With nothing added
56 Ping or zing
58 Swedish diva Jenny
59 Makeup applicator
64 "Puppy Love" singer Paul
65 Ye — Curiosity Shoppe
66 Magical wish granter
67 Trueheart of the comics
68 Paths
69 Glue

DOWN

1 Spoil
2 Prefix with -metric
3 Sow's pen
4 Pitcher's stat.
5 Deodorant type
6 — of Capri
7 Butter maker
8 Snap course
9 "Quiet!"
10 River in a Strauss waltz
11 Fred's dancing sister
12 Money, in slang
13 German industrial city
18 Celebration
21 Laid-back sort
22 Toss out
23 Simmer, as eggs
24 Trojan War epic
25 Mount Olympus dwellers
27 Flower holder
29 Took off
33 Rd. or hwy.
34 "I get it," humorously
35 The "R" of R.F.D.
36 Al — (not too soft)
37 Strong point
39 Have dinner at home
40 "As advertised —!"
41 Tackle box item

45 Nike rival
47 Sit for a photo
48 Come into view
49 Water balloon sound
50 "A Fish Called Wanda" Oscar winner
51 Americans, to Brits
52 — Gay (W.W. II plane)
53 Rambunctious
57 Middle of March
59 Comic book punch sound

60 Get-up-and-go
61 Numero —
62 Repair
63 Hardly macho

ACROSS

1 Sound at a fun house
5 Channel for political types
10 Ones found near home
14 Music halls
15 San Antonio site, with "the"
16 Marinate
17 "Against All __"
18 They need to be in order at a border
19 "Holy __!"
20 Fleeting success
23 Longing
24 Thousand __, Calif.
25 Kudrow and Bonet
28 Ukr. and Lat., once
29 Hip person
31 Member of the House of Lords
34 Instant, briefly
35 Coach Parseghian
36 Start of a child's rhyme
41 Myrna of "Love Crazy"
42 Utter
43 __ stealer
44 Made "glub-glub" sounds
47 Vampire's act
49 Wear down
50 Top-notch
51 Danny's "Do the Right Thing" role
54 Rustic film couple

58 Try not to be taken by surprise
60 Hopping mad
61 Opera solo
62 Certain atoms
63 More gracious
64 Bunk
65 Icky stuff
66 Copyists
67 Fr. honorees: Abbr.

DOWN

1 Mickey Mouse chum
2 Confuse
3 Roomy vehicle
4 Quarterback's move
5 Pricey spread
6 Moves stealthily
7 They may be checkered
8 Wet nurse
9 Schnozz
10 Inscription on a letter box
11 It's full of craters
12 Chum
13 It's up there
21 Egypt's Mubarak
22 Mideast inits.
26 Composer Copland
27 Governor's domain
28 Costa del __
29 Epcot center?
30 World Series mo.
31 Nonsense
32 Love affair
33 Big cheese in TV comedy?

Puzzle 64 by Elizabeth C. Gorski

34	Like some winks
37	Mao —-tung
38	Bit
39	Cosmetician Lauder
40	Expert
45	City where Lech Walesa rose to prominence
46	Meadow
47	Yachtsman
48	Print shop folks
50	Quickly
51	Pompous walk
52	"Get —!"
53	Pages (through)
55	Zagat of restaurant guide fame
56	Faucet problem
57	Price indicators
58	Corkscrew-tailed animal
59	British john

ACROSS

1 Secy.
5 The South, in the Civil War: Abbr.
8 Nickname for Montana
14 Den
15 Possess
16 Nobody in particular
17 Actress Swenson of "Benson"
18 1950's–60's TV western
20 Noted Louisiana-born concert pianist
22 Chooses
23 Pennsylvania home of Lafayette College
24 Appear
26 "__ pig's eye!"
28 Wheat keeper
33 Garments that moths may eat
38 "__ and the Pussycats" (old TV cartoon)
39 Guest-room furniture
42 To have, in Le Havre
43 Santa's bagful
44 Mosaic component
47 Feedbag bit
48 Broccoli __ (leafy vegetable)
50 Actress Kidman
55 Baths
59 Seat carried on poles
61 "Come here often?," e.g.

63 On the bounding main
64 Cut into
65 LP successors
66 Fivers
67 Caught
68 "__ the season . . ."
69 In __ (existing)

DOWN

1 Not dead
2 Yemen's capital
3 Zodiac divisions
4 Piece of land
5 Sharer of a prize
6 Q-tip, e.g.
7 Black __ (cattle breed)
8 Headline
9 Amt. compounded at a bank
10 Toy that whirls
11 "General Hospital," e.g.
12 Make 33-Across, say
13 Longings
19 Wash. neighbor
21 One who may be arrested for doing nothing
25 Grand
27 Paintings
29 Narrow victory margin
30 "Unto us __ is given"
31 Fissure
32 Supporting votes
33 "Shoo!"
34 Used a loom

Puzzle 65 by Gail A. MacLean

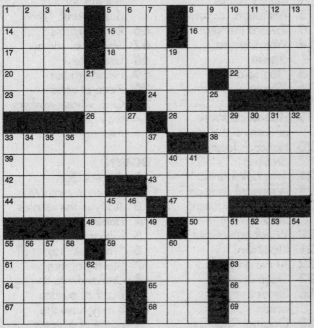

35 Baseball's Slaughter
36 Hertz rival
37 Drink, as hot tea
40 Sibling for sis
41 Quality of good
   ground beef
45 Spoke scratchily
46 First fratricide victim
49 Government order
51 Rub raw
52 Where camels stop
   for refreshment
53 Mortgages, e.g.
54 Clear the slate

55 Whirl
56 Ponderosa __
57 Brokerage file: Abbr.
58 Playlet
60 "Me, myself __"
62 Expend

ACROSS

1 Quirky habits
5 Ars longa, __ brevis
9 Toward the stern
14 Wax-covered cheese
15 "You said it!"
16 "Stompin' at the __"
17 Bug spray
19 Hollywood Walk of Fame sights
20 Hancock Tower architect
21 ". . . baked in __"
23 A musical Jackson
24 "Lord of the Rings" actor
27 Windbag's output
31 "Take this!"
32 At the drop of __
33 Stage opening
36 Speck in the ocean
40 Original "Star Trek" actress
43 Boarded
44 Arabian Peninsula land
45 Creative spark
46 Farm sounds
48 Enter the picture
50 Short or long, in phonetics
55 Plug of tobacco
56 One-named New Ager
57 Straight: Prefix
62 Jewish sectist

64 2001–2 sitcom, or an apt title for this puzzle, with "The"
66 Really steamed
67 Sounds of sorrow
68 Useful item
69 Hikers' routes
70 Piece of cake
71 Org. whose workers may be left carrying the bag

DOWN

1 Actress Garr
2 Same, in footnotes
3 Andy in the funnies
4 Hook's underling
5 Kilmer of "The Doors"
6 "That is to say . . ."
7 News hr., maybe
8 Unfriendly to Beijing
9 Beast of burden
10 It may have the name of a state
11 Be of use
12 Strong point
13 Iron Mike
18 Chapter 53
22 __ out (just manage)
25 Asia's shrinking __ Sea
26 McCormack of "Will & Grace"
27 Suspend
28 John Glenn's state
29 Diplomat's asset
30 Handling comfortably
34 Proximity

Puzzle 66 by M. Francis Vuolo

35 Pro — (for now)
37 Miner's strike
38 Home of Zeno
39 Bygone despot
41 Organic compound
42 — the finish
47 Ring cheer
49 Sound: Prefix
50 TV screening device
51 Tara family name
52 Attended
53 Stocking material
54 Emperor after Nero
58 Queue after Q

59 Pres. Jefferson
60 Earring style
61 Hooters
63 — Plaines
65 John Edward's supposed ability

ACROSS

1 Spike Lee's "She's —
Have It"
6 Ship's front
10 Singer Sylvia
14 Shun
15 Right-hand person
16 Butcher's stock
17 39-Across in Rome
20 Schubert's
"The — King"
21 Club — (resort)
22 Old-time comedian
Red
23 Gen. Lee's side: Abbr.
25 Whitney or Wallach
27 Inclined
28 39-Across in New York
32 Change, as the
Constitution
33 Mauna — (volcano)
34 Word repeated after
"Que" in a song
38 Nancy Drew's
boyfriend
39 Theme of this puzzle
43 Vietnamese New Year
44 She, in Italy
46 Ghost's cry
47 "You — Beautiful"
49 39-Across in
Mexico City
53 "— luck!"
56 Its slogan is "The
Racer's Edge"
57 Explosive letters
58 Playwright John who
wrote "Look Back in
Anger"

61 Slugger Williams
63 24-hr. banking
convenience
65 39-Across in Paris
68 Parsley or sage
69 Russian leader
before 1917
70 Not yet rented
71 Talk back to
72 Daughters'
counterparts
73 Hopalong Cassidy
actor and others

DOWN

1 Storm wind
2 Conquers
3 Backyard buildings
4 Sn, chemically
speaking
5 Genesis man
6 Ping-Pong ball whacker
7 "Flying Down to —"
8 3:1 or 4:1, e.g.
9 Unconvincing,
as an argument
10 Happy face symbols
11 Busybody
12 City in Georgia
13 Tour of duty
18 Stink
19 South African
grassland
24 Late columnist Landers
26 Old-fashioned pen
receptacles
28 John or — Doe
29 Federal regulatory
grp.

Puzzle 67 by Sarah Keller

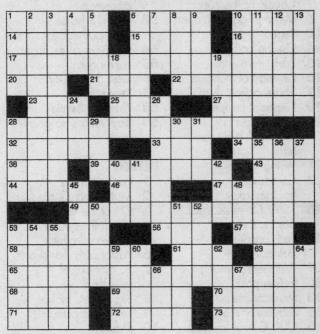

30 Prefix with classic
31 Sound receiver
35 Forever
36 Moved to
a new home
37 The gamut
40 __ Saud (Saudi
Arabia's founder)
41 "Vive le __!"
42 Follower of sigma
45 Works like a sponge
48 Stoolie
50 Nobleman
51 Aquatic animals

52 Computer image file
format
53 Scottish bodies of
water
54 Irish-born actor Milo
55 Ski lifts
59 Volleyball court
dividers
60 Old U.S. gas brand
62 Smear
64 Shea team
66 Dapper __
67 Family card game

ACROSS

1 Cousin of the cobra
6 Metal in galvanization
10 Yearn
14 On the ball
15 Early Peruvian
16 Perlman of "Cheers"
17 Share acting duties?
19 Elephant flappers
20 "— Always a Woman" (Billy Joel hit)
21 Within earshot
23 Computer troublemaker
26 1992 Olympic track star — Devers
28 Fed. property manager
29 Oklahoma wealth
30 Indian post
33 Mexican friend
35 Mayberry man
36 O.K. Corral lawman
39 Delineate again
40 Roll of dough
41 Taj —
42 Ball girls
43 Huge mouths
44 Football site
45 Machine
48 Cutting tool
49 Alert to squad cars, briefly
51 Mayberry man
52 Football sites
54 Small cavern
56 Poetic tributes
57 Sound of crowd approval
58 Golf 18 holes sans golf cart?
64 Replacer of the franc
65 Love god
66 Sign on a door
67 Water swirl
68 "Lovely" Beatles girl
69 Boy Scouts do good ones

DOWN

1 Pas' partners
2 Matterhorn, e.g.
3 Ott of the Giants
4 Like fall weather
5 Above all others
6 Postal aids, for short
7 — manner of speaking
8 Big A.T.M. maker
9 Feline attractants
10 Region
11 Assess per person?
12 Rosemary and thyme
13 No-stress class
18 Commercial prefix with star
22 "Evil Woman" grp.
23 Squirrel away
24 Anouk of film
25 Prepare to surf?
26 Discover how to do something?
27 Surrounded by
31 In the direction of
32 Shakespearean king

Puzzle 68 by Denise M. Neuendorf

34 Sound of astonishment
37 "Amazing" magician
38 City square
41 Achieved expertise in
43 Early Thoroughbred champ
46 Butter square
47 Org. that rejects bad eggs
49 Concur
50 Like a new parent
53 In unison
55 Legendary Greek conquest
56 Gumbo vegetable
59 French friend
60 Auction unit
61 Comanche enemy, once
62 Beatty of "Deliverance"
63 Stethoscope users: Abbr.

ACROSS

1 The "L" of A.F.L.–C.I.O.
6 Merriment
10 Baghdad's land
14 Popular pain reliever
15 Red gem
16 Spiritual guide
17 Perfect
18 Musical instrument that's blown into
19 Celebrity's wheels
20 Public speaker's goal
23 Way out sign
24 Musician Yoko
25 Ran into
28 Useless
31 English TV–radio inits.
34 Neighborhoods
37 Polite words at an entrance
39 Knocked
42 Beginning to awake
43 "The Divine Comedy" writer
44 Brick carrier
45 Mistake remover
48 Double curve
49 Industrious insect
50 Fishing aids
53 Like a sarong
59 Incarcerate
61 Gooey stuff
62 Impressive display
63 Helper
64 Gumbo pods
65 Shipping container
66 Small songbird
67 Backside
68 Mary — Moore

DOWN

1 Den
2 Alan of "M*A*S*H"
3 When repeated, the Road Runner's cry
4 Egg-shaped
5 Take it easy
6 Cave
7 Garage job
8 Black, to poets
9 Canine
10 Dome-shaped home
11 Destroy
12 Elbow's site
13 Quid pro —
21 The — Man ("The Wizard of Oz" character)
22 Truly
25 Reedy place
26 Poetry Muse
27 Lukewarm
29 Groups of troublemakers
30 Frequently, in verse
31 When an office worker may have to be back from lunch
32 Galoshes
33 Remedies
35 Mar. follower
36 Venus's tennis-playing sister

Puzzle 69 by Nancy Kavanaugh

38 Nutritional inits.
40 Poverty-stricken
41 Swear ___ stack of Bibles
46 Be pleasing (to)
47 Stephen of "The Crying Game"
49 Sen. Specter
51 Piece of land
52 Rueful
53 Not narrow
54 Jab
55 Poet Pound
56 Russian river

57 Son on "Six Feet Under"
58 Textile worker
59 What the teeth are connected to
60 Breathable stuff

ACROSS

1 High berth
6 Napkin holders?
10 — one's time (wait)
14 Artillery burst
15 Leave out
16 Skunk's defense
17 See 41-Across
19 Move like sludge
20 "Now I see!"
21 Rummy cake
22 Spots for spats
24 Glaswegian gals
26 Slobs' homes
28 Ticks off
30 Falling upon deaf ears
34 "Follow me!"
37 — Bator, Mongolia
39 Place to store mukluks
40 Pizazz
41 17- and 65-Across, and 10- and 25-Down
43 Note on a Post-it, maybe
44 Press conference attendee, at times
46 Civil wrong
47 Crammer's worry
48 Repeat, as a theme
50 Planted
52 Marina walkways
54 Cuomo's successor as New York governor
58 "Wheel of Fortune" category
61 Tel —
63 Coffee, slangily
64 Tooth part
65 See 41-Across
68 Assist in crime
69 Zoo houseful
70 Mercury and Saturn, e.g.
71 Jellystone Park denizen
72 Toad feature
73 Guilt-producing meeting, maybe

DOWN

1 Customary
2 Bygone Turkish title
3 Calls for donations
4 Actress — Marie Saint
5 Robin Hood, for one
6 Leopold's celebrated murder co-defendant of the 1920's
7 Oscars org.
8 Epitome of easiness?
9 Cause of muscle ache
10 See 41-Across
11 Subject of adoration
12 Catch a few Z's
13 "— Tu" (1974 hit)
18 Slacken
23 Classic soft drink
25 See 41-Across
27 Stereo components
29 Christian of Hollywood
31 TV's Trebek
32 Italia's capital

33 Dire fate
34 Industry big shot
35 — en scène (stage setting)
36 Making a mess in the army?
38 Many moons —
42 "That's enough!"
45 Social reformer Jacob
49 Playground equipment
51 Signal by hand
53 More rational
55 Friendship
56 Word of praise

57 Words of clarification
58 Say the rosary
59 King of the road
60 "The Witches" director Nicolas
62 Seemingly boundless
66 Air quality tester, for short
67 Gold: Prefix

ACROSS

1 Slacken
6 Disparaging remark
10 Dog —
   (G.I. identifiers)
14 Speeder's bane
15 Sukiyaki ingredient
16 Cain's victim
17 Actress Verdugo
18 Shortly
19 Divorce mecca
20 Like doggerel, often
22 Chamber group,
   maybe
24 Make the first moves,
   in dancing
25 Former Italian money
26 Dogie catchers
29 Game with an
   onomatopoeic name
33 Frigid
34 Company with a
   once-famous catalog
36 Mister in Mexico
37 Ripsnorter
39 Chastise
41 Country music's
   McEntire
42 Skip the usual
   wedding preparations
44 Stagnant
46 Sitcom alien
47 Crackpot
49 Little fjord
51 Went off, as a bell
52 IV+IV
53 Grand — (island east
   of Florida)

56 Film sensation
   of 1933
60 Wished undone
61 Remained in bed
63 Shortwave, e.g.
64 — Lackawanna
   Railroad
65 Watch at a strip club,
   maybe
66 Confuse
67 Voting district
68 Hair goops
69 Red Sea parter

DOWN

1 Mars' counterpart
2 Island near Java
3 Yemeni port
4 What a comb undoes
5 Pencil features
6 Witness-box
7 Men's jacket size
8 Martian's craft,
   for short
9 Takes to the station
   house
10 Roofing base
11 Help in piracy, e.g.
12 Heredity carrier
13 Piggy-bank aperture
21 Desert stops
23 Metric work units
25 Stocking material
26 Angry, with "up"
27 Latin eyes
28 Aircraft course marker
29 Fork tine
30 Tatum of Tinseltown

Puzzle 71 by John Greenman

31 Chivalrous
32 Add on, as to a plant
35 Making a hole in one
38 Moved to first class
40 Bathtub feature
43 Dutch cheese
45 Any three-letter sequence
48 Where to find a bump, in a phrase
50 Gilbert & Sullivan work, with "The"
52 Grape holders
53 Beer or ale

54 Mystique
55 Estate receiver
56 "A View to a —" (Bond film)
57 Chances
58 Cairo's waterway
59 Travels
62 A dog's — (long spell)

ACROSS

1 Ocean motion
5 Epistle apostle
9 Get-go
14 Words of confidence
15 "Dirty" Cajun dish
16 Makes some music, like the Stones
17 Tape for a music exec
18 WWW addresses
19 Aerodynamically designed
20 Fish playing a woodwind?
23 "May — now?"
24 PBS funder
25 To no avail
28 Not relaxed
30 Auctioneer's cry
33 Cube maker Rubik
34 Unmannered sort
36 Outdated atlas abbr.
37 Pride member
38 Looney Tunes horse-drawn conveyance?
42 — Hari (spy)
43 La preceder
44 — gratia artis (MGM motto)
45 Per unit
46 Banjoist Scruggs
48 Chance for a hit
52 Force
54 Will Smith biopic
56 Expose, in verse
57 Dirigible party?
61 Hillside
63 Prayer addressee
64 Look up and down
65 Red Sea land
66 Score for Mia Hamm
67 Cheery tune
68 Actress Winger
69 Fork over, with "up"
70 Many August births

DOWN

1 Morsel
2 Frigid time
3 Plum variety
4 Slaughter of Cooperstown
5 Danish filler
6 Crash cushioner
7 The Bruins of the N.C.A.A.
8 Not as much
9 Bean on the screen
10 Ill feelings
11 Screenwriter's creation
12 Barely make, with "out"
13 "For shame!"
21 — a time
22 — Nevadas
26 Get — a good thing
27 Prefix with profit
29 Doodler's aid
31 Coveted statue
32 Fed. hush-hush group
35 "I'm all ears!"

Puzzle 72 by Harvey Estes

38 Mafia bigwig
39 Mushroom cloud producer
40 Pro-gun rights org.
41 Bring up the rear
42 Brit's raincoat
47 Maze scurrier, maybe
49 Dance energetically
50 Famed Harlem theater
51 Religious principles
53 Spanish princess
55 Soup scoop

58 Gymnast Korbut
59 "High" time
60 Take it easy
61 Barrett of Pink Floyd
62 General in gray

ACROSS

1 Pitcher
5 Fresh-mouthed
10 Irish Spring alternative
14 The Crimson Tide, familiarly
15 Perform better than
16 Fashion magazine
17 Corrosive liquid
18 Unwanted loss of intellectual workers
20 Jellystone Park resident
22 Caught at a rodeo
23 Engine sounds
24 1968 hit "Harper Valley —"
26 Chicago-to-Miami dir.
27 Grass units
29 Sir's partner
30 Announcement at J.F.K.: Abbr.
31 Fragrant oil
32 Airport surface
34 Deuce topper
35 They can follow the starts of 18- and 56-Across and 4- and 33-Down
36 Turnpike turnoff
40 Molded
42 Scrooge
43 Jar part
46 Mideast's Gulf of —
47 Zoological classification
48 Ginger —
49 A's opposite, in England
50 Fathers
51 Finish second
53 Birthday party serving
56 Jefferson Memorial site in Washington
59 Prefix with dynamic
60 Wallet fillers
61 Church council
62 Ike & — Turner (1960's–70's duo)
63 Baby girls may be dressed in it
64 Ages and ages
65 School on the Thames

DOWN

1 Online auction site
2 City on the Brazos
3 Move to a new land
4 1987 Woody Allen movie
5 Recovers from drinking, with "up"
6 Surrounding glows
7 Christmas tree topper
8 Reagan-era mil. program
9 Hither and —
10 Goose egg
11 Pass, as time
12 Most cunning
13 Kept an eye on
19 Pulitzer Prize category
21 1930's boxing champ Max
24 Trimmed

Puzzle 73 by Barry Silk

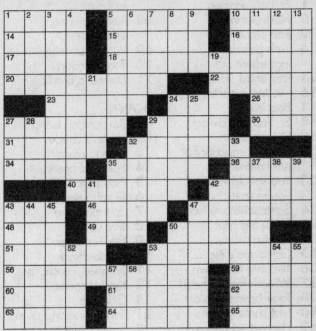

25 Skye caps
27 Dracula transformation
28 Env. contents
29 Expert
32 Not live
33 F.B.I. statistic
35 Walk in water
37 Opinion opener
38 Actor Gibson
39 Meddle
41 Eye color
42 Painter Chagall
43 Portable computer

44 The Big Ten's Fighting —
45 Muffle
47 Ogres
50 Grafting shoot
52 Wine holder
53 "Money — object"
54 Florence's river
55 Express regret
57 Jamboree grp.
58 Sailor's yes

ACROSS

1 Fr. holy women
5 Nut's partner
9 Rite place
14 Bath powder ingredient
15 Tom Joad, for one
16 Mr. Moto portrayer
17 Boorish
18 St. Paul's architect
19 Shoe blemish
20 Flexible educational environment
23 You should worry if you're in it
24 Suffix with auction
25 Lobbying grp.
28 "Smile!" show
33 California's Big —
36 Teutonic turndown
37 Wreath for the head
38 Took advantage of
40 Like some organs
42 Herbert sci-fi classic
43 Dracula portrayer
45 Burned-out ship, e.g.
47 Amigo
48 "Guys and Dolls" composer
51 Car loan fig.
52 They, in Tours
53 Simoleons
57 Payee's convenience
62 False move
64 Mate's greeting
65 False move
66 Best Actress winner for "Blue Sky"
67 Mountain-climbing aid
68 Just manages, with "out"
69 Pushed strongly
70 Took to court
71 Deliver a tirade

DOWN

1 Barbershop band?
2 Hosiery shade
3 One to respect
4 Postcard-pretty
5 Play in the alley
6 Gumbo pod
7 Epitaph word
8 Got uptight
9 Election loser
10 Plumb crazy
11 Falsified, as charges
12 Kennel sound
13 Officiate
21 Tartan-wearing group
22 Some California political moves
26 Place to fight
27 Sahara transport
29 Britain's Chamberlain
30 Early sixth-century date
31 — dark (clueless)
32 "Spy vs. Spy" magazine
33 — drug (infection fighter)
34 Take forcibly
35 With respect to
39 Put on

Puzzle 74 by Alan Arbesfeld

41 Neighbor of Ger.
44 Sidestepped
46 Gridder-turned-politician Jack
49 Back-to-back awards for Hanks
50 Top contractor?
54 Honshu port
55 Compare
56 Bikini event, in old headlines
58 "Picnic" playwright
59 10 C-notes
60 Inside info

61 Checked out
62 Winter bug
63 Musical perception

ACROSS

1 Coffee with body
6 Greta who said, "I vant to be alone"
11 Relaxing resort
14 Sing like Crosby
15 Ancient Greek marketplace
16 President Coolidge
17 "Peter Pan" villain
19 Assayer's material
20 Dressed
21 Suggestions on food labels: Abbr.
22 Three-toed animal
24 "There's a problem!"
26 Flock leader
27 Country dance
32 Demean
33 Missing companionship
37 Droop
38 Cope with
40 Write quickly
41 More reliable
44 Abstract visual images
46 Efficient manufacturing process
49 Dwarfed tree
52 Ascent
53 Less cordial
54 Fiendish
56 Artist Salvador
60 Comic's bit
61 Water locator
64 Encouragement at the bullring
65 Big ape
66 Christopher who played the Man of Steel
67 __ and feather
68 Horse features
69 Horse relatives

DOWN

1 1300 on a cornerstone
2 Spoken
3 Nightclub in a Manilow song
4 Ballpark vendors' offerings
5 Actress __ Alicia
6 The Father of India
7 Turkish leader
8 Down Under hoppers
9 Friend in the 'hood
10 Yellow ribbon site
11 Listerine alternative
12 Plaster of __
13 Warn
18 Multivitamin supplement
23 Is not well
25 Hasten
26 Remain unsettled
27 Widespread
28 Letter-shaped building beam
29 Pasta sauce maker
30 Security feature
31 Howard of "Happy Days"
34 City east of Santa Barbara

35 "September __" (Neil Diamond hit)
36 Suffix with disk or novel
38 Answer to a señor
39 Golfer's gadget
42 Business letter encl.
43 Russian ruler's domain
44 Pained cries
45 Fraternity candidates
47 Fetches
48 Title role for Leslie Caron
49 Intolerant one

50 City between Gainesville and Orlando
51 West African river
54 Novelist Hunter
55 Climber
57 Son of Hera
58 Honey
59 Fateful day in March
62 A Gershwin brother
63 Gun owners' grp.

ACROSS

1 Starting four
5 Arm or leg
9 Goes on the fritz
14 Whopper maker
15 Teen ___
16 River of Pakistan
17 Fill beyond full
18 First name in scat
19 Bailout button
20 Horse-racing financial system?
23 Dairy airs?
24 Striped antelope
25 Jean on the screen
28 Young newts
29 Company that makes Wite-Out
32 At full speed
33 Lotion additive
34 Actor's pursuit
35 Races horses to gain authority?
38 Music player, for short
39 "What time ___?"
40 Put up with
41 Receiver of many Apr. checks
42 Closely related
43 Is on the same page, so to speak
44 Gave lines to
45 Peter Fonda role
46 Government support for horse-racing equipment?
51 Plant life
52 Sharer's word
53 Abbr. before ZIP code 10001
55 Oscar winner Marisa
56 Word processor option
57 Toledo's lake
58 Primitive fishing tool
59 Comedic Laurel
60 Iron pumper's count

DOWN

1 Rev. Sharpton and others
2 Prejudice
3 Suffragist Carrie Chapman ___
4 Surrealistic
5 Stay out of sight
6 Runs without moving
7 Suburban tunneler
8 Great Plains Indian
9 Maniacs
10 Certain pear
11 The same, in bibliographies
12 Desi loved her
13 Retired speedster
21 Trailblazing Daniel
22 External
25 Pilgrim to Mecca
26 Love in l'après-midi
27 Oven appurtenances
28 Pixie-sized
29 Jim at the Alamo
30 ___-France
31 First known asteroid
33 Hard-working

Puzzle 76 by M. Francis Vuolo

34 "All in the Family" co-star
36 "Egads!"
37 Beeped
42 Domestic from overseas
43 Grammy winner Krauss
44 Jazz's Chick
45 Abbr. on a food label
46 Horse's footfall
47 Seven Hills city
48 Minor hit
49 Brontë heroine
50 Short cut?
51 Knox and Dix: Abbr.
54 "You bet!"

ACROSS

1. Event attended by Cinderella
5. Dumbbells
10. Totally unexciting
14. Black-and-white cookie
15. W.W. II plane — Gay
16. Plumb crazy
17. Song from Sondheim's "A Little Night Music"
20. Aria flourishes
21. Start
22. Sound repeated while marching
23. Company with a crocodile logo
25. Soft shade
29. High rank
33. Cast member
34. Kukla, — and Ollie
35. "Eureka!"
36. Scene of dazzling goings-on
40. Loving murmur
41. Toledo's lake
42. Vermont city
43. Catcher's position
46. Drives back
47. — liquor
48. Disfigure
49. Stream
52. Scale interval
57. "The Greatest Show on Earth" purveyors
60. "Holy Toledo!"
61. Bar patron's request, with "the"

62. Edward who popularized the limerick
63. Old bandleader Columbo
64. — roof
65. Dashed

DOWN

1. Pear variety
2. Vicinity
3. Allow temporary use of
4. Ore's locale
5. Washington of Hollywood
6. Alternative to "in a bottle"
7. Cries from Homer Simpson
8. Spanish cheer
9. Baglike structure
10. Mae West, for one
11. Temperature extremes
12. Clearasil target
13. Party-giver
18. Be a natural part
19. Diving bird with a weird call
23. Public persona
24. Multivitamin additive
25. Quilt part
26. Sneezer's cry
27. Late Sen. Thurmond
28. Stubbed item
29. "Sesame Street" Muppet
30. Button material

31 Rude person
32 Simplifies
34 Blue-ribbon position
37 True
38 Spain and Portugal
39 Eminem's music
44 Corrects
45 Azerbaijan's capital
46 Walk aimlessly
48 Olympic award
49 "Good buddy"
50 Spaghetti sauce brand
51 Historical times

52 Social rebuff
53 Pinball error
54 Yellow sub?
55 Close in on
56 Brontë's "Jane ___"
58 Root beer order
59 Happy ___ lark

ACROSS

1 Othello, for one
5 Indian prince
10 — no. (bank info)
14 Helper
15 Like a gymnast
16 Became tattered
17 Trudge
18 King portrayer on stage and screen
20 Neighbor of Israel
22 Sailing
23 Suffix with hotel
24 Carte starter
26 Deceptive
28 Spokesperson who liked "wild hickory nuts"
34 Co. with a plant
35 Tennis serving whiz
36 Brazilian dance
40 State of mind
42 Speeder's bane
44 Wine label info
45 Silk-producing region
47 "Shake a leg!"
48 Baseball stat.
49 Annual winter celebration
53 Sweater material
56 Shelley's "— Skylark"
57 Goose pimples producer
58 Fluster
62 Looks at lustfully
66 Possible comment before an embarrassing admission
69 Give marks to
70 Army NCO
71 Ventriloquist Bergen
72 Book before Nehemiah
73 Burpee unit
74 Not just words
75 One taking a gander

DOWN

1 Cartographic products
2 Like unwashed hair, maybe
3 Scent
4 Phone feature
5 Beam of light
6 Lago contents
7 Reject, as a beau
8 Priestly wear
9 Regarding this point
10 Barley bristle
11 Like highway traffic markers
12 Rural swimming place
13 Robe fabric
19 Tall tales
21 Everybody
25 Petri dish filler
27 Brit's exclamation
28 Meddlesome heroine of an 1816 novel
29 Some streaking lights, briefly
30 Ardent love

31 Start of Caesar's boast
32 — roses
33 Atlanta player
37 "Jeopardy!" creator — Griffin
38 Rum-soaked cake
39 Seed covering
41 Belafonte song catchword
43 Musical mark
46 Many a commissioned artwork
50 Served, as soup
51 Unduly

52 "You have my support"
53 Bottomless chasm
54 Lasso part
55 Overcharge
59 Miami-— County
60 Winter Olympics sport
61 Quaint cry of horror
63 Do-nothing
64 Raison d'—
65 Burn
67 Old Ford model
68 Mins. and mins.

ACROSS

1 Overabundance
5 Party pooper
9 Excited, in dialect
14 Viking letter
15 Counterpart of a count
16 Wipe off, as a slate
17 Person in the '00 class, e.g.
18 ___ cost (free)
19 King or czar
20 Very tight, as 38-Across
23 Peacock's pride
24 Torched
25 Departure's opposite: Abbr.
28 Put back in office
31 At wit's ___
34 Seashore
36 Sidewalk stand drink
37 Jai ___
38 Subject of frequent reports by helicopter
42 Catch sight of
43 Old cloth
44 It helps you get a leg up
45 Mudhole
46 Welsh ___
49 Hush-hush org.
50 "Can't Help Lovin' ___ Man"
51 Old-fashioned verses
53 Auto commuter's companion
60 Paris's river

61 "Mamma Mia" group
62 A deadly sin
63 Number of deadly sins
64 Convene
65 Cut like a letter opener
66 Lock of hair
67 Raison d'___
68 Additionally

DOWN

1 Get, as a cab
2 Doozie
3 E pluribus ___
4 Entice
5 Honeybunch
6 Noisy toy
7 River through Florence
8 Amount squeezed from a tube
9 Loner
10 Blow one's top
11 Fable
12 Customer
13 Pay-___-view
21 Third rock from the sun
22 Problem of the stomach lining
25 Fields are measured in them
26 Push out of bed
27 Hoarse
29 The "L" of XXL
30 Summer hrs., in N.Y.C.
31 Spritelike

32 Symbols of hardness
33 Judicial declarations
35 Like a wallflower
37 Toward the stern
39 Preach
40 Former Mideast alliance: Abbr.
41 Fall flower
46 Baltimore 11
47 Plane on a mission
48 Put on one's thinking cap
50 Has supper
52 Chip dip
53 Bucks and does
54 Split
55 Easily calmed
56 Sarcastic reply to an assurance
57 Uninteresting
58 Egyptian fertility goddess
59 Director Preminger
60 Champagne-flight jet, once

ACROSS

1 Louganis who did gainers
5 Gelled garnish
10 Greenish-blue
14 Back
15 Animal life
16 Vice president under Jefferson
17 Gymnast Korbut
18 Place to say "I do"
19 Lacking spring or curl, as hair
20 Eloquent
23 He's no bull
24 Kind of sign
25 Uncooked
28 Reason to call a plumber
31 Jeweled headdress
33 "60 Minutes" network
36 Like a fast driver
40 Way to learn, after "by"
42 Concur
43 Prime-time time
44 Tyrannical
46 Real heel
47 __ Gras
48 Invitation notation
51 Computer program suffix
52 Wicked
56 Wipe out
60 Possible title for this puzzle
64 Famous cookie guy
66 Mischievous one
67 Stopgap measure for a 28-Across
68 Sticky stuff
69 Tourist's aid
70 "__ homo" (Pilate's words)
71 Television award
72 Playful animal
73 Suggestive look

DOWN

1 "Ewww!"
2 Like twice-smoked cigars
3 American symbol
4 Driveway surface
5 Off in the distance
6 Sodium chloride
7 Pretense
8 Foolish
9 Freight
10 Competent
11 Algebraic equation
12 Large coffee holder
13 Biblical boat
21 Before, once
22 Golden rule word
26 Sports venue
27 Went in ankle-deep
29 __ Mountains, near the Tian Shan range
30 They're found under the counter at bars
32 Charged particle
33 Arson, e.g.
34 Cleansing agent
35 Pantry

Puzzle 80 by Nancy Kavanaugh

37 "If the — is concealed, it succeeds": Ovid
38 Bambi, for one
39 D.E.A. employees, e.g.
41 Butt
45 Feudal land
49 Neckline type
50 Urge onward
53 Sign of summer
54 Going either direction
55 Kosher
57 Swiftly

58 Pie portion
59 Sniggler
61 Spot
62 Dapper fellow
63 Equal
64 Get older
65 May honoree

ACROSS

1 Unwanted e-mail
5 Top spot
9 Stupid jerk
14 Attire for Caesar
15 Get-out-of-jail money
16 Toward the back
17 Writer Waugh
18 "Coffee, Tea __?" (1960's best seller)
19 Light bulb holders
20 "Vanilla Sky" actress
23 Young 'un
24 "I Like __"
25 Carryall
29 Dead-on
31 How often Santa checks his list
33 Pie __ mode
34 "I found it!"
36 Tic-tac-toe win
37 One who's close-mouthed
38 Maiden voyage preceder
43 City near Osaka
44 Live
45 "__ the ramparts . . ."
46 Human's cousin
47 Old-time oath
49 1960's tripper Timothy
53 Best Picture of 1997
55 3 on a sundial
57 Grassy area
58 Ballpark maintenance groups
61 Pulitzer winner __ Jefferson
64 Unaccompanied
65 Bush's __ of Evil
66 Be of use
67 Swear
68 Nothing more than
69 Crown sparkler
70 Zany Martha
71 Waterfront walkway

DOWN

1 Paper clip alternative
2 Medieval weapon
3 Meeting plan
4 Nutmeg spice
5 "You can't judge __ by its cover"
6 Wall-to-wall installation
7 Charades player
8 November event
9 Military action?
10 Fad
11 Skirt stitching
12 Atlas page
13 Hosp. areas
21 Supple
22 Highly ornate
26 "__ Ha'i"
27 "Oh, woe!"
28 Charades, e.g.
30 Wedding reception centerpiece
32 Impressed, and how!

Puzzle 81 by Allan E. Parrish

35 Slowly, to a conductor
37 Medical breakthrough
38 It's played with a deck of 32 cards
39 Arizona Indian
40 Aid in crime
41 Delphic
42 Thing from the past
47 Sign up
48 Actor Poitier
50 Soviet leader ___ Kosygin
51 Provide with new cable

52 Late P.L.O. head Arafat
54 Texas A & M athlete
56 Grenoble's river
59 Popular PBS science series
60 Interstate exit
61 Rank below Lt. Col.
62 "___ Maria"
63 Like crunchy carrots

ACROSS

1 Be sweet on
6 "Quiet!"
9 Boy Scout unit
14 The Bates __, in "Psycho"
15 Soccer star Hamm
16 Baseball Hall-of-Famer Combs
17 Poolside wear
20 Flat formation
21 Harold Gray's Annie, for one
22 Louse-to-be
23 Mountain debris
25 Gate pivots
27 Bird of 29-Down
30 Smart-mouthed
32 Prefix with -asian
33 A, B, C, D or E
35 Marsh plant
39 Giveaway: Var.
41 Place for butts
43 Final authority
44 Copycat's words
46 Auction ending?
47 Race marker
49 Be a buttinsky
51 Disco flasher
54 Put a stop to
56 Jackie's second
57 Available, as a doctor
59 Org. for Annika Sorenstam
63 House wear
66 Kosher
67 Narc's grp.
68 Place for rouge
69 Idyllic places
70 Map rtes.
71 Acts the stool pigeon

DOWN

1 Radio letters
2 1996 Republican standard-bearer
3 Elevator maker
4 Meal
5 Polar helper
6 Campfire treat
7 Maximally cool
8 Truck stop fare
9 Court wear
10 "Awesome!"
11 Sumatra swinger
12 Pal of Kukla and Fran
13 Royal pains
18 Country singer Morgan
19 Contented sighs
24 Ranch wear
26 Russian's refusal
27 Gridiron "zebras"
28 Heavenly glow
29 Mouse, to a 27-Across
31 At the drop of __
34 Audition tape
36 __ Scott Decision
37 Celt or Highlander
38 Brontë's Jane
40 Hockey great Phil, familiarly

Puzzle 82 by Kent Lorentzen

42 Mogadishu resident
45 Placed in a box, say
48 Late-night Jay
50 Oracle site
51 Fine fur
52 In a tough spot
53 Chain of hills
55 Fitzgerald and others
58 U.S.N. rank below Capt.
60 Hammer's end
61 Cyclist LeMond
62 Questions

64 __ Tin Tin
65 I.B.M.-compatibles

ACROSS

1 Birds' homes
6 Order (around)
10 Quaint cry of shock
14 Not bottled, as beer
15 Choir voice
16 Knot
17 Writer — Rogers St. Johns
18 Nay opposers
19 Coin opening
20 Nursery rhyme bakery item
23 Rap's Dr. —
24 Theater alert
25 More down and out
27 Omaha's home: Abbr.
30 Burden
33 Letters and packages
34 Make, in arithmetic
35 Reception with open arms
39 Was a passenger
41 Play on the radio
42 Supply-and-demand subj.
43 Tidy Lotto prize
48 Mary — cosmetics
49 Sweet Spanish dessert
50 Suffix with kitchen
51 Railroad stop: Abbr.
52 Once-fashionable card game
55 PanAm rival
57 Doctors' org.
58 Scarce consolation
64 Pompeii, e.g., today
66 Writer Ephron
67 Anouk of "La Dolce Vita"
68 Capital NNW of Copenhagen
69 Slaughter of the 1940's–50's Cardinals
70 —-fatty acid
71 Taking the blue ribbon
72 Fall mo.
73 Elephant groups

DOWN

1 Ark builder
2 Prefix with derm
3 Leave in, as text
4 Bathroom powders
5 Songbird
6 Seabiscuit and Citation, e.g.
7 Barcelona cheers
8 Pierces
9 Flip response to a complaint
10 Naval rank: Abbr.
11 Famous bed tester
12 Love to pieces
13 Keep (from)
21 Mrs. Chaplin
22 Patricia who won an Oscar for "Hud"
26 Backgammon equipment
27 Drug cop
28 Suffix with switch
29 Not the most comfortable place to sleep
31 Russia's — Mountains

32 Grin
36 Lawyer's document
37 Palace protector
38 "A Day Without Rain" singer, 2000
40 Singer Fitzgerald
44 Fem. opposite
45 Recites
46 Germany's — von Bismarck
47 Educational innovation of the 1960's
52 Tree with pods
53 Entertain

54 By oneself
56 Blazing
59 Let go
60 Play group?
61 Bridge master Sharif
62 Tear
63 "— of the D'Urbervilles"
65 Word in most of the Commandments

ACROSS

1 Bongo or conga
5 Bellhop's burden
8 Integra maker
13 Diarist Frank
14 Concert halls
16 "Vacancy" sign site
17 Star of 59-Across
20 Got 100 on
21 Extinct bird
22 Brazilian hot spot
23 Director of 59-Across
27 Pampering, briefly
28 Olive __
29 Saragossa's river
30 Circusgoers' sounds
32 Understand
34 "__ Irish Rose"
38 Music featured in 59-Across
42 English assignment
43 Slangy refusal
44 Classic soda brand
45 Tiff
48 PBS funder
50 III, to Jr.
51 Author of 59-Across
56 A.F.L. former partner
57 Suffix with Peking
58 "__ #1!"
59 Theme of this puzzle, with "A"
65 Like bell-bottoms, nowadays
66 Claudius's successor
67 Highlander

68 Bus. aides
69 Little bit
70 Fair-hiring org.

DOWN

1 River regulator
2 Genetic stuff
3 Opens, as a gate
4 Hajji's destination
5 Proceed à la Captain Kirk?
6 Nimitz or Halsey: Abbr.
7 Glittering, like a diamond
8 Latin 101 verb
9 It's no bull
10 Wombs
11 Archaeologist's find
12 Free of problems
15 "Have __ and a smile" (old slogan)
18 Wine: Prefix
19 Paint crudely
23 Plumlike fruits
24 Mtn. stat
25 Fiber source
26 Radio personality __ Quivers
27 Repeated words in a famous soliloquy
31 Narc's discovery
33 Hamilton's bill
35 Fundamentally
36 Group values
37 Tibia's locale
39 Doc's needle

Puzzle 84 by M. Francis Vuolo

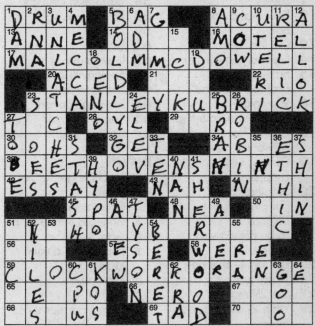

D	R	U	M		B	A	G			A	C	U	R	A
A	N	N	E		O	D		15		M	O	T	E	L
M	A	L	C	O	L	M	M	C	D	O	W	E	L	L
		A	C	E	D		21				R	I	O	
S	T	A	N	L	E	Y	K	U	B	R	I	C	K	
I		C		D	Y	L		29		R	O			
O	D	H	S		G	E	T		A	B		E	S	
B	E	E	T	H	O	V	E	N	S	N	I	N	T	H
E	S	S	A	Y			N	A	H		N	H	I	
		S	P	A	T		N	E	A			I	N	
K	I	40		Y	B	R						C		
I		E	S	E		W	E	R	E					
C	L	O	C	K	W	O	R	K	O	R	A	N	G	E
E	S	P	Q		N	E	R	O			O			
S	U	S		A	D						O			

40 Half an Orkan farewell
41 Forest name
46 From the top
47 Ex-champ Mike
49 Antiquing agent
51 Capital of Ghana
52 Frasier's brother
53 Whistle blasts
54 Special Forces cap
55 Wipe clean
60 PC component
61 Ring victories, for short

62 Malay Peninsula's Isthmus of __
63 Gloppy stuff
64 List ender

ACROSS

1 Layers
7 Sound of a lightning bolt
10 Cut the hair of
14 Main argument
15 Frank Sinatra's "__ Fool to Want You"
16 Top-notch
17 Losses, in accounting
18 Charlie Rose's network
19 Serving with chop suey
20 Jonathan Swift pamphlet about Ireland
23 To be given away
24 Court
25 The whole shebang
26 Twisty turn
27 See 29-Across
29 With 27-Across, get hitched
31 Cigarette residue
34 Ukr., once
35 Flight paths
37 Reason for turning down an invitation
41 Capulet rival
42 Stars and Stripes land
43 Ocean
44 Guess: Abbr.
45 Film director Craven
46 Nightwear, for short
49 Helios' Roman counterpart
51 Calf's mother
53 Jai __
54 2003 teen comedy
59 Practice, as skills
60 Apply
61 Territory
62 In addition
63 Spy novelist Deighton
64 Show clearly
65 Spelling contests
66 "Acid"
67 Caught, as fish

DOWN

1 Machine-gun by plane
2 One's wife, slangily
3 Changes the decor of
4 Actor's whisper
5 Point at the dinner table?
6 Implores
7 Nothin'
8 Olympian repast
9 El __, Tex.
10 Noel
11 Clark Kent's gal
12 Ancient Peruvian
13 Speed away, with "out"
21 Number of teeth Goofy has
22 Popular discount shoe store
27 Tel Aviv native
28 Worthless part
30 Bandy words
32 Capitol Hill V.I.P.: Abbr.

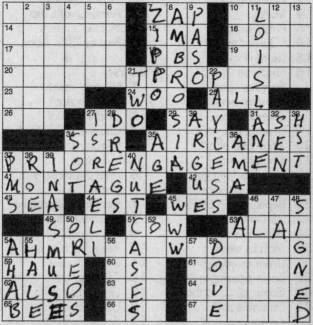

33 President after F.D.R.
34 Drunkard
35 Get better, as wine
36 Drs.' group
37 Afternoons and evenings, briefly
38 Caviar
39 Kinda
40 Wackos
45 Internet start-up?
46 Flexible
47 Actress Rule
48 Like finished contracts
50 Nabisco cookies

52 Continuously
53 Come clean
54 Ishmael's captain
55 Spy
56 Select
57 First lady's residence
58 Hawk's opposite

ACROSS

1 Punching tool
4 Minus
8 Purity units
14 "Quiet down!"
15 Lie next to
16 Supreme Egyptian god
17 Summer weather phenomenon
19 Dreadlocks wearers
20 With little effort
21 Itinerary word
23 Nervous twitches
24 Like an old cigar
25 Repel, as an attack
27 25-Down, e.g.
29 Within view
30 Marina event
35 Drum majors' props
39 Basin accompanier
40 Coeur d'___, Idaho
42 Feminine suffix
43 Arnaz and Ball's studio
45 Eat quickly
47 Pick up
49 Bering, e.g.: Abbr.
50 Dark, heavy type
53 A black key
58 Colombian city
59 Bruised item, maybe
60 Automat, e.g.
61 Ersatz gold
63 Winter weather phenomenon
65 Launderer, at times
66 Sheriff Taylor's son
67 Former New York City mayor Beame
68 Admits, with "up"
69 Not very much
70 Part of CBS: Abbr.

DOWN

1 Hibachi residue
2 Toast choice
3 Tibet's capital
4 Like the Wild West
5 Popular site for collectors
6 Ford Explorer, e.g.: Abbr.
7 Martin of "Roxanne"
8 Martial arts wear
9 "I ___ Rock" (1966 hit)
10 Went back to the top
11 Bit of silliness
12 CD segment
13 Get snippy with
18 Up to, briefly
22 Actor Holm
25 High school subj.
26 Ovine utterance
28 Some prom night drivers
30 Hospital unit
31 Have markers out
32 Loser to D.D.E.
33 Lots and lots and lots
34 A browser browses it, with "the"
36 Lennon's lady
37 Compass heading
38 Six-yr. term holder
41 It smells

Note: The circled letters will show a "change in the weather."

44 Topper
46 Like most tires
48 Baseball put-out
50 Ballet rail
51 "Stand and Deliver" star
52 Après-ski drink
54 McHenry and Sumter: Abbr.
55 Olin and Horne
56 Sheikdom of song
57 Pounds on an Underwood
58 Salon creation
60 Director Kazan
62 Jackie Onassis' sister
64 Make a choice

ACROSS

1 Manila envelope closer
6 Computer screen image
10 "Spare tire"
14 Dominican Republic neighbor
15 Italia's capital
16 Interlude
17 Luggage clip-on
18 "Amo, amas, — . . ."
19 Prod
20 It made Leary bleary
22 Rizzuto of the 1940's–50's Yankees
24 Fire, as from a job
25 Unruffled
28 Laid on generously
30 Tot's wheels
32 Hwy. mishap respondent
33 Med school subj.
34 Driveway occupant
36 Becomes a domehead
40 Skirt that shows off legs
41 Pasture
43 Forsaken
44 Fossil fuel blocks
46 Harry Potter's lightning bolt, e.g.
47 Suffix with buck
48 Piercing site
50 Exceed the bounds of
52 Summary holder?

56 With resolute spirit
57 WSW's opposite
58 Party for lei wearers
59 — Lanka
60 — Jay Lerner of Lerner & Loewe
62 Jolt
64 Jazz's James and Jones
68 Fall's opposite
69 Sea eagle
70 System utilizing grates
71 Editor's mark
72 Space capsule insignia
73 Rulers before Lenin

DOWN

1 Greek X
2 Boy
3 River island
4 Downers?
5 Farm pen
6 Tax deferral means: Abbr.
7 Connectors?
8 Nebraska city
9 Not an emigré
10 Winter ailment
11 Leave in the —
12 Pond growths
13 Mix
21 Joe that won't keep you up
23 Arm or leg
25 Envelope sticker

Puzzle 87 by Patrick Merrell

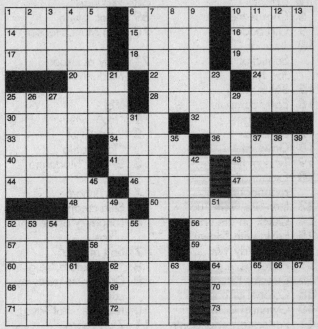

26 Bert's Muppet pal
27 Late Princess of Wales
29 Uppers?
31 San __ Obispo, Calif.
35 Norway's patron saint
37 Peter of "Casablanca"
38 Slobber
39 Like a winter wonderland
42 Wine residue
45 Comedian Mort
49 Sandwich with sauerkraut

51 Least seen
52 Closes in on
53 Dark
54 Pull one's leg
55 Mrs. Bush
61 Volleyball equipment
63 Small coal size
65 Intl. flier, once
66 __ Lingus
67 Last year's jrs.

ACROSS

1 Cripple
5 Chorus member
9 Old adders
14 Alan of "The Seduction of Joe Tynan"
15 Ballet move
16 Early computer language
17 Light gas
18 Gawk at
19 Type of type
20 Examination, redundantly
23 Increase, with "up"
24 Quick on the uptake
25 Frisk, with "down"
28 "The Way We __"
31 Perfectos, e.g.
36 Director Kazan
38 Colonel or captain
40 Gymnast Comaneci
41 Pestering, redundantly
44 Uniform shade
45 Student driver, usually
46 Slugger Sammy
47 Gets smart with
49 Try for a part
51 One of 100 in D.C.
52 Conquistador's prize
54 Whisper sweet nothings
56 Angry outburst, redundantly
63 Oscar winner Foster
64 Unable to decide
65 Took off

67 Maine college town
68 "Zounds!"
69 Jacob's twin
70 Von Münchhausen, e.g.
71 Lady of Lisbon
72 Medium-__

DOWN

1 "Hoo-ey!"
2 Baldwin of "Talk Radio"
3 Elvis or Madonna, e.g.
4 Lord's home
5 Skin cream ingredient
6 Longevity at the box office
7 Soft mineral
8 "Il Trovatore," e.g.
9 Driving the getaway car for
10 Island east of Java
11 Z — zebra
12 Like lowest-mileage driving
13 Diamonds, slangily
21 Stitch up
22 Bars at the checkout counter: Abbr.
25 Eats like a bird
26 Maui greeting
27 Louise and Turner
29 Carry on
30 Keyboard key
32 Comedian's stock
33 Sonora "so long"
34 Washer cycle

Puzzle 88 by Randall J. Hartman

35 "Contact" author Carl
37 Invites
39 Patella's place
42 Get snockered
43 It puts the squeeze on
48 Hindu title
50 Singer McLean
53 Made a choice
55 Put forward
56 Mrs. Dithers
57 Dump problem
58 El __ (weather factor)
59 Like some pizza orders
60 Gulf land
61 Rick's love in "Casablanca"
62 Something shed
63 Applicant's goal
66 Expected in

ACROSS

1 Homebuilder's strip
5 Bruins of the Pac 10
9 Unflashy
14 "Can you hear me? . . . hear me? . . . hear me?"
15 Horse in a 60's sitcom
16 Ralph — Emerson
17 "What a shame!"
18 Laser light
19 Go in
20 Overly florid writing
23 Acorn maker
24 Before, to Byron
25 Recharges one's batteries, so to speak
27 Bucky Beaver's toothpaste, in old ads
31 Switchblade
33 Weapons of — destruction
37 Pesos
39 Prefix with metric or tonic
40 Author Ferber
41 1951 Alec Guinness film, with "The"
44 City west of Tulsa
45 Night before
46 Go on Social Security, maybe
47 One-and-only
48 Mouth off to
50 September bloom
51 Frisbee, e.g.
53 Some univ. instructors

55 "I knew it!"
58 The 1890's
64 Reaction to the Beatles, once
66 Flying: Prefix
67 Pitch
68 "Git — Little Dogies"
69 Section of seats
70 58-Across and others
71 "Death Be Not Proud" poet John
72 North Carolina college
73 Hourly pay

DOWN

1 — year (2004, e.g.)
2 Legal rights grp.
3 In that direction, to a whaler
4 The "H" in "M*A*S*H": Abbr.
5 Brownish
6 Thin pancakes
7 "All in the Family" producer Norman
8 Call on the carpet
9 Clean the carpet
10 Brownish
11 Choir voice
12 Notion
13 Social misfit
21 Memorize
22 —-faire
26 Gets the lead out?
27 Runs in neutral
28 Upright or baby grand

29 Blacksmith's block
30 Had to have
32 Root beer brand
34 Fess up to
35 Sound of slumber
36 Cavalry blade
38 Texas oil city
42 Clear out, as before a hurricane
43 Renter's paper
49 Alternative to mono
52 Likeness
54 Decorate

55 "Diary of ___ Housewife" (1970 film)
56 Angel's headwear
57 Unattributed: Abbr.
59 Bridal wear
60 Grind with the teeth
61 Distinctive quality
62 Quarter-mile race, e.g.
63 In addition
65 Holiday ___

ACROSS

1 Sagittarius, with "the"
7 "My gal" et al.
11 Any ship
14 Aplenty
15 Apple product
16 Wee one
17 Goddess of love's love
18 Washroom
20 "— the season . . ."
21 Roof part
23 Certain refrigerators
24 Broke ground
26 Chicken order
28 Pub stock
29 Showy annual
31 This puzzle has a secret one, starting with the third letter of 4-Down
34 Prefix with classical
36 "— we forget . . ."
37 Salon stiffener
38 "Unbelievable!"
42 Patient people
44 "Exodus" hero
45 Misses the mark
47 Govt. code crackers
48 What to do to read the secret message (going diagonally down, then diagonally back up the under side)
51 Inputs into a computer
55 Afternoon affairs
56 Say — (refuse)
58 Smarmy
59 Throat part
61 Scent
63 "If I Ruled the World" rapper
64 "Is everything all right?"
66 Manage, slangily
68 Dogfaces
69 Scruff
70 Regal fur
71 Plea at sea
72 Took action against
73 Cash in

DOWN

1 First name in mystery
2 Contacts from space
3 Skeleton site
4 Sweetie pie
5 Old railroad name
6 Cut again
7 Llama's head?
8 Docs' grp.
9 Hot issue
10 Con guy
11 "The Flintstones" setting
12 More than a pest
13 Popular ice cream
19 Locker room supply
22 Nobleman above a baron: Abbr.
25 Disavow

Puzzle 90 by J. Bower and N. Salomon

27 Greek Mother Earth
30 Booms' opposites
32 ID in a library
33 Overhead trains
35 __ cloud (cosmic debris)
38 Monopoly token
39 Choral work
40 Portrait, e.g.
41 St. Paul's architect
43 Belafonte song opener
46 Scared a bit
49 "Calm down . . ."

50 Part of E.S.T.: Abbr.
52 Small digit
53 "Seinfeld" role
54 Modus operandi
57 Awed one
59 Marks
60 Island get-together
62 Hard to find
65 Reveal, poetically
67 Mil. authority

ACROSS

1 People who make you yawn
6 Tibetan monk
10 British fellow
14 Crème de la crème
15 Had payments due
16 Part of a Valentine bouquet
17 Greek marketplace
18 Glenn Miller's "In the __"
19 Leave out
20 Testifier in a court case
23 Sea eagles
24 "__ will be done . . ."
25 Event with floats
29 Female in a pride
33 Hebrew prophet
34 Be enraptured
36 Animal that beats its chest
37 Pleasant excursion
41 Golf peg
42 Abominates
43 Gillette razor
44 Regards highly
46 Mother of Joseph
48 Wayne film "__ Bravo"
49 Prayer's end
51 Top of a tall building, maybe
59 After-bath powder
60 Fed chairman Greenspan
61 Harold who composed "Over the Rainbow"
62 Gait faster than a walk
63 Film part
64 Cotton thread
65 Disastrous marks for a gymnast
66 Gardener's spring purchase
67 Outpouring

DOWN

1 Smile widely
2 Korbut of the 1972 Olympics
3 Very funny person
4 Raison d'__
5 Charred
6 Fictional salesman Willy
7 M.P.'s hunt them
8 Pussy's cry
9 Building wing
10 Actor Hume
11 Where the heart is, they say
12 Sale tag caution
13 Dogs, but rarely hogs
21 Anger
22 Daring bikini
25 Stickum
26 French girlfriends
27 Synonym man
28 Cigarette's end
29 Colleague of Clark at The Daily Planet

Puzzle 91 by Robert Dillman

30 Our planet
31 Steeple
32 Flower part
34 Film designers' designs
35 Tiny
38 Not our
39 Tea urns
40 Tic-__-toe
45 Builds
46 __ Speedwagon
47 Chronicles
49 "It is __ told by an idiot": Macbeth

50 Dug up
51 __ the Great (10th-century king)
52 Building near a silo
53 __ gin fizz
54 __ vera
55 What icicles do
56 Lohengrin's love
57 Boston cager, informally
58 Leg's middle

ACROSS

1 Let out the waist of, e.g.
6 Ark or bark
10 Mexican Mlle.
14 Pet —
15 Up to it
16 Rattler's posture
17 Supporter of the arts?
18 Title start of a 2003 Al Franken best seller
19 Still pink
20 Fool a onetime child actor?
23 Tiebreakers, briefly
25 Clean-air org.
26 Elite group
27 Cause a sleepy old man to stumble?
32 Car owner's document
33 With respect to
34 Toe the line
35 Black Russian ingredient
37 20's dispensers
41 "See ya!"
42 Orderly grouping
43 Express gratitude to a country singer?
47 Greasy —
49 Rip-roaring time
50 Frisk, with "down"
51 Tie up a Midwest senator?
56 Wholly absorbed
57 Show opener
58 Like a luxury car
61 Suit to —

62 Guitarist Atkins
63 Give a wide berth
64 Garden intruder
65 Unabridged dictionary, e.g.
66 The out crowd

DOWN

1 Mock, in a way
2 Grazing locale
3 Bikini atoll, once
4 At any time
5 Take over for, as a pitcher
6 Europe's — Peninsula
7 Eastern sashes
8 A Baldwin
9 New-Ager John
10 Dead Sea document
11 Band hand
12 Gets pooped
13 Heads-up
21 Number cruncher, for short
22 Croupier's tool
23 "Beetle Bailey" dog
24 Chicago paper, familiarly, with "the"
28 Panel layer
29 Lehár's "The Merry —"
30 Publicity, slangily
31 Org. whose members are packing?
35 Chablis, for one
36 — Park, Ill.
37 "Exodus" hero
38 Secret exit, perhaps

Puzzle 92 by Seth A. Abel

39 Doll's cry
40 Part of CBS: Abbr.
41 Gives the boot
42 Election loser
43 Rug, so to speak
44 Emceed
45 Set off
46 Fall behind
47 Scarecrow stuffing
48 Chatter idly
52 It's true
53 Bounce back
54 Agenda unit
55 Zero, on a court

59 —-Atlantic
60 QB's pickups

ACROSS

1 Chances
5 Wires on a bicycle wheel
11 Tavern
14 In __ of (substituting for)
15 One of Jerry's pals on "Seinfeld"
16 Down Under bird
17 Bejeweled president?
19 Mo. of Presidents' Day
20 "Much __ About Nothing"
21 Dine
22 Planet
24 Pale, aging president?
28 Most elderly
31 Hang around for
32 Place to store valuables
33 Hair colorer
34 __ and hearty
38 Devoted follower
40 Demolisher
42 More's opposite
43 Opening for a tab
45 Zeal
46 Burning up
48 Disinfects
49 Comic president?
53 Wheel turners
54 Tint
55 Historic period
58 Compete (for)
59 Hirsute president?
64 Mont Blanc, e.g.
65 Money earned
66 Communicate by hand
67 Tennis court divider
68 Check receivers
69 Neighborhood

DOWN

1 Gymnast Korbut
2 Stopped working, as an engine
3 Showroom model
4 Total
5 Trigonometric ratio
6 Ancient Greek thinker
7 Paddle
8 Set of tools
9 WSW's reverse
10 Composer Rachmaninoff
11 Obscure
12 Tiny creature
13 "American Idol" winner __ Studdard
18 Frothy
23 One using lots of soap
24 Object of a dowser's search
25 Reclined
26 Lived
27 Like hen's teeth
28 The White House's __ Office
29 Delicate fabric
30 Performing twosomes
33 "We love to fly, and it shows" airline

Puzzle 93 by Charles Barasch

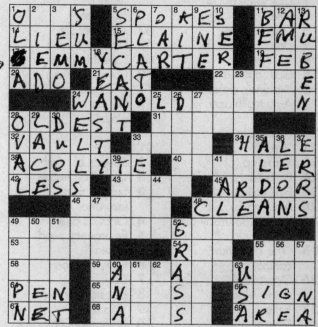

G

35 Alan of "M*A*S*H"
36 Ponce de —
37 Goofs
39 Nicholas I or II
41 Appraiser
44 "— the land of the free . . ."
47 Send again
48 Slides
49 From Jakarta, e.g.
50 Kick out of the country
51 Snoozed
52 Lemon — (herb)
55 Kuwaiti ruler
56 Fury
57 "— and the King of Siam"
60 Santa — winds
61 Wintry
62 Shad product
63 Land between Can. and Mex.

ACROSS

1 Like some appliances, electrically
5 Field of work
9 Daft
14 Bailiwick
15 Gossip tidbit
16 Wahine's welcome
17 Auto trailblazer
19 Eatery
20 Small sofa
21 "Drat!"
23 Wrap up
24 Ltr. holders
26 First course, often
28 Auto trailblazer
34 Kid-___ (Saturday a.m. fare)
35 "The Thin Man" canine
36 Operation at the Alamo
37 Yalies
39 Slangy denial
42 Protein bean
43 Freeze over
45 Self-identifying word
47 "All Things Considered" network
48 Auto trailblazer
52 Slip on the galley
53 Dead against
54 Little shaver
57 Suffragist Carrie
59 Plays the role of
63 Geologic period
65 What 17-, 28- and 48-Across were, so to speak
67 Alphabet set
68 Director Kazan
69 Equestrian's grip
70 Camera setting
71 Withhold from
72 Hot Springs and others

DOWN

1 Sounds of relief
2 Canadian native
3 Subject of an insurance appraisal
4 OPEC is one
5 Emergency need at sea
6 Skater Midori
7 Dork
8 Ellipsis alternative
9 Villains
10 Poetry-spouting pugilist
11 Muscle quality
12 Ergo
13 Prison exercise area
18 Gossipmonger
22 Here-there connector
25 Young lady of Sp.
27 Trident-shaped letters
28 Radioer's "Good as done!"
29 Toulouse "Toodleoo"
30 "The Cider House Rules" co-star, 1999

Puzzle 94 by B. Frank and N. Salomon

31 Sierra ___
32 Land from which Moses came
33 Bring up
34 Bride hider
38 Spades or clubs
40 Explosive star
41 Refuse admission to
44 Prep mentally
46 Lumberjack's first cut
49 Reviewer of books, for short
50 Place of rapid growth
51 Soda bottle units

54 Fall faller
55 Gibbons and gorillas
56 "Go ahead!"
58 Scrabble piece
60 Trickle
61 Inter ___
62 Workers' ID's
64 Sound in a barn rafter
66 Martini ingredient

ACROSS

1 Shade trees
5 Consent (to)
10 Baby bottle contents
14 "See you later!"
15 Senior dances
16 Assert
17 Flimflam
19 Roman cloak
20 __ of a kind
21 Warp-resistant wood
22 Temptress
23 One who went to tell the king the sky was falling
26 Not just ask
29 Commotions
30 Family data
31 Juicy tropical fruit
33 Watering hole
36 Perform a dance with a shake
40 WNW's opposite
41 Hackneyed
42 Wall Street inits.
43 Wearisome one
44 Archipelago parts
46 Some messing around
49 Narrative
51 The "A" of ABM
52 Just great
55 Royal attendant
56 Mishmash
59 Asia's shrinking __ Sea
60 County north of San Francisco

61 Where a stream may run
62 Lots of
63 Clay pigeon shoot
64 Final word

DOWN

1 Talk back?
2 Big cat
3 Nutmeg relative
4 Not worth a __
5 Tack on
6 Bad pun response
7 Having lots of ups and downs
8 Cousin of an ostrich
9 Road curve
10 Morning prayers
11 Off-white
12 Theater section
13 Skating champ Michelle
18 British gun
22 Busybody
23 Dish of leftovers
24 Group of jurors
25 Jittery
26 Florida's Miami-__ County
27 Selves
28 Apportion, with "out"
31 Miser's hoarding
32 Alias
33 __ terrier
34 Nuisance
35 One side of a vote
37 Jet black
38 "Listen!"

Puzzle 95 by Anne Garelick

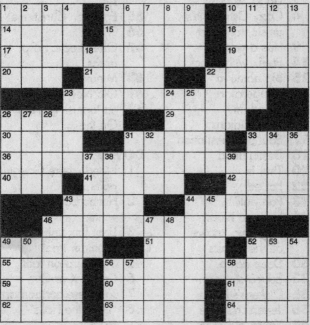

39 Exclusively
43 By the skin of one's teeth
44 Purpose
45 Omit
46 Title colonel in a 1960's sitcom
47 Military chaplain
48 Actress Dickinson
49 Unsolicited e-mail
50 "Gone With the Wind" estate
52 Man cast out of paradise

53 Girl-watch, e.g.
54 Sharp
56 — Pinafore
57 Acorn's source
58 Reproductive cells

ACROSS

1 Up to, in ads
4 Ozzy Osbourne's music, for short
9 Has a yen
14 Prefix with puncture
15 Big name in refrigerators
16 Good, in Guadalajara
17 Sound of hesitation
18 Desilu head
20 That is
22 Posted
23 Pan pal?
26 Ham, to Noah
29 One who knows all the secrets
30 Deep down
33 Educators' org.
35 Dickens's Heep
36 Jefferson's note
42 Yours, old-style
43 Suffix with expert
44 Spoiled
47 Austere
53 With 36-Down, "Next . . ."
54 Weevil's hatching place
56 Pennsylvania's — Mountains
59 Usher's locale
60 Michael Jordan, for years

64 Rest and relaxation site
65 Egyptian Christians
66 Pi, e.g.
67 Often-hectic hosp. areas
68 Minute —
69 Old New Yorker cartoonist William
70 On the —

DOWN

1 Island where Gauguin painted
2 Harborbound, in winter
3 Light flux units
4 Fountain treat
5 Swift bird on foot
6 Center X or O
7 Japanese cartoon art
8 "Deck the Halls" syllables
9 Genesis brother
10 Rubik creation
11 Foremast attachment
12 Big picture?: Abbr.
13 Our sun
19 Cheery song
21 Move among the moguls
24 Former Attorney General
25 Composer Jacques
27 Test type
28 Utmost

Puzzle 96 by Alan Arbesfeld

31 Airline's home base
32 "— tu" (Verdi aria)
34 Frazier foe
36 See 53-Across
37 Trachea
38 Que. neighbor
39 Cotillion girl
40 — prof.
41 Bank take-back
42 Former flying inits.
45 Slip — (blunder)
46 Bloodmobile visitors
48 Not digital

49 Sacrifice fly stat.
50 Ejected
51 Elite N.F.L.er
52 N.Y. Mets' div.
55 Go — for (support)
57 Eight: Prefix
58 Wine holder
60 Syringe amts.
61 All the rage
62 Colorado native
63 XXVI doubled

ACROSS

1 Continental currency
5 Give off
9 Assumed name
14 Jazz's Kenton
15 Go (over) carefully
16 Officer's shield
17 Easy wins
19 With 62-Across, a possible title for this puzzle
20 Long sandwich
21 Regarding
23 Word after ready or petty
24 Web addresses, for short
26 List-ending abbr.
28 Young hospital helpers
33 Capone and Capp
34 Always, poetically
35 Predicament
37 Where a car may end up after an accident
40 Have dinner
42 Talent
43 Says "cheese"
45 Part of a baseball uniform
47 Tic-__-toe
48 Credits for doing nice things
52 The writing __ the wall
53 Choir voice

54 Play parts
57 Fishhook feature
59 Corporate money managers: Abbr.
62 See 19-Across
64 Some USA Today graphics
67 The "V" of VCR
68 "Good grief!"
69 "Uh-huh"
70 Snoozer's sound
71 Old salts
72 Italia's capital

DOWN

1 PC key
2 The Beehive State
3 Yard tool
4 Small winning margin, in baseball
5 Ecol. watchdog
6 Baked beans ingredient
7 Bothers
8 Teacher, at times
9 Middle muscles, for short
10 Legal assistant
11 Brainstorm
12 Mellows, as wine
13 Adam's third
18 Basic dictionary entry
22 Soul singer Redding
25 Caustic substance
27 Rental units: Abbr.
28 Get to the top of

Puzzle 97 by Gail Grabowski

29 Up and about
30 It may be called on the battlefield
31 Singer Bonnie
32 "___ Marner"
33 Computer pop-ups
36 R.N.'s forte
38 Religious site
39 Chops
41 Goldilocks sat in his chair
44 Snooty person
46 Campaigner, in brief

49 All worked up
50 Hankering
51 "That's cheating!"
54 Ones heading for the hills?: Abbr.
55 Nickel or dime
56 Commotion
58 Latvia's capital
60 Approximately
61 Flower stalk
63 Tiller's tool
65 S. & L. offerings
66 Baltic or Bering

ACROSS

1 One of five Norwegian kings
5 Times in history
9 Longed
14 Bit of mockery
15 Cancel
16 Spoils
17 Breezes through, as a test
18 Chanel competitor
19 Boxer Roberto
20 Story written by 38-Across
23 1960's radical grp.
24 Cities Service competitor
25 And
26 Quaker —
28 1960's–70's baseball All-Star — Santo
30 It's sometimes hard to make them meet
33 Nicks
35 "— does what Nintendon't" (old slogan)
37 — polloi
38 Writer born March 2, 1904
41 Gooey green substance in the title of a 38-Across story
43 Professional org.
44 It often thickens
46 Thief's "savings"
47 Goes on and on
49 Summer mo.
50 Dueler of 1804
51 Verve
53 Pitcher
55 Took a load off
58 Birthplace of 38-Across
62 Fleeced
63 — Minor
64 Service org. since the 1850's
65 Emerged
66 Verve
67 Hammer-wielding deity
68 Fellows
69 "Do it, or —!"
70 Have the — for

DOWN

1 1973 "Love Train" singers, with "the"
2 Ripped (into)
3 Tautology spoken by the title character in 11-Down
4 Jacket accompanier
5 Overage
6 Cheers (for)
7 38-Across and others
8 Eye malady
9 Singer Paula
10 18 holes, say
11 Book written by 38-Across
12 And others, for short
13 Unit of force
21 Eases
22 Dance for two

Puzzle 98 by Charles Barasch

27 Carbon dating determination
29 Fair-hiring agcy.
31 43-Across members
32 Religious person with a turban
33 Do-or-die time
34 Cookbook writer Rombauer
36 Crazy
39 70-Across, e.g.
40 Former franc part
42 P.O. delivery

45 38-Across's real name, in brief
48 Most clever
50 Miss the start
52 Aconcagua is their tallest peak
54 "Marat/Sade" playwright Peter
56 Fancy tie
57 Romanov V.I.P.'s
58 Kind of carpet
59 Site of a sweat bead
60 Disconcert
61 Fable

ACROSS

1 Fed. food inspectors
5 Raindrop sound
9 Songwriters' grp.
14 Lecherous look
15 Cleveland cagers, briefly
16 Weigher
17 Co-star of 36-Down
19 Jabs
20 It's heard on the grapevine
21 I. M. Pei, for one
23 Red flag, e.g.
24 Lyricist Lorenz —
25 See 41-Down
29 Online film maker
33 Star of 36-Down
38 Stallone title role
39 Out of port
40 January in Juárez
42 "— delighted!"
43 Brouhahas
45 Co-star of 36-Down
47 Knock over
49 Fencing blade
50 The "Y" of B.Y.O.B.
52 Barge's route
57 100% incorrect
62 Whooping —
63 50's candidate Stevenson
64 Setting for 36-Down
66 — breath (flower)
67 "Guilty" or "not guilty"
68 Flex
69 Boffo show
70 Gardener's bagful
71 Counts up

DOWN

1 Part of UHF
2 Capital of South Korea
3 Film director Jonathan
4 Shady spot
5 Alternatives to Macs
6 Syllables in "Deck the Halls"
7 Finished
8 Intimidate, with "out"
9 Person with goals
10 Co-star of 36-Down
11 Wedding reception centerpiece
12 Writer Waugh
13 Exterminator's target
18 Garden products name
22 "Hee —"
26 —-inspiring
27 Lois of "Superman"
28 "— Jacques" (children's song)
30 Naval leader: Abbr.
31 "Dancing Queen" quartet
32 Big name in water faucets
33 Makeshift river conveyance
34 Norway's capital
35 Certain tide
36 TV series that premiered in 1974

Puzzle 99 by Allan E. Parrish

37 Cause for a plumber
41 With 25-Across, 50%
44 Molasseslike
46 Muhammad's birthplace
48 Where Switz. is
51 Easy wins
53 Popular Caribbean island
54 Sans clothing
55 Put __ to (halt)
56 English city NE of Manchester
57 Applies lightly

58 Dutch cheese
59 "Duchess of __" (Goya work)
60 Cairo's river
61 Elation
65 Mouthful of gum

ACROSS

1 Certain iron setting
6 Govt. bill
11 Mars or Milky Way
14 Really, really want
15 Toiled in the galley
16 "I love," to Livy
17 Old "Tonight Show" intro
19 Transcript fig.
20 CPR giver
21 Have a late meal
22 Unlit?
24 Scale of mineral hardness
26 Lions' lairs
29 Tee cry
30 Zeno of __
31 Atmospheric region with a "hole"
34 Ladies of Spain
36 Word repeated after "Que," in song
37 Draft letters
38 Head honcho
42 Blood-typing letters
45 When repeated, a fish
46 Hose woes
50 Loofah, e.g.
54 Neighbor of Yemen
55 "__ girl!"
56 Hymn start
57 Fodder's place
58 Follower of Zeno
60 U-Haul rental
62 Make public
63 Haw's partner
64 Women's tennis immortal
69 Historic period
70 1940's–50's slugger Ralph
71 More despicable
72 Thesaurus entry: Abbr.
73 Big name in printers
74 Goes up and down and . . .

DOWN

1 Connived
2 Vibrating effect
3 Made of clay
4 "__ Maria"
5 Many a teen's room
6 Saint-__ (French resort)
7 Japanese drama
8 Hold title to
9 Half a score
10 Breyers competitor
11 Supermarket helpers
12 Current units
13 Lions, at times
18 Self-defense sport
23 Son–gun link
25 Swedish auto
27 Having a snack
28 Snick-a-__
32 Poet's preposition
33 Laddie's love
35 Jazzman Zoot
39 Letterman dental feature
40 Half a train?

Puzzle 100 by Sarah Keller

41 Son of Seth
42 Makes ashamed
43 9-volt, e.g.
44 Cushioned footrest
47 In a friendly manner
48 1600's stargazer
49 "Z" makers, in comics
51 "Bali —"
52 Wield authority
53 Dutch seaport
59 Word that can follow the ends of 17-, 31-, 38-, 50- and 64-Across

61 Blue shade
65 Place to put gloss
66 Elected officials
67 Corporate V.I.P.
68 "Flying Down to —"

ACROSS

1 Opposite of highs
5 Big stingers
10 Concert blasters
14 Hawaiian island
15 Maximum poker bet
16 Bob who lost to Bill Clinton
17 Warner's statement after the fact
19 "Roots" author Haley
20 "Julius Caesar," e.g.
22 __-fi
23 Bird's home
24 Fire leftover
27 Eve's predecessor
30 Tortilla chip dip
34 Fateful day in a 20-Across
38 Ringer
39 Not so good
40 Egg: Prefix
41 Baseball hit just beyond the infield
42 Bard of __
43 Fateful day in a 20-Across
45 Pays a landlord
47 Require
48 "I get it"
49 Guys-only
52 Cry to a mouse
54 "Et tu, Brute? Then fall, Caesar!," e.g.
62 Building beam
63 One who warned Caesar
64 Bronx cheer
65 Golfer Palmer, familiarly
66 Liberals, with "the"
67 __-bitsy
68 Fabric colorers
69 Schnauzer in Dashiell Hammett books

DOWN

1 __ Lane, admirer of Superman
2 Inauguration Day recital
3 Command to a horse
4 Broods
5 Land next to a road
6 Crooked
7 Turn on a pivot
8 Resident near the Leaning Tower
9 Make a nighttime ruckus
10 Not limited to one use
11 Gangster's gal
12 Defendant's declaration at an arraignment
13 Alluring
18 The 60's or 70's, e.g.
21 Road section requiring caution
24 Battling
25 Rudely push
26 Long-billed wader
28 __ this minute
29 "The Jeffersons" theme "__ On Up"
31 Hotelier Helmsley

Puzzle 101 by Patrick Merrell

32 Laziness
33 Omega's opposite
35 Feels no remorse
36 Drum accompanier
37 John Philip Sousa offering
41 Moistens with droplets
43 "Little Women" family name
44 Grows chewers
46 VW predecessors?
50 Syrian president
51 "Mine eyes have seen the __ . . ."

53 Australian "bear"
54 Land SW of Samoa
55 Assist in crime
56 Fannie __ (securities)
57 Top-notch
58 Mix (up)
59 Deli loaves
60 Adept
61 Sp. miss

ACROSS

1 Talk like Jimmy Stewart
6 Minnelli of "Cabaret"
10 Frozen waffle brand
14 Noted Montague
15 First father
16 Potting need
17 Jellied garnish
18 Glazier's unit
19 Ditto, with "the"
20 Kingdom's dock?
23 Suffix with musket
24 Tic-tac-toe winner
25 Poet Elinor
27 Invent
30 Enzyme suffix
32 Baseball playoffs mo.
33 Mikhail of chess
34 Adage
35 Home of the Blue Devils
36 Municipality's dock?
40 Part of a financial portfolio
41 Yale, for one
42 Q-tip target
43 Put down, on the street
44 Place where you can get into hot water
45 No less than
49 Looks out for, at a heist
51 Commotion
52 Early Beatle Sutcliffe
53 Country's dock?
58 Diva Gluck
59 Breakfast food chain
60 Back, at the track
61 Depend (on)
62 Barrel of laughs
63 Hosiery hue
64 Breyers competitor
65 Adds (up)
66 Photographer Adams

DOWN

1 Hung loosely
2 More upbeat
3 Fuse unit
4 Small dam
5 Lead-in to motion
6 Traveler's work aid
7 Potato state
8 Billy of "Titanic"
9 From the U.S.
10 Composition with a viewpoint
11 Give 100%
12 Gadget-laden
13 Grand __ Opry
21 Ball that may hit an umpire
22 Meadow mother
26 Summer in Suisse
28 Just slightly
29 Indianapolis 500 time
30 Sound of relief
31 Fond of
34 Farm pen

Puzzle 102 by Ron Sweet

35 Calamitous
36 Nitpicked
37 Socially improper
38 Future aves?
39 Record-setting Ripken
40 Pharmaceutical-safety org.
44 Retired flier
45 Changes to fit
46 "The way things are . . ."
47 One of a slapstick trio

48 Prison escape route, maybe
50 Cafeteria carriers
51 Underway
54 "Java" player Al
55 Home to Columbus
56 "Chiquitita" quartet
57 Freshman, usually
58 "You __ here"

ACROSS

1 1953 Leslie Caron title role
5 Water pitcher
9 Companion for Snow White
14 Garden of —
15 Bad habit
16 At the proper time
17 Meteorologist's favorite movie of 1939?
20 Longtime buddy
21 Metals from the earth
22 Drunk's problem
23 One of the Jackson 5
25 Quaker —
27 "Pow!"
30 "— the night before Christmas . . ."
32 Lumberjack's "Heads up!"
36 Lotion ingredient
38 "Now it all makes sense!"
40 Dinero
41 Meteorologist's favorite movie of 1952?
44 Tennis champ Chris
45 London district
46 Jazz singer — James
47 Dislike with a passion
49 Writer Philip
51 "Game, —, match!"
52 Kite part
54 Trade

56 Co. that merged with Time Warner
59 Consider
61 Meeting schedule
65 Meteorologist's favorite movie of 2000?
68 Miss America's crown
69 Scotch —
70 Forest unit
71 Sing in the Alps
72 Speak unclearly
73 [Been there, done that]

DOWN

1 Toy block company
2 TV's "American —"
3 Give temporarily
4 Bumbling
5 Easily-blamed alter ego
6 Mental quickness
7 Canyon effect
8 Fashionably outdated
9 Chills in the cooler
10 ESE's reverse
11 Etching liquid
12 Little squirt
13 Government agents
18 "Hold on!"
19 Miami basketball team
24 Desert resting place
26 Campfire treat popular with Scouts
27 — on a true story

Puzzle 103 by Kyle Mahowald

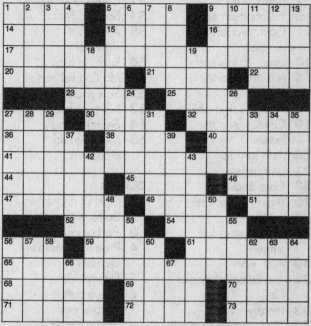

28 Full of energy
29 "Water Lilies" painter Claude
31 Mexican Mister
33 Marina sights
34 Cream of the crop
35 Charged
37 Everglades wader
39 Cultural values
42 Words with a handshake
43 Deep trouble
48 Seating level
50 Crones

53 About half of all turns
55 Trifling
56 Lawyer: Abbr.
57 Birthplace of seven U.S. presidents
58 Its symbol is Pb
60 Breakfast, lunch or dinner
62 Author Ephron
63 Sketched
64 "You can say that again!"
66 Opposite of post-
67 PC core: Abbr.

ACROSS

1 Minty drink
6 Fallback strategy
11 Govt. property overseer
14 Loud, as the surf
15 Martini's partner
16 Mantra syllables
17 Author's sign-off?
19 College sweater letters
20 Add zest to
21 Like helium
23 Cold and wet
26 Ave. intersectors
27 Smells
28 One-named folk singer
30 A.D. part
32 "__ Bulba" (Brynner film)
33 Hardly tanned
34 Tiny fraction of a min.
37 Designer Cassini
38 One of the Osmonds
39 "Ignorance __ excuse"
40 LP's and CD's: Abbr.
41 Microwave, e.g.
42 Yegg's job
43 Mary Hartman portrayer Louise
45 Is currently selling
46 Cellos' little cousins
48 Pricing word
49 PBS supporter
50 Keypad key
51 Compound of gold
54 Sort of: Suffix
55 Astronaut's sign-off?
60 Born, in bios
61 Mailing list items
62 Sole material
63 Norm: Abbr.
64 Search blindly
65 Mentholated cigarettes

DOWN

1 Start of a one-two
2 Suffix with strict
3 Part of PRNDL
4 Prominent donkey features
5 Unwed fathers
6 Use a button
7 Timber wolf
8 Simile center
9 Defense advisory org.
10 Two-piece wear
11 Nuclear physicist's sign-off?
12 Blue cartoon character
13 Bus. aides
18 "Later!"
22 Chuckleheads
23 Chopper part
24 Allan-__
25 Tailor's sign-off?

Puzzle 104 by Fred Piscop

27 Captain Hook's henchman
29 Bargain hunter's stop
30 Risk taker
31 Lena of "Chocolat"
33 Do roadwork
35 Come after
36 Terra ___
38 Trunk growth
42 Five-time Kentucky Derby winner Bill
44 South Seas attire
45 Make well

46 Lines on leaves
47 Map enlargement
48 Plain writing
51 Spherical opening?
52 Lone Star State sch.
53 Money on the Continent
56 Former Mideast org.
57 Opposite of paleo-
58 An N.C.O.
59 Cocks and bulls

ACROSS

1 Apple computers
5 1:00, e.g.
9 Eye color
14 Hideous
15 In __ (actual)
16 New York's __ Fisher Hall
17 Time for a Wild West shootout
18 "Excuse me . . ."
19 Pointing device
20 Fancy term for a 36-Across
23 Hornswoggled
24 Tetley product
25 Regretted
26 London's Big __
27 Shopping place
28 Quick punch
31 Self-evident truth
34 __ fide
35 Coke or Pepsi
36 Puzzling person?
39 Goldie of "Laugh-In" fame
40 Party giver
41 Atlas blow-up
42 Needle hole
43 Yappy dog, briefly
44 Colorado native
45 Kodak product
46 Explosive letters
47 Put down, slangily
50 Fancy term for a 36-Across

54 Secluded valleys
55 Actress Winslet
56 Stage part
57 W.W. II vessel
58 Split personalities?
59 Think tank output
60 Hairy-chested
61 Edges
62 Work station

DOWN

1 Chew (on)
2 Ancient marketplace
3 Cirrus or cumulus
4 Lip-__ (not really sing)
5 Realm for St. Peter
6 Actor Milo
7 One who takes drugs, e.g.
8 "The Night Watch" painter
9 Tiny village
10 Steer clear of
11 Mount Olympus chief
12 Formerly, once
13 Caustic substance
21 Tabloid twosomes
22 Surrounding glows
26 Cap'n's mate
27 Samuel with a code
28 Scribbles (down)
29 Cream ingredient
30 Quarterback Starr
31 Flu symptom
32 Picture of health?

33 "__ Russia $1200" (Bob Hope book)
34 Gambling professional
35 Art movie theater
37 Overcome utterly
38 "Same here!"
43 Boar's abode
44 Except if
45 Important exam
46 __ pole
47 Electron tube
48 Cruise stopovers

49 T-bone, e.g.
50 Site of Napoleon's exile
51 Light on Broadway
52 Prepare for takeoff
53 Lines on a radar screen
54 Doublemint, e.g.

ACROSS

1 Pleasant to look at
7 "Hold on a ___!"
10 Abba of Israel
14 Promgoer's rental
15 Airport monitor abbr.
16 Nathan of stage and screen
17 Colorful ring
18 Pal in the 'hood
19 Toggery, informally
20 Christmas tree
21 Grade booster
24 Big bash
26 Helps with the dishes
27 Make even smoother
30 The late Sen. Thurmond
34 "Folsom Prison Blues" singer
38 ___-Locka, Fla.
39 Oneness
40 Chews the scenery
43 Fr. holy woman
44 Luggage receipt
48 Synagogue scroll
51 Achieve
52 Snapple competitor
54 Galley gear
58 Sub sinker
63 It may be loaded at the casino
64 Word-of-mouth
65 Fam. member
66 Assail, as a reputation
68 Not prerecorded
69 ___ y Plata (Montana's motto)
70 Puts on a happy face
71 Sly glance
72 "Spring ahead" hrs.
73 Be a snitch

DOWN

1 Office crew
2 Radium discoverer
3 Put forth, as effort
4 Prefix with classical
5 Like some chatter
6 Sweet-talk
7 Audrey Hepburn title role
8 Gofers' tasks
9 Long reptiles, in short
10 First-born
11 Modem speed unit
12 "The King ___"
13 Egg holder
22 ___ II (razor brand)
23 Apt., e.g.
25 Seaside soarers
28 Brian of the early Roxy Music
29 Harmony
31 Classroom drudgery
32 Oil grp.
33 Mardi Gras wear
34 "___ do it"
35 Not fooled by

Puzzle 106 by Sarah Keller

36 Yesterday: Fr.
37 Blood: Prefix
41 — WorldCom
42 "This can't be!"
45 Prepares to shave
46 Gorged oneself
47 —-Tass (Russian news agency)
49 Branch in a trophy room
50 Snickering syllable
53 New England catch
55 Not for kids

56 Star in Orion
57 Taste or touch
58 "Mama" sayer
59 Canal of song
60 Finish a drive?
61 Main idea
62 Lazarus or Goldman
67 Orchestra area

ACROSS

1 Tough spots to get out of
5 City leader
10 Ego
14 Old radio word for the letter O
15 "___ there yet?"
16 Half a sextet
17 Charlton Heston epic, with "The"
20 Ratfink
21 Ray of the Kinks
22 Essential
25 Witherspoon of "Legally Blonde"
26 "Holy smokes!"
29 Marked, as a survey square
31 Whodunit board game
32 New Guinea native
34 C.E.O.'s degree
37 Home for Pooh and Tigger
40 Baseballer Mel
41 Large system of newsgroups
42 Smog
43 Unappetizing dishes
44 Try to pick up, as at a bar
45 Laissez-___
48 Join forces (with)
51 Popular Honda
53 Runs full speed

57 Chain in the upper St. Lawrence River
60 Ages and ages
61 False move
62 Jazzy improv style
63 One bit of medicine
64 Hot dog picker-upper
65 Amerada ___ (oil giant)

DOWN

1 Writes (down)
2 Assist in wrongdoing
3 Pre-stereo sound
4 Supported, as a motion
5 Mrs. Eisenhower
6 Like gunmen and octopuses
7 Nay's opposite
8 Possess
9 Foxx of "Sanford and Son"
10 Filmmaker Spielberg
11 Bert's roommate on "Sesame Street"
12 Reduced-calorie beers
13 "All That Jazz" choreographer Bob
18 Bullfight cheers
19 Corps member
23 Wide area
24 Two of cards
26 Sound in a big, empty room
27 Excess supply

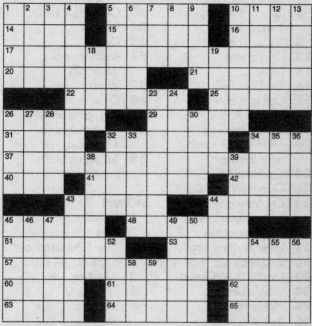

28 Uncle's partner
30 It's thrown at a bull's-eye
32 Mexican money
33 Good (at)
34 Castle encircler
35 Old TV clown
36 Chief Yemeni port
38 Kings and queens
39 Auto accident injury
43 Complain
44 Hockey great Bobby
45 Destined

46 Sound preceding "God bless"
47 Desktop pictures
49 Growing older
50 Sail supports
52 Loony
54 Formerly
55 Some handhelds: Abbr.
56 Speedy fliers, for short
58 Modern: Prefix
59 Kipling's "Gunga __"

ACROSS

1 Big stinger
5 Org. whose approval is much sought
8 "Le — Prince"
13 Opera solo
14 Costa —
16 The O in FeO
17 Call in a bakery
18 Tennis's Arthur
19 Slangy send-off
20 1986 Prince movie, after 29-Down
23 Calendar box
25 Opponent's vote
26 Cry from a butterfingers
27 Map miniatures
29 Letter carriers' org.
30 "No seats left" sign
33 Martin or McQueen
34 Initial stake
35 Not at home
36 By night, with 29-Down
39 Rightmost column
40 Suffix with young or old
41 Smallest
42 Thesaurus feature: Abbr.
43 Minnesota Twin, e.g., briefly
44 Dance at 23-Down
45 Set-to
46 Not dis, in Brooklyn
47 Sun. talk

48 Business sign, after 29-Down
53 Orangeish shade
54 Respite
55 Grub
58 Popular vodka, informally
59 Wash
60 Oscar winner Sorvino
61 Has, as a party
62 Place to hear a 13-Across, with "the"
63 Taking care of business

DOWN

1 Pallid
2 Exist
3 Year "The Graduate" came out, in short
4 Walkway
5 Set-to
6 Like good gossip columns
7 Overexerciser's woe
8 Growths that may be removed by surgery
9 Tests
10 — Puente, the Mambo King
11 Prefix with logical
12 Beach bird
15 Former Ford minivan
21 Type in
22 Rodeo performer
23 Studio 54 and Xenon, famously
24 Cleopatra's paramour

Puzzle 108 by Tony Orbach

28 Preceding nights
29 See 20-, 36- and 48-Across
30 Laundry challenge for a gymgoer
31 Fight down and dirty
32 Food in a shell
34 In the end
35 Hydrocarbon suffixes
37 Singer K. T. __
38 Movie for which Jane Fonda won an Oscar
43 Some old computers
44 Classic Olivier role

45 Silvery food fish
46 Dig (into)
48 Snack
49 Prefix with plasm
50 "Look __ Talking"
51 U.S. Pacific island
52 Captain of fiction
56 Prefix with color or cycle
57 Posed

ACROSS

1 Subdued color
7 Lift in Aspen
11 Height: Abbr.
14 Title girl in Kay Thompson books
15 "Othello" villain
16 Pastoral place
17 Golf locale
19 Prohibit
20 Letters on a Cardinal's cap
21 Rock musician Brian
22 Diving board's part of a swimming pool
24 Ambles (along)
27 Johnson of "Laugh-In"
28 Thom __ shoes
30 Extremely low, as prices
34 Strokes on a green
36 Game authority
37 Brays
40 Views, as through binoculars
44 Online correspondence
46 Quick bite
47 Informal group discussion
52 Choir voice
53 Roundish
54 Walks about looking for prey
56 Frog's seat
60 Figure skater Midori __
61 __ Lingus
64 On the __ (fleeing)

65 Pivoting span on a river
68 Summer in Montréal
69 Encl. with a manuscript
70 Give, as duties
71 One side in checkers
72 Little 'un
73 Tyrannical leader

DOWN

1 Chest muscles, briefly
2 Tremendously
3 One's special person in life
4 __ Lizzie (Model T)
5 __ Park, Colo.
6 Loewe's partner on Broadway
7 The first O of O-O-O
8 Like Yul Brynner or Telly Savalas
9 Tropical fever
10 Justice's attire
11 Queen Victoria's prince
12 Shack
13 Two-trailer rig
18 Toy that does tricks
23 Fatherly
25 Furtively
26 Jr. high, e.g.
28 Speedometer letters
29 Billiards rod
31 Keystone officer
32 Automatic tournament advance
33 Bullring hurrahs

Puzzle 109 by Gail Grabowski

35 Identical
38 "What __ I saying?"
39 __-boom-bah
41 Spicy chip topping
42 Malfunction,
   with "up"
43 Bout ender, for short
45 Place for gloss
47 Hair salon item
48 Fly
49 Picked up stealthily
50 It goes on a
   photocopier: Abbr.
51 "Pretty good!"

55 Poorer
57 "Hey, you!"
58 Not at home
59 Part of the spine
62 Frozen waffle brand
63 Apartment payment
66 Previously named
67 Magazine no.

ACROSS

1 Play lookout for, for example
5 Praises
10 Vegetarian's no-no
14 Lollapalooza
15 Beginning
16 "Cogito, — sum"
17 V.I.P. #1
20 Blazing, as the eyes
21 Stirs up
22 Forest rangers' worries
25 U.F.O. fliers
26 Ammo holder
28 Fizzler
30 Like zoo animals
34 Very, in Versailles
35 Maze goal
37 "Where —?"
38 V.I.P. #2
41 Dr. J's org., once
42 Unit
43 James who wrote "A Death in the Family"
44 Marooned, maybe
46 Chicago-to-Tampa dir.
47 Pants part
48 Barely lit
50 Blue eyes or curly hair
52 The "E" of PETA
56 Turn
60 V.I.P. #3
63 Group in a spies' network
64 Harden
65 Property right
66 London's — Park
67 Jargons
68 Actress Heche

DOWN

1 Aquatic plant
2 Small town
3 Carrier to Israel
4 Sushi staple
5 Running horse
6 Bibliographical suffix
7 Part of the Defense Dept.
8 — vu
9 Gaze intently
10 One of the Gorgons
11 Botches one
12 Chills and fever
13 Male turkeys
18 Mr. Unexciting
19 Cut irregularly
23 Decrees
24 Orange label
26 Corn holders
27 Over 18, say
29 One on the Atkins plan
31 Railroad measure
32 Roastmaster
33 It holds back the sea

34 Spicy cuisine
35 When said three times, a 1964 Beach Boys hit
36 Pigpen
39 Noble Italian family name
40 Spanish scarf
45 Fit to serve
47 Fuzzy fruit
49 Wizardry
51 "Angela's —" (1996 best seller)

52 Inscribe permanently
53 "If — only knew!"
54 Grasped
55 Musical Horne
57 Conceited
58 1950's British P.M.
59 The Beatles' "Penny —"
61 Sister
62 TV screen: Abbr.

ACROSS

1 Timber wolf
5 Gymnast Comaneci
10 Little tricksters
14 Grad
15 Addicts
16 One who nabs 15-Across
17 Nothing more than
18 Eats elegantly
19 French cheese
20 Like some Christians
22 Four-door
23 Do cross-country
24 When the stomach starts grumbling
26 Air conditioner capacity, for short
29 Co. name completer
31 Boar's mate
32 Not behaving conservatively
39 Genesis garden
40 French sea
41 Dublin's land
42 Not just gone
47 ___ Jima
48 Science guy Bill
49 CD predecessors
50 Does a U-turn
55 Place to relax
57 Enlighten
58 Utterance that sums up 20-, 32- and 42-Across
63 Misshapen citrus
64 Chicago airport
65 "A Clockwork Orange" protagonist
66 Unload, as stock
67 Voting machine part
68 5,280 feet
69 Dutch cheese
70 Clothe
71 Quaker ___

DOWN

1 Gentle animal
2 Toast spread
3 Famous duelist
4 Black cats, traditionally speaking
5 Prodding
6 One side of the Urals
7 Overalls material
8 "Me, Myself & ___" (2000 flick)
9 Ninny
10 Not on one side or the other
11 ___ Gras
12 Trojan War king
13 Verona, in "Romeo and Juliet"
21 Related
22 ___ gin fizz
25 Arson aftermath
26 Ran, as colors
27 Seashore washer
28 Eye layer
30 Deep sleep
33 Sundance entry, informally
34 Actor Beatty
35 1982 Disney film

Puzzle 111 by Michael Doran

36 Use a rotary phone
37 Basic of golf instruction
38 Lampreys, e.g.
43 Twisted
44 Letters of distress
45 Dish sometimes served "on the half-shell"
46 Officials elected for two yrs.
50 Employ again
51 Nosed (out)
52 Mediterranean estate

53 Old-fashioned anesthetic
54 Trim
56 Site of an 1836 massacre
59 Son of Zeus
60 Russian gold medalist __ Kulik
61 Had emotions
62 Alimony receivers
64 On in years

ACROSS

1 Tupperware sound
5 Viva — (by word of mouth)
9 Jazz genre
14 State firmly
15 Skeptic's scoff
16 Unescorted
17 Where to get hitched in a hurry
18 Brummell or Bridges
19 Laundry soap introduced in 1918
20 See 40-Across
23 Cozy room
24 Demagnetize, as a tape
25 "Heads up!" and others
27 Run-of-the-mill
30 Kingdom divisions, in biology
31 "What have we here?!"
32 Jill of "Diamonds Are Forever"
35 Stash
38 "Please," in Potsdam
40 Clue to 20- and 55-Across and 11- and 29-Down
41 Paris's river
42 Crude sort
43 Acela Express runner
45 17-Across's state: Abbr.
46 Breaks in relations
48 Hair snarl

50 Cloak's partner
52 Sudden outpouring
54 Make a miscue
55 See 40-Across
60 Regional flora and fauna
62 — Domini
63 General or major
64 Run-of-the-mill
65 Frees (of)
66 X-rated
67 Great Plains home
68 Ripken Sr. and Jr.
69 Thanksgiving dish

DOWN

1 Cutting remark
2 Iris's place
3 Patronize Hertz or Avis
4 Like some presidents
5 Pulsing with energy
6 Takes orders from
7 Stop
8 Needle case
9 Just
10 — Lilly and Company
11 See 40-Across
12 Beginning
13 Lowly workers
21 Irregularly notched, as a leaf
22 Paula of CNN
26 Ultimatum ender
27 Ty of Cooperstown
28 Kent State state
29 See 40-Across
30 Rx dispenser: Abbr.

Puzzle 112 by Allan E. Parrish

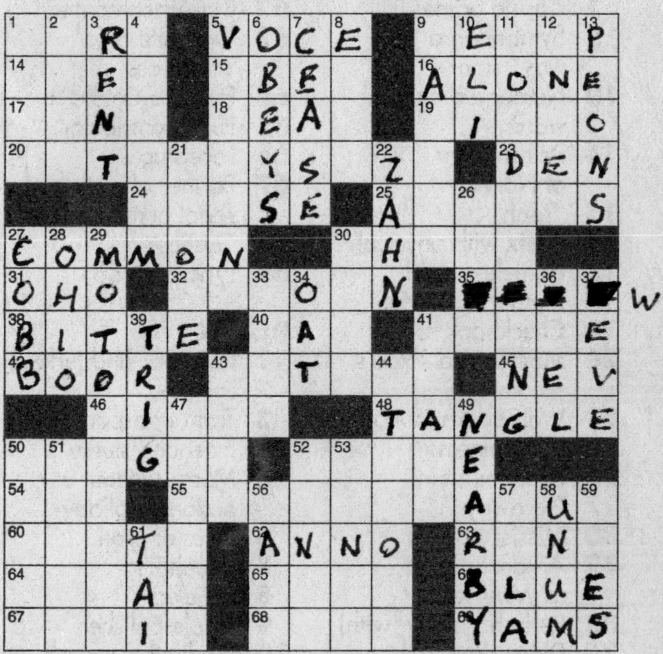

A crossword grid with handwritten answers (partially filled):

- 1: R E N T
- 5: V O C E / B E A / E A / Y S / S É
- 9: E / A L O N E / I / D E N S
- 16: A L O N E
- 22: Z A H N
- 27: C O M M O N
- 31: O H O
- 32: O A T
- 35: (scratched out) W / E
- 38: B I T T E
- 40: A T
- 42: B O O R I / G
- 45: N E V
- 46: R I G / T A I
- 48: T A N G L E / E A R N
- 62: A N N O
- 63: B L U E
- 66: Y A M S

Clues (continued):

33 Photocopier problems
34 Cereal grain
36 Scott Turow title
37 "__ Only Just Begun"
39 H.S. math class
41 Do figure eights, say
43 Longfellow's bell town
44 Totally baffled
47 Like fillies but not billies
49 Close at hand
50 Coming-out
51 Get up
52 Braga of film

53 Gearshift sequence
56 Pusher's pursuer
57 Hearty party
58 E pluribus __
59 Squeaks (out)
61 __-Bo (exercise system)

ACROSS

1 Casino game
5 Symbol on a "one way" sign
10 Numbered musical work
14 Patron saint of Norway
15 "Yeah"
16 Prefix with physical
17 Homeless child
18 Mother — stories
19 Checkbook record
20 Mother in a 1960's sitcom
23 Web address: Abbr.
24 Naturalness
25 Sen. Feinstein
27 Go away
30 Mississippi city
32 Arkansas's — Mountains
33 Be in harmony (with)
34 Diner sign
37 Vessel for ashes
38 Thirst quenchers
41 Poker prize
42 Historical
44 Pinnacle
45 Port-au-Prince's land
47 It's a bore
49 Los Angeles base-baller
50 Golden period
52 Drop of sweat
53 "Hold On Tight" band
54 1965 Natalie Wood title role
60 Emcee's need
62 Big African critter
63 Opposite of 15-Across
64 France's Cote d'—
65 Fund contributor
66 Laced up
67 Partner of rank and serial number
68 Gushes
69 Lyric poems

DOWN

1 Chickens and turkeys
2 Jai —
3 Train transport
4 Extended slump
5 Month without a national holiday
6 River of Lyon
7 Greek R's
8 Un-elect
9 Apple-polisher
10 Meditative sounds
11 Merrie Melodies "co-star"
12 Reversal
13 Valuable fur
21 Pre-euro German money
22 — Bravo
26 Paul Bunyan's tool
27 Arrange, as the hair
28 Book before Nehemiah
29 "Li'l Abner" mother
30 Gang member, maybe

31 Wild goat
33 Make sport of
35 Lug
36 Recipe direction
39 Holders of referee whistles
40 River hazard
43 Small amount
46 Extend, as a house
48 Roll of bills
49 Styles
50 Charles Atlas, for one
51 "My Fair Lady" lady
52 Already

55 Breakfast restaurant chain
56 Trig function
57 Empty space
58 Fencing blade
59 Wines that aren't whites
61 Afore

ACROSS

1 Job detail, briefly
5 24/7 auction site
9 Jazz group
14 Sledder's spot
15 Sub builder?
16 Burger layer
17 Pastel shade
18 Loafing
19 Pottery finish
20 Bad place for the modest
23 Tractor name
24 Many-headed serpent
25 __ Lanka
28 Since 1/1, to a C.P.A.
29 It has 21 spots
31 Orchestra's percussion or strings, e.g.
33 Coniferous tree
35 Library ID
36 Band with the 1998 #1 hit "One Week"
42 Bard's river
43 Chief exec
44 Played a knight game?
48 __ Amin
49 Chum
52 Leave speechless
53 "Peachy!"
55 Met offering
57 1997 steelworkers-turned-dancers film
59 Red River capital
62 Calvary letters
63 Pond gunk
64 Shady spot
65 Like eggs
66 Beget
67 Meager
68 Therefore
69 North Carolina university

DOWN

1 Sterne's "Tristram __"
2 Card game for two
3 Gave the slip to
4 "__ de Lune"
5 Trim to fit, maybe
6 Nighttime inspection
7 Brass or pewter
8 Rates of return
9 French brandy
10 Just
11 Hamm of soccer
12 Dickens's pen name
13 "That's __ for the books!"
21 Family auto
22 Smelter input
25 "Certainly!," south of the border
26 Boxer's wear
27 Vacationers' stops
30 Nest-egg letters
32 In good order
33 Fisheye __
34 With it
36 Mexican peninsula
37 Declare openly
38 Philandering sort
39 Oil company structure

Puzzle 114 by Janet R. Bender

40 Played first
41 Self-evident truth
45 Casual top
46 Ram's mate
47 Desecrate
49 Tentatively schedule, with "in"
50 Conductor Toscanini
51 Nonprofessionals
54 Like some eclipses
56 Oater group
57 Animator's creation
58 Italian resort
59 Suffers from

60 Circle segment
61 Magic and Wizards org.

ACROSS

1 Did laps in a pool
5 Foolhardy
9 "She loves me . . . she loves me not" flower
14 "Horrors!"
15 "Cómo — usted?"
16 Blast from the past
17 Spick-and-span
18 Genesis twin
19 F.B.I. worker
20 Achieve initial success
23 Singletons
24 Bullfight cheer
25 Suffix with lion
28 Oar-powered ship
31 Like a fiddle
34 "Scratch and win" game
36 Pub brew
37 Sweep under the rug
38 Estimates
42 Intl. oil group
43 Take to court
44 Use crib notes
45 Cheyenne's locale: Abbr.
46 Kind of underwear
49 Foxy
50 "— Drives Me Crazy" (Fine Young Cannibals hit)
51 Western tribe
53 Completely mistaken
60 Improperly long sentence
61 Risk-free
62 Number not on a grandfather clock
63 Space shuttle gasket
64 With warts and all
65 Elm or elder
66 — Park, Colo.
67 Camper's cover
68 Hankerings

DOWN

1 Spiritual, e.g.
2 Cry on a roller coaster
3 Med. school class
4 E pluribus unum, for instance
5 "— Madness" (1936 antidrug film)
6 Whence St. Francis
7 Night twinkler
8 Düsseldorf dwelling
9 Within one's power
10 Pond buildup
11 March 15, e.g.
12 Trig term
13 "Are we there —?"
21 In first place
22 Marisa of "My Cousin Vinny"
25 Arm joint
26 Unrinsed, maybe
27 Fifth-century pope
29 Autumn yard worker
30 Santa's little helper
31 Pink-slips
32 Perfect
33 Short-tempered
35 Nurse's skill, for short

Puzzle 115 by Gregory E. Paul

37 "What'd you say?"
39 Gray
40 Feel sorry about
41 Symbol at the head of a musical staff
46 First __ first
47 Breakfast bread
48 Swear (to)
50 Masonry
52 Nearing retirement age, maybe
53 Yours and mine
54 The "U" in I.C.U.
55 Future atty.'s exam

56 Facilitate
57 Dublin's land
58 Legal claim
59 Goes kaput
60 Salmon eggs

ACROSS

1 Spain and Portugal
7 ___ alai
10 Amtrak stop: Abbr.
13 Vietnamese port
14 End abruptly
16 Tense
17 Source of a cry at night
18 Wound
19 ___ Maria
20 Tree-lined road: Abbr.
21 Contribute
22 Uses the HOV lanes, perhaps
24 Butt of jokes
27 Blond shade
29 Krypton or radon
30 Security numbers
33 Groovy
36 ___ apso (dog)
37 It's south of Eur.
38 Sylvester's co-star in "Rocky"
40 Lay turf
41 "As luck would have it . . ."
44 Chemin de ___ (French railway)
45 Med. care provider
46 With a discount of
47 Victoria's Secret item
51 Hush-hush D.C. org.
53 Lena of "The Unbearable Lightness of Being"
54 Guitarist Nugent
55 Seasonal mall employees
59 "Praise be to God!"
61 After-class aides
62 Inclination
63 Even (with)
64 Seattle-to-Las Vegas dir.
65 Rhoda's TV mom
66 Talk show groups

DOWN

1 Person on a poster
2 Undoing
3 Chemical endings
4 Gives off, as heat
5 ___ We Trust
6 Slates
7 Louis-Dreyfus of "Seinfeld"
8 Not yet apprehended
9 Suffix with expert
10 Simply smashing
11 Shrimper's net
12 Courtroom figs.
14 Shore dinner special
15 Some needles
23 Trattoria course
24 Women, casually
25 Dos cubed
26 Military sch.
28 Leave a permanent mark on
31 Bank features
32 Large barrel
33 Run away
34 Is unwell

Puzzle 116 by Eric Berlin

35 Howls like a dog
39 Brave, for instance
42 Rich, as a voice
43 24-hour
44 Penalized,
 as a speeder
47 Paint layers
48 "Deutschland über
 ___"
49 Creator of Pooh and
 Piglet
50 Nikon rival
52 Place for sweaters?
56 Hit the bottle

57 ___ Sea, east of the
 Caspian
58 Lith. and Lat., once
60 Wreath

ACROSS

1 Likely
4 Hot dish with beans
9 Bridge maven Charles
14 Justice Sandra __ O'Connor
15 Appealingly shocking
16 Licorice flavoring
17 Antique auto
19 Frank of rock's Mothers of Invention
20 Vegetable oil component
21 The "S" of CBS
23 Black currant
25 Humiliated
29 Tea server's question
33 Out of one's mind
36 Van Susteren of Fox News
37 Alternative to a nail
38 "That's __!" (angry denial)
40 Conductor's stick
42 Long-eared hopper
43 Neuters
45 Danger
47 Fashion inits.
48 Cause of an out
51 Refuses
52 Smoothed
56 Drops
60 Baghdad resident
61 __ Mongolia
64 Small frosted cake
66 Item confiscated at an airport
67 Goofy
68 Wrestler's locale
69 Seasoned sailors
70 Parachute pulls
71 They: Fr.

DOWN

1 __ committee
2 Newswoman Zahn
3 Varieties
4 Asexual reproduction
5 Where spokes meet
6 Showy flower
7 Showy flower
8 "Beware the __ . . ."
9 Park shelters
10 Parading . . . or a hint to this puzzle's theme
11 __ Van Winkle
12 Psychic's claim
13 Educators' org.
18 Japanese soup
22 Punch out, as Morse code
24 Kosovo war participant
26 Not stay on the path
27 Pitchers
28 Wooden pin
30 Bounded
31 Absolute
32 New Zealand native
33 A brig has two
34 __ male (top dog)
35 Locked book
39 Command to people who are 10-Down
41 "Just do it" sloganeer
44 Gentlemen of España

46 An original tribe of Israel
49 Scatter, as seeds
50 Feudal figure
53 Ashley's country-singing mother
54 Sweet'N Low rival
55 Mud, dust and grime
57 Like "The Lord of the Rings"
58 It's north of Carson City
59 Movie rating unit

61 Approves
62 Spanish article
63 Up to, informally
65 Polit. maverick

ACROSS

1 Trunk item
6 Job seeker's success
11 Gridlock
14 Poe's middle name
15 Bisect
16 Mentalist Geller
17 All-freshman team?
19 Zero
20 Ugly Duckling, in reality
21 Reflect (on)
22 Arcade coin
24 So-so
26 Bridle's partner
27 Peter Cottontail?
32 Tonsil neighbor
33 Smallish field
34 Put on TV
37 Boone, to rustics
38 Have a ball?
40 Blue Triangle org.
41 Inventor Whitney
42 Fill-in
43 Heart of France
44 Answer to "Who wrote 'The Highwayman'?"
48 Historical Scottish county
50 Summoned Jeeves
51 M-1, for one
52 Tokyo ties
54 Charlie Chaplin's widow
58 60's muscle car
59 Milliner on the move?
62 Poet's preposition
63 Zoo critter
64 Campfire treat
65 "Shame on you"
66 Supersized
67 Tournament favorites

DOWN

1 __-serif
2 Furrow former
3 Thomas __ Edison
4 Drops from on high
5 Letter accompanier: Abbr.
6 "Yeah, right"
7 Web site sect. for newbies
8 Chimney channel
9 Zsa Zsa's sister
10 Bureaucratic tangle
11 Place for miscellaneous stuff
12 Sharon of Israel
13 Eeyore's creator
18 Oscar winner Jannings
23 Lyrical lines
25 Dr. J's old league: Abbr.
26 Nimble
27 Au naturel
28 Horse course
29 Item in a musician's pocket
30 Arthur Marx, familiarly
31 Columbus Day mo.
35 Hosp. areas
36 Like a compliant cat

Puzzle 118 by L. Glickstein and N. Salomon

38 Banana waste
39 Early hrs.
40 "Dunno"
42 Aspirin alternative
43 Bamboozle
45 Olive in the comics
46 Milk container?
47 Redeem, with "in"
48 Insiders' vocabulary
49 Priests' administrations
52 "Rubáiyát" poet
53 Screen door sound
55 Oklahoma Indian
56 One who's unhip

57 Aphrodite's lover
60 — pro nobis
61 Big jerk

ACROSS

1 Boeing 747's and 767's
5 The Monkees' "__ Believer"
8 "Am not!" rejoinder
14 Forced out
16 Wash receptacles
17 With 56-Across, lawyer who argued in 19- and 49-Across
18 Pre-Mexican Indians
19 With 49-Across, noted decision made 5/17/54
21 Buying binge
24 Musical talent
25 Eight: Fr.
26 Stuart queen
29 Went after congers
34 Aged
35 On the briny
36 Curious thing
37 Decision reversed by 19- and 49-Across
40 One sailing under a skull and crossbones
41 Locust or larch
42 Spanish aunt
43 Belgian painter James
44 Chief Justice __ Warren, who wrote the opinion for 19- and 49-Across
45 Rolodex nos.
46 Select, with "for"
48 Stanford-__ test

49 See 19-Across
55 Sitting room
56 See 17-Across
60 Groups of starting players
61 Forebodes
62 Vice President Dick
63 Ave. crossers
64 Mary __ Lincoln

DOWN

1 Stick (out)
2 Book after Galatians: Abbr.
3 Capote, for short
4 Iced dessert
5 Langston Hughes poem
6 Cat's cry
7 Annex: Abbr.
8 Addis __, Ethiopia
9 Symbol of sharpness
10 "Cómo __ usted?"
11 Echelon
12 How a lot of modern music is sold
13 Secret W.W. II agcy.
15 Brute
20 Flying geese formation
21 Quaint establishment
22 Arrive, as by car
23 Passengers
26 "__ sow, so shall . . ."
27 Reno's state: Abbr.
28 U.S./Can./Mex. pact
30 University URL ending
31 Pay attention
32 French star

Puzzle 119 by Ethan Cooper

33 Ruler by birth
35 Houston landmark
36 Pitcher Hershiser
38 __ Paulo, Brazil
39 Go off track
44 And so forth
45 Soldier's helmet, slangily
47 Short-winded
48 Bruce Springsteen, with "the"
49 __ of office
50 Gratis
51 Flair

52 Concert equipment
53 Pucker-inducing
54 Angers
55 __-Man (arcade game)
57 Past
58 Was ahead
59 "Acid"

ACROSS

1 Wise competitor
5 Quack
10 On vacation
14 Snack sold in a stack
15 Crystal set
16 Lens holders
17 Soccer commentator's cry
18 Shelley's "Adonais" is one
19 List-ending abbr.
20 "Aha!"
23 Caper
24 Little one
25 Four-bagger
27 Hosp. workers
28 Top worn with shorts
30 "All in the Family" network
32 Arctic bird
33 Soccer star Hamm
34 — correspondent
35 Singer/songwriter Laura
36 Honky-tonk instruments
40 Mountaintop
41 Aurora's counterpart
42 Wonderment
43 Deli sandwich, for short
44 Corots, Monets and such
45 Sp. Mrs.
46 Qualifiers
49 Red Sea peninsula
51 Cartoon collectible
53 Spokes, e.g.

55 Passable
58 Some drive-thru features, briefly
59 Not as friendly
60 Tennis score after deuce
61 Old-fashioned dance
62 "— luck!"
63 Evening, in ads
64 Retailer's gds.
65 "Mmm, mmm!"
66 Leave in, to an editor

DOWN

1 River blockage
2 In the vicinity
3 Bakery supplies
4 Longtime Chicago Symphony maestro
5 Air Force One passenger: Abbr.
6 Soft, white mineral
7 Keats's "— a Nightingale"
8 Bedtime drink
9 Ma with a bow
10 "All systems —!"
11 How a 43-Across is usually prepared
12 All Olympians, once
13 Designer monogram
21 Play segment
22 Sounds of doubt
26 "King Kong" studio
29 Raring to go
31 Hare's habitat
33 Mystery man
34 Scale amts.

Puzzle 120 by Elizabeth C. Gorski

35 Del.-to-Vt. direction
36 Elated
37 Spot and Felix, e.g.
38 Après-ski treat
39 Tony, Oscar or Hugo
40 Middle manager's focus?
44 Balloon filler
45 Most guileful
46 "Hurray for me!"
47 Limited
48 Major paperback publisher
50 Bridal path

52 Gives off
54 Bates and King
56 Pinball stopper
57 Horse-drawn vehicle
58 Pitching __

ACROSS

1 Dreadful, as circumstances
5 One not of high morals
10 Spanish house
14 TV's "American __"
15 Come back
16 Shakespeare, the Bard of __
17 1970 Richard Thomas film adapted from a Richard Bradford novel
20 Mao __-tung
21 Hula shakers
22 To no __ (uselessly)
23 Outlaws
24 Wall Street business
26 Jumped
29 Long baths
30 Ayatollah's land
31 Kunta __ of "Roots"
32 Duo
35 1975 Al Pacino film
39 Lamb's mother
40 Landlord payments
41 Shrek, for one
42 Slight hangups
43 Reveries
45 Oilless paint
48 Cure
49 Lily family plants
50 Arias, usually
51 King topper
54 1941 Priscilla Lane film whose title was a #1 song

58 Advance, as money
59 Lollapalooza
60 Bridle strap
61 Football positions
62 "I'm innocent!"
63 Poet __ St. Vincent Millay

DOWN

1 Earth
2 Midmonth date
3 Was transported
4 Raised railroads
5 Difficult
6 Harvests
7 Intermissions separate them
8 Silent
9 __-am (sports competition)
10 Sail material
11 Birdlike
12 __ boom
13 Corner
18 Mongol title
19 Fouler
23 Wedding reception staple
24 Type assortments
25 "I can't believe __ . . ." (old ad catchphrase)
26 Lateral part
27 Ship's front
28 Fury
29 Sorts (through)
31 Australian hopper, for short

32 "Gladiator" garment
33 Fish bait
34 Halves of a 32-Across
36 James of "Gunsmoke"
37 Wine vintage
38 Christmas song
42 Zips (along)
43 X out
44 Cause for umbrellas
45 Billiards furniture
46 Actress Burstyn
47 Knoll
48 Yawn-inducing
50 Yards rushing, e.g.

51 Elderly
52 Goatee site
53 Sicilian volcano
55 Son of, in Arabic names
56 Recent: Prefix
57 Fury

ACROSS

1 Doze (off)
4 Following
9 Infield fly
14 Pub offering
15 "Death, Be Not Proud" poet
16 "Maria —," 1940's hit
17 At leisure: Abbr.
18 Pact made at The Hague?
20 Legacy sharer
22 Directors Spike and Ang
23 Co., in France
24 Talks wildly
26 One more
28 Emulated O. Henry?
31 Many eras
32 Distress signal
33 — to go
37 Six-time U.S. Open tennis champ
40 Fool
42 Dweeb
43 Longing
45 Onetime neighbor of Israel: Abbr.
47 Neckline style
48 Where chocolate candy is made?
52 Procession
55 Sensation
56 Mancinelli opera "— e Leandro"
57 They're welcome on the back

59 Epoch of 50 million years ago
62 Part of a shirtmaker's education?
65 Female rabbit
66 Place to moor
67 Stan's foil, in old films
68 Not well
69 Reluctant
70 Interminably
71 Taboos

DOWN

1 D.E.A. agent
2 Butter alternative
3 Removes from power
4 Summing
5 Quarters
6 Explosive
7 Abbr. at the bottom of a business letter
8 Consider again
9 Kind of ad
10 Corrida cry
11 Miss — of the comics
12 Loosen
13 Reimburser
19 Pavarotti, notably
21 — de Cologne
25 Portico in Athens
27 Beginner
28 Work in the garden
29 Wander
30 Promulgate
34 Gets elected
35 —-do-well
36 Joel of "Cabaret"
38 Estrangement

Puzzle 122 by Richard Chisholm

39 God's way, in religion
41 Umpire's call
44 Mystery writer's award
46 Arrived quickly
49 Mounts
50 Was too sweet
51 Middle X or O
52 Rhodes of Rhodesia
53 College town on the Penobscot River
54 University of Missouri locale
58 W.W. II battle town

60 __ contendere
61 Fish caught in pots
63 Tennis call
64 Suffix with mod-

ACROSS

1 Gun-toting gal
5 __ vu
9 Put forth, as a theory
14 Singer Brickell
15 Greek counterpart of 27-Down
16 Wonderland girl
17 Mediocre
18 "__, vidi, vici" (Caesar's boast)
19 Ohio birthplace of William McKinley
20 Bridge
23 Widespread
24 April 15 deadline agcy.
25 Fond du __, Wis.
28 Take the witness stand
31 Classic muscle car
34 Caribbean resort island
36 "__ we having fun yet?"
37 Conclude, with "up"
38 Bridge
42 Spew
43 Washington's __ Stadium
44 Below
45 Young fellow
46 Feature of Texaco's logo, once
49 Period in history
50 Sawbuck
51 Periods in history
53 Bridge
61 Ancient Greek marketplace

62 Prayer's end
63 Govern
64 Laser printer powder
65 Left, at sea
66 Vicinity
67 War horse
68 Some Father's Day callers
69 Sign of boredom

DOWN

1 Flat-topped hill
2 Reason to say "Pee-yew!"
3 "Schindler's __"
4 Sainted ninth-century pope
5 Concoct
6 Puts up, as a tower
7 Mitchell who sang "Big Yellow Taxi"
8 India's locale
9 Kitchen closet
10 Miscellanies
11 Building next to a barn
12 Noted rapper/actor
13 Radio host John
21 Deadly
22 Prisoner who'll never get out
25 Sports jacket feature
26 Inviting smell
27 Roman counterpart of 15-Across
29 Bulletin board stickers
30 Savings for old age: Abbr.
31 Exam mark

Puzzle 123 by Gregory E. Paul

32 Worker with circus lions
33 "La Bohème," e.g.
35 Except that
37 Chicago-based Superstation
39 Where the action is
40 TV's "Mayberry —"
41 German engraver Albrecht
46 Offer on a "Wanted" poster
47 Alehouse
48 C.I.A. operatives

50 Number of points for a field goal
52 Deodorant type
53 Stetsons, e.g.
54 Gershwin's "— Rhythm"
55 Sold, to an auctioneer
56 Puppy sounds
57 1847 Melville novel
58 Mysterious quality
59 Whole bunch
60 Actor Connery

ACROSS

1 Verboten: Var.
5 Boats' backbones
10 "The Nazarene" writer Sholem
14 Park and Lexington, e.g., in N.Y.C.
15 Decorated Murphy
16 Starlet's goal
17 Ceremony for inventors?
19 In alignment
20 Off the track
21 Rankled
23 Lager holder
24 Burlesque star Lili St. ___
25 One of Alcott's "Little Women"
26 Jean Arp's art
28 Stair part
31 Greeting for a villain
34 Holy Iraqi
37 In reserve
38 Bat material
39 Is headed for a fall
41 Baseball rarity
42 Ill will
44 Lantern-jawed celeb
45 Hide's partner
46 High-strung
47 Shiites or Amish
49 Easy card game
50 Place to relax
52 Sophisticates they're not
56 Soak through
59 Coin flipper's phrase
60 "How sweet ___!"
61 Low-cal beer in reserve?
63 Ides of March rebuke
64 Actor Delon
65 In perpetuity
66 Leak slowly
67 Jack who was famously frugal
68 Laura of "I Am Sam"

DOWN

1 Spanish appetizers
2 Sailor's "Stop!"
3 Midler of stage and screen
4 Cyber-handles
5 Name in a stuttered 1918 song title
6 Where Lux. is
7 Uplift spiritually
8 Pepsi bottle amount
9 Meets, as a bet
10 Sister of Apollo
11 Bad place to build?
12 Whodunit board game
13 Pay mind to
18 "Peter Pan" dog
22 Gogol's "___ Bulba"
24 Caravan beast
27 Conk out
29 Falco of "The Sopranos"
30 Need a bath badly
31 Dish that's "slung"
32 Culp/Cosby TV series

Puzzle 124 by Fred Piscop

33 Word processor
for sailors?
35 Munched on
36 Brainy group
39 — Haute, Ind.
40 Sturgeon delicacy
43 Joins forces (with)
45 Silenced
48 Crack from the
cold
50 Played out
51 Praline nut
53 Critic Barnes
54 Check falsifier

55 Howard of morning
radio
56 They're cut into
wedges
57 Sermon ending?
58 Simple rhyme scheme
59 Big Apple college
inits.
62 They're related

ACROSS

1 True-blue
6 Toy gun poppers
10 Smooch
14 "Good Night" girl of song
15 Arthur __ Stadium in Queens
16 Peak
17 River triangle
18 Signify
19 Horn's sound
20 Logic
23 __ capita
24 Buffalo's lake
25 Money in the bank, e.g.
30 Declare
33 Seizes without authority
34 Old what's-__-name
35 George W. Bush's alma mater
36 Michael who starred in "Dirty Rotten Scoundrels"
37 Snorkeling accessory
38 Wolf calls
39 Broadway hit with 7,000+ performances
40 With it
41 Immobilize
42 Swelling reducer
43 Highway stops
45 Ritzy
46 Little rascal
47 Question of concern, with a hint to 20-, 25- and 43-Across
54 Corner square in Monopoly
55 Den
56 Unsophisticated
57 Loafing
58 Dublin's home
59 Lyrics accompany them
60 2000 "subway series" losers
61 Toy used on hills
62 Commence

DOWN

1 Eyeball covers
2 Nabisco cookie
3 Shout
4 Against
5 Weapon in the game of Clue
6 Tripod topper
7 On the open water
8 Adds gradually
9 Mexican misters
10 Couric of "Today"
11 Computer symbol
12 Haze
13 Movie backdrop
21 Commies
22 Tiny criticism
25 Emmy-winner (finally!) Susan
26 Author __ Bashevis Singer
27 Truly

Puzzle 125 by Lynn Lempel

28 Vases
29 Harbor sights
30 Took care of
31 Totally tired
32 Sí and oui
35 Quotable Yank
37 Swerve back and forth, as a car's rear end
38 Very short shorts
40 Big bothers
41 Soccer star Mia
43 Caught
44 In layers

45 Sees a ghost, maybe
47 Walk through water
48 Sword handle
49 Put on the payroll
50 Tightly stretched
51 Turner who sang "I Don't Wanna Fight"
52 At any time
53 Sabbath activity
54 __-dandy

ACROSS

1 10K, e.g.
5 Wheedler's tactic
10 Jungle crushers
14 — Bator
15 Land of a billion
16 Basilica area
17 Start of an Oscar Wilde quote
20 Revolutionary Allen
21 Comics shriek
22 Out of bed
23 Bakers' wares
25 Strange sightings
27 Quote, part 2
31 Cost-controlling W.W. II agcy.
34 Jacob's twin
35 Et — (and the following)
36 Cozy spots
38 "I cannot — lie"
40 Make a knight, e.g.
42 Utter disorder
43 See 61-Down
45 Dr. Seuss's Sam —
47 "Rule Britannia" composer
48 Spain's Juan Carlos, for one
49 Quote, part 3
52 — En-lai
53 Slinky's shape
54 Bawdyhouse manager
57 Bleachers cry
59 — Jean Baker (Marilyn Monroe)
63 End of the quote
66 Excursion
67 Met offering
68 Civil wrong
69 Coin flip
70 Theroux's "endless night"
71 Summers in Québec

DOWN

1 Deserving a slap, maybe
2 Touched down
3 Country singer Johnny
4 Summarize
5 Tonic's partner
6 Brand-new
7 — fixe (obsession)
8 Meeting of spacecraft
9 "Mangia!"
10 Groundwork
11 Chooses, with "for"
12 1975 Wimbledon winner
13 Perceived
18 "Sleep —"
19 Like many an O. Henry story
24 Pothook shape
26 Half a sawbuck
27 Awful smell
28 Grenoble's river
29 Come from behind
30 Furnish with gear
31 Midwest air hub
32 Hacienda drudges
33 Pack animals
37 A Brontë sister

Puzzle 126 by Ed Early

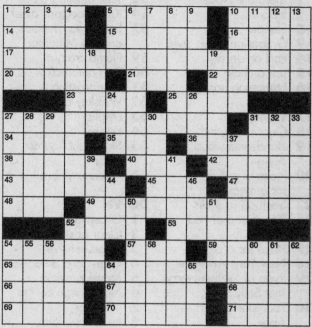

39 Cause of wheezing
41 Graph with rectangular areas
44 "__ 'nuff!"
46 Meadow call
50 The Continent
51 Actress Lollobrigida
52 Roughs it
54 Feminist Lucretia
55 Michael Jackson's old do
56 Honored guest's spot
58 Neighborhood
60 Knee-slapper
61 With 43-Across, approximately
62 Little scurriers
64 Auction assent
65 "Uh-uh!"

ACROSS

1 Literature Nobelist Bellow
5 Slender
9 Gregorian music style
14 Port or claret
15 Left a chair
16 Edmonton hockey player
17 Vicinity
18 Out of the wind
19 Handsome wood design
20 Place to pull in for a meal
23 Seafood in shells
24 Site of one-armed bandits
27 Place for a pig
28 New York ballplayer
29 Ryan of "When Harry Met Sally"
30 Four-star officer: Abbr.
31 F.D.R. radio broadcast
34 As well
37 Responses to a masseur
38 German chancellor — von Bismarck
39 Highest-priced boxing ticket
44 It may be served with crumpets
45 Snoop around
46 Old cable inits.
47 "Sesame Street" broadcaster

50 Modern affluent type
52 Teen meeting place
54 Kindly doctor's asset
57 Setting for Theseus and the Minotaur
59 Plumb crazy
60 Skin outbreak
61 Broadcasting
62 Whiskey drink
63 Display
64 Desires
65 Statement figures: Abbr.
66 "Bonanza" brother

DOWN

1 Groups of bees
2 Clear of stale smells
3 Apprehensive
4 Clues, to a detective
5 Movie preview
6 Not change course
7 "Gotcha"
8 Must-have item
9 Just-made-up word
10 Actor/dancer Gregory
11 O.K.
12 Org. that funds exhibits
13 Have a go at
21 Big rig
22 Decorated, as a cake
25 Well-groomed
26 Not fooled by
29 Fail to qualify, as for a team
31 London weather, often

Puzzle 127 by Craig Kasper

32 That girl
33 Barracks bunk
34 Bohemian
35 In — of (replacing)
36 Vegetable in a crisp pod
40 Tarantulas, e.g.
41 Angers
42 Captivates
43 Tennis star Kournikova
47 Pullover raincoat
48 — Aires
49 Scatters, as petals
51 Mini, in Marseille

53 Grind, as teeth
55 Rick's love in "Casablanca"
56 Fate
57 It may be put out to pasture
58 Genetic stuff

ACROSS

1 Rugged rock
5 Incite
9 Unlike a dirt road
14 Whopper
15 White-tailed eagle
16 Spry
17 Fusses
18 Makes lace
19 Like maples but not firs
20 Area between two scrimmage lines
23 Jul. follower
24 Largest of the British Virgin Islands
29 Chemical process also called hyperfiltration
33 Attention-getter
34 Radio feature
35 Successful
36 Flared-spout pitcher
38 Military newbie
41 Heredity unit
42 Grief
44 Rotators under the hood
46 __ Lingus
47 Make crazy
51 Increased
52 Took off
53 Yellowstone employees
59 Video game pioneer
63 Bluish green
64 "The Grapes of Wrath" figure
65 Get ready for Web-surfing
66 Northern Oklahoma city
67 Take a break
68 Hard stuff
69 Lightning catchers
70 Inquires

DOWN

1 Family group
2 Obnoxious
3 Baseball brothers' name
4 Holst who composed "The Planets"
5 "Stop living in your fantasy world!"
6 Kind of hygiene
7 1998 animated film with the voice of Woody Allen
8 Spanish explorer who discovered the Mississippi
9 Capital of Sicily
10 Get on in years
11 By way of
12 Keebler worker?
13 Susan of "L.A. Law"
21 Regretted
22 Rejections
25 Chinese mafia
26 Bony
27 Toy train maker
28 "__ your instructions . . ."
29 Express differently
30 Lash site
31 Mineo of "Exodus"

Puzzle 128 by Nancy Kavanaugh

32 Vote in
33 Gossipy Hopper
37 Gad about
39 Relative of "Phooey!"
40 Green gems
43 Timber from Maine
45 Long-necked bird
48 Hagen of Broadway
49 Luggage carrier
50 Some wool
54 Gambler's game
55 Police cry
56 Stretches (out)
57 Hazard

58 Nears the western horizon
59 Vestment for a priest
60 As well
61 Back then
62 Role on "Frasier"

ACROSS
1 End-of-week cry
5 Makes, as tea
10 Wise __ owl
14 Folk singer Guthrie
15 Soprano Callas
16 Popular building block
17 1959 Doris Day/Rock Hudson comedy
19 Actress Singer of "Footloose"
20 Victor's entitlement
21 Errors
23 See 24-Across
24 With 23-Across, Neptune, e.g.
26 Back street
27 Clearance item's caveat
29 Wrestler's win
30 Had a bite
31 Disposable pen maker
32 Davenport
33 Church official
37 What a full insurance policy offers
40 Bronze and stainless steel
41 Bed size smaller than full
42 __ Paul's seafood
43 Spider's prey
44 Conger or moray
45 Mosquito repellent ingredient
46 First lady after Hillary
49 Put two and two together?

50 California's Big __
51 Evidence in court
53 Tetley competitor
56 Radio tuner
57 Piano player's aid
60 France, under Caesar
61 "__ Doone" (1869 novel)
62 Not us
63 Building additions
64 Vote into office
65 Jekyll's alter ego

DOWN
1 Bugler's evening call
2 Hang on tight?
3 Not according to Mr. Spock
4 Shakespearean volumes
5 Some luxury cars
6 Squealer
7 Time in history
8 "The Flintstones" mother
9 Pseudonym of H. H. Munro
10 Post-danger signal
11 1988 Olympics host
12 Be of one mind
13 Clamorous
18 Outdated
22 Lustrous fabric
24 Go (through), as evidence
25 Made into law
27 "Mamma Mia" pop group

Puzzle 129 by Craig Kasper

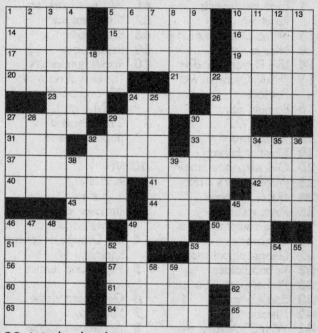

28 Window box location
29 Verse-writing
30 Tablet with ibuprofen
32 Bygone space station
34 Averse to picture-taking
35 Meanie
36 Home in a tree
38 Without any extras
39 Was beholden to
45 University of Minnesota campus site
46 Overhang

47 Like some symmetry
48 Mover's rental
49 Playwright — Fugard
50 Uncle —
52 Ireland, the Emerald —
53 Ballpark figure?
54 Went out, as a fire
55 Pinnacle
58 Before, in 29-Down
59 Business letter abbr.

ACROSS
1 Luau instruments, for short
5 Noted plus-size model
9 Nice to wear
14 Like Playboy models
15 "Hud" Oscar winner Patricia
16 Be nuts about
17 Qatari V.I.P.
18 Turns abruptly
19 Novelist Ephron
20 Old telephone feature
23 Proofreader's mark
24 G.P.A., slangily
25 Put a value on
27 When summer starts
30 Cry over
32 Geographical septet
33 Kabob holder
35 Pitcher part
38 See 41-Across
40 Historic time
41 With 38-Across, what the four key parts of this puzzle are
43 Uno + due
44 Conductor Toscanini
47 State openly
48 Brawl site in a western
50 Horrifies
52 Yalta's peninsula
54 Stowe equipment
55 Hearty party
56 Gymgoer's goal
62 Earth's — layer
64 19-Across's sister

65 Medieval chest
66 Wades across, say
67 "The heat —!"
68 Bring up
69 Rendezvous
70 Rock's Rundgren
71 The end of each of 20- and 56-Across and 11- and 29-Down is a popular one

DOWN
1 Addict
2 — sabe
3 Turnpike toll-paying locale
4 Big Orange of college sports
5 Pepsin and rennin, for two
6 Gettysburg victor
7 Yule trio
8 Adamson's lioness
9 Crude dude
10 Ukrainian port
11 Fuji flow
12 Part of a Happy Meal
13 "The Second Coming" poet
21 Seek a seat
22 Poor, as excuses go
26 Put into slots
27 "— that special?!"
28 Within earshot
29 "Howards End" director

Puzzle 130 by Allan E. Parrish

30 Kicked off
31 Fancy pitcher
34 Green Hornet's sidekick
36 Hit Fox show, in headlines
37 Mass seating
39 Mall attraction
42 Eminem and Dr. Dre, for two
45 Gad about
46 Bay Area city
49 Makes right
51 Pizza order
52 Video game heroine Lara —
53 Stubble remover
54 New England catch
57 Complex dwelling
58 "Eh"
59 Black-and-white treat
60 Final Four org.
61 Tombstone lawman
63 Ballpark fig.

SOLUTIONS

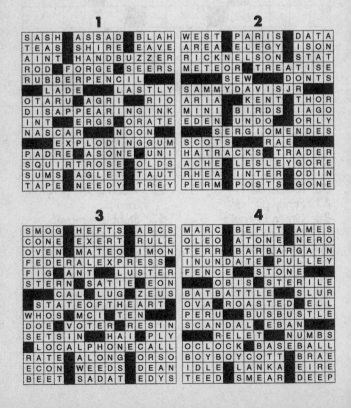

1

S	A	S	H		A	S	S	A	D		B	L	A	H
T	E	A	S		S	H	I	R	E		E	A	V	E
A	I	N	T		H	A	N	D	B	U	Z	Z	E	R
R	O	D		F	O	R	G	E		S	E	E	R	S
R	U	B	B	E	R	P	E	N	C	I	L			
		L	A	D	E				L	A	S	T	L	Y
O	T	A	R	U		A	G	R	I			R	I	O
D	I	S	A	P	P	E	A	R	I	N	G	I	N	K
I	N	T			E	R	G	S		O	R	A	T	E
N	A	S	C	A	R				N	O	O	N		
			E	X	P	L	O	D	I	N	G	G	U	M
P	A	D	R	E		A	S	O	N	E		U	N	I
S	Q	U	I	R	T	R	O	S	E		O	L	D	S
S	U	M	S		A	G	L	E	T		T	A	U	T
T	A	P	E		N	E	E	D	Y		T	R	E	Y

2

W	E	S	T		P	A	R	I	S			D	A	T	A
A	R	E	A		E	L	E	G	Y		I	S	O	N	
R	I	C	K	N	E	L	S	O	N		S	T	A	T	
M	E	T	E	O	R		T	R	E	A	T	I	S	E	
			S	E	W					D	O	N	T	S	
S	A	M	M	Y	D	A	V	I	S	J	R				
A	R	I	A			K	E	N	T			T	H	O	R
M	I	N	I		B	I	R	D	S		I	A	G	O	
E	D	E	N		U	N	D	O		O	R	L	Y		
			S	E	R	G	I	O	M	E	N	D	E	S	
S	C	O	T	S					R	A	E				
H	A	T	R	A	C	K	S		T	R	A	D	E	R	
A	C	H	E		L	E	S	L	E	Y	G	O	R	E	
R	H	E	A		I	N	T	E	R			O	D	I	N
P	E	R	M		P	O	S	T	S			G	O	N	E

3

S	M	O	G		H	E	F	T	S		A	B	C	S
C	O	N	E		E	X	E	R	T		R	U	L	E
O	V	E	N		M	A	T	E	O		I	M	O	N
F	E	D	E	R	A	L	E	X	P	R	E	S	S	
F	I	G		A	N	T			L	U	S	T	E	R
S	T	E	R	N		S	A	T	I	E		E	O	N
		C	A	L		L	U	G		Z	E	U	S	
S	T	A	T	E	O	F	T	H	E	A	R	T		
W	H	O	S		M	C	I		T	E	N			
D	O	E		V	O	T	E	R		R	E	S	I	N
S	E	T	S	I	N			H	A	I		P	L	Y
	L	O	C	A	L	P	H	O	N	E	C	A	L	L
R	A	T	E		A	L	O	N	G		O	R	S	O
E	C	O	N		W	E	E	D	S		D	E	A	N
B	E	E	T		S	A	D	A	T		E	D	Y	S

4

M	A	R	C		B	E	F	I	T		A	M	E	S
O	L	E	O		A	T	O	N	E		N	E	R	O
T	E	R	R		B	A	R	B	A	R	G	A	I	N
I	N	U	N	D	A	T	E			P	U	L	L	E	Y
F	E	N	C	E			S	T	O	N	E				
			O	B	I	S		S	T	E	R	I	L	E	
B	A	T	B	A	T	T	L	E				S	L	U	R
O	V	A		R	O	A	S	T	E	D		E	L	L	
P	E	R	U		B	U	S	B	U	S	T	L	E		
S	C	A	N	D	A	L		E	B	A	N				
			R	E	L	E	T			N	U	M	B	S	
O	C	L	O	C	K		B	A	S	E	B	A	L	L	
B	O	Y	B	O	Y	C	O	T	T		B	R	A	E	
I	D	L	E		L	A	N	K	A		E	I	R	E	
T	E	E	D		S	M	E	A	R		D	E	E	P	

5

```
S A V O R # C A B I N # J E W
T R I P E # A M A N A # E P A
O G L E S # P A N T Y R A I D
P U E R T O R I C O # O N C E
S E R A # P A N # N A T # # #
# # # S E T # D E V I L L E #
S H A # L I B Y A # A N A I S
P U B L I C R E L A T I O N S
A G L E T # A R E N A # S O O
T E E T E R S # G R R # # # #
# T S E # T O E # E L A N # #
O D I E # P A U L R E V E R E
P O T R O A S T S # M I N C E
A G E # D I T T O # I V I E D
L E M # D R A I N # R E N D S
```

6

```
S N O W # S N I P S # A C E D
R E D O # H O M E O # N A M E
S E E M # R E E L S # A N I L
# # # B U I L T T O S C A L E
A B A # R V S # # R A I L E D
S U N D A E # A A R O N # # #
H O T E L L O B B Y # # C U B
E Y E S # # J O E # # V O T E
S S S # P A I D A V I S I T #
# # # B A S I L # D I A B L O
S H E I L A # R O D # Y E N #
H I D D E N O P E R A S # # #
I N G E # D R A P E # L A D Y
N E A R # Q A T A R # A R I A
S S R S # S L E D S # T E E M
```

7

```
B A S E R # H I P S # S L A W
A H O R A # E R S E # Y A L E
J E N N Y C R A I G # S N A P
A M S # G O E S # M U T A N T
# O U T S # S E R E # # # # #
# H E N N Y Y O U N G M A N #
F I S T S # C I T E # V O W #
O T T O # K E A T S # B A B E
R U E # S E L L # T R I E D #
# P E N N Y M A R S H A L L #
# # # # A A H S # O T I S # #
I N D I G O # G U A M # F I B
V I A L # L E N N Y B R U C E
A N T E # E G A D # L E M O N
N E E D # S O W S # E V E N T
```

8

```
B R U T # B U D S # S A L E M
L U T E # I T I N # E R O D E
U P I N # G A G A # E E R I E
R E C O R D H I G H S # A N T
B E A N I E # T S A R I N A S
# # # S P A M # Z E N # # # #
G Y M # S L I P P E D D I S K
N O A H # L E I # # Y O R E #
P U P U P L A T T E R # N O G
# # # G E O # A D A M # # # #
R E C H E C K S # A N E M I A
E T A # V I N Y L S I D I N G
M U L T I # O R A N # U L N A
I D L E S # T U N E # S K I M
T E A C H # S P A R # A S E A
```

9

```
A D E P T # A M I S # P S S T
P A Y E E # T O R I # A H O Y
O N E A M # B O A R D W A L K
P A R K P L A C E # A N G I E
# # # L A T H # E N E # # # #
F A B L E S # S N I D E S T #
E R L E # T O P P L E # P H I
R E A D I N G R A I L R O A D
M A N # S A L O N S # A C M E
# I R K S O M E # T I T H E S
# # # A B E # S T E N # # # #
S C A L A # S H O R T L I N E
L U X U R Y T A X # R A C E R
O B I T # A L L I # A M O C O
E A S E # K O L N # Y A N K S
```

10

```
A S T A # A L S O # K A T I E
B A A S # D I E M # I M A G E
A N K A # D O R A # N Y L O N
S T E P H E N F R O S T E R #
H A T # O D E # A K A # # # #
# H A R O L D P R I N T E R #
P I E P A N # I R S # # E R A
T A R T S # A N Y # T R A I T
A G A # P R E # S A U T E S #
# S O P H I E T R U C K E R #
# # # # E S E # P O E # O R B
P H Y L L I S D R I L L E R #
S U E D E # N E A P # A L E E
T R E A T # T A T I # N E V E
P E P Y S # O R E O # D Y E D
```

The bonus word is MONOPOLY.

11

```
S A W N   S L A S H   C U B A
I N R E   K O R E A   O V E R
K N I T P I C K E R   V E N T
H A T   O N U S   S L E A Z Y
      B E S S   C H E R
A L A R M   D O N A T I O N
S A F E   G R I M E S   R N A
K N O W G R E A T S H A K E S
E A U   A I S L E S   B E N T
D I L E M M A S   B U D D Y
      I M A Y   M E E T
F R U G A L   K A T E   B E E
E A C H   K N I G H T C L U B
S I L T   I R E N E   A U R A
S L A Y   N A V A L   T R O Y
```

12

```
S P A R T A   S U R G E
L I N E A R   C H O I C E S T
A T T I C S   O U T F O X E S
T H I N K O F T H A T   C E O
      S O N E S   E W E R S
O F F   N S W   Y O D E L
R E A C T   H U B   A L D A
C A N Y O U B E L I E V E I T
A T T N   F A X   G E N O A
A D I O S   A T O   T N T
R E S I N   F L A M E
O A T   J U S T I M A G I N E
T R I B U N A L   E N A M O R
E N C I R C L E   S I D I N G
      T E H E E   T A S T E S
```

13

```
T W A   C H A O S   A B A S E
W A D   H E L L O   R O P E R
A L I   I S L E O F C A P R I
I D E S   T O N I   A V E
N O U R I S H   E N S U R E S
      I D L E   R E A T A
B A A   E A R N   G E T U P
I L L H A V E T H E U S U A L
D E P O T   H O L A   S R O
      I T E M S   C A R E
D I N E D I N   K N O W H O W
I D I   L A O S   E A C H
A I S L E L I G H T S   N E E
N O T E R   L E O N A   O A T
A T S E A   S E P T S   I N S
```

14

```
S P E C   S T R A P   B A B A
F A R O   T A U P E   A L E S
P A R K R A N G E R   E K E S
D R S E U S S   S T R A F E
      S H H   L A I R   L E T
A H A   R E V E R S E B I D S
F U S S   D I G I T A L
T E P E E   T A O   D O G M A
      C L E A N S E   B O I L
N E U T R A L Z O N E   T A P
O D S   O S S A   T R A
T I E D Y E   E R I T R E A
O T R A   D R I V E C R A Z Y
N E I L   I N D I E   A C R E
E D D Y   N A I L S   P E A S
```

15

```
R E P A I R   U M P S   A D S
A M A N D A   G E R E   S O L
T U R K E Y S H O O T   T O E
      B L A S E   H M O   E W E
F L O E S   L E M O N D R O P
L U I S   D E N Y   I S P Y
A L L   D O C S   H A S
B U S T O U T L A U G H I N G
      R A G   A S T O   L E A
A B B A   A V I S   F L O G
F L O P E A R E D   S I G N S
R O D   M B A   E S T E E
A W E   B O M B S H E L T E R
M U G   E D I E   I N D I G O
E P A   R E S T   P O S T O N
```

16

```
D E A T H   J A W S   B O O K
A R T O O   A L A N   L O D E
M A T Z O M   I A T A   I Z O D
P T A   P A L   E P O N Y M S
S O R E L Y   G R U N T
      T A T A R   P U Z Z L E
T A C O   A S I P   S K O A L
A R O N   G O D O T   R O M E
R E A C H   F L O E   I T E M
P A T H O S   O H A R E
      A N N E X   P E G L E G
N E W L E A F   O O P   O S U
O P E L   T R E N T L A T K E
R E B A   C E D E   A P S E S
M E S H   H M O S   Y E A R S
```

17

```
S A N G   R A V E   H E M E N
C L I O   E D E N   A L I C E
R O C K   F O R T H R I G H T
A H E A D     N E E D   S O S
M A R R I A G E R I T E
    T E A R   R O A M E D
A I R S T R I P S   P R O X Y
I R E   P E L T S     P I E
L A N D S   G O A L P O S T S
S N O O T S   R E A R
    W I L B U R W R I G H T
O A R   L O O N     E E R I E
G H O S T W R I T E   N E L L
R E V U E   E T A L   T A L E
E M E N D   S E R F   S T Y X
```

18

```
M A P S   T A D A   F I F T Y
A L O P   A T O M   I N U S E
G A P E   N E W Y O R K S P A
I M P L Y   I S S U E   S S R
C O A L M I N E   N T H
      S A D   A C R E A G E
A R C   S T A T E A B B R S
R O R E M   A D O   P E R O T
T W O L E T T E R S   A W E
S E C E D E S   A R A
    C A P   L A N D D E A L
E S C   L I L A C   S A M O A
F L O R I D A K I N   G O R Y
F O C U S   M E D E   E T T E
S T A R T   E R S E   S E A R
```

19

```
B O R E S   D E L I   B A N G
A B U S E   O V E N   O R C A
B O S S A   D E N T   D I A L
Y E T   B R O N Z E M E D A L
    B E E T S   R A G
C O U L E E   P E N T A C L E
R A C K S   T R I E S   O A R
A S K S   S A I N T   S P C A
T I E   E T U D E   R O P E S
E S T I M A T E   T A L E S E
    G I G   O U T E R
A U B U R N T I G E R   H I S
W H O A   A W O L   A G E N T
N U N N   N O T E   C E A S E
S H E A   T S A R   E N D O W
```

20

```
E L M S   A C M E   B A L E S
B E E T   G A I T   A C E L A
A N N A   A L L T E R R A I N
Y O U B E T Y O U R L I F E
      L E X   R E D
G R I L L S   T R O Y   M A B
E E R I E   S E E R   B A D E
T H E P R I C E I S R I G H T
T A N S   D A M N   O R N O T
O B E   P E N S   S O L A C E
    E R A   S T S
T O T E L L T H E T R U T H
L I G H T S A B E R   E P E E
E G R E T   V A I N   B O N D
B E E R Y   A R K S   A N D Y
```

21

```
G R A P E   L A S T S   W A N
A T L A S   E S T E E   A B E
B E A T T H E H E A T   L B S
    T A U   E A S T   K I T
L E T I T B E   D E L E T E S
A N A   E R A S   S E T H
I N K   S I G H S   S T E M S
R U E D   S L A T E   U T A H
S I T U P   E L A N D   A R A
    H O R S   L I M E   L I D
P R E S O A K   D E B A K E Y
L I C   F L I P   S E T
O N A   F I L L T H E B I L L
T S K   E N L A I   R A D I O
Z O E   R E S T S   S T O U T
```

22

```
F I R   I T S M E   K I C K
A M A T   G O T O N   E T O N
U P T O N O G O O D   L A M E
N A T T E R S O N   I L L B E
A L L O W     P E N N Y
S E E   A F T   D O T   C O P
    I D I O M   T H R O N E
C O U L D N T B E B E T T E R
C A M E R A   A N A M E
S R S   E L M   O D O   S H E
    A S S A M   N A T A L
B L O T S   N O I S E L E S S
R O U E   S U N D A Y B E S T
E C R U   O A T E N   A R L O
W I S P   B L E A K   S E N
```

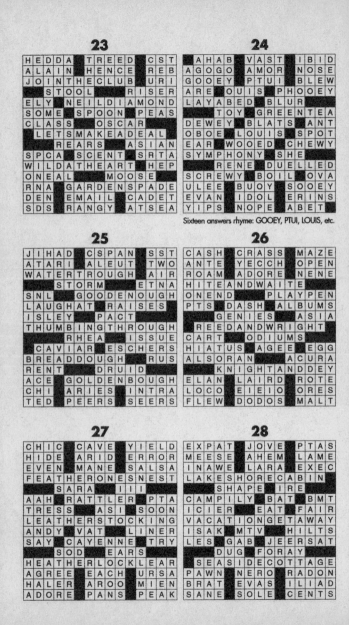

23

H	E	D	D	A		T	R	E	E	D		C	S	T
A	L	A	I	N		H	E	N	C	E		R	E	B
J	O	I	N	T	H	E	C	L	U	B		U	R	I
		S	T	O	O	L			R	I	S	E	R	
E	L	Y		N	E	I	L	D	I	A	M	O	N	D
S	O	M	E		S	P	O	O	N		P	E	A	S
C	L	A	S	S		O	S	C	A	R				
	L	E	T	S	M	A	K	E	A	D	E	A	L	
			R	E	A	R	S			A	S	I	A	N
S	P	C	A		S	C	E	N	T		S	R	T	A
W	I	L	D	A	T	H	E	A	R	T		H	E	P
O	N	E	A	L			M	O	O	S	E			
R	N	A		G	A	R	D	E	N	S	P	A	D	E
D	E	N		E	M	A	I	L		C	A	D	E	T
S	D	S		R	A	N	G	Y		A	T	S	E	A

24

	A	H	A	B		V	A	S	T		I	B	I	D
A	G	O	G	O		A	M	O	R		N	O	S	E
G	O	O	E	Y		P	T	U	I		B	L	E	W
A	R	E		O	U	I	S		P	H	O	O	E	Y
L	A	Y	A	B	E	D		B	L	U	R			
			T	O	Y		G	R	E	E	N	T	E	A
D	E	W	E	Y		B	L	A	T	S		A	N	T
O	B	O	E		L	O	U	I	S		S	P	O	T
E	A	R		W	O	O	E	D		C	H	E	W	Y
S	Y	M	P	H	O	N	Y		S	H	E			
	R	E	N	E		D	U	E	L	L	E	D		
S	C	R	E	W	Y		B	O	I	L		O	V	A
U	L	E	E		B	U	O	Y		S	O	O	E	Y
E	V	A	N		I	D	O	L		E	R	I	N	S
Y	I	P	S		N	O	P	E		A	B	E	T	

Sixteen answers rhyme: GOOEY, PTUI, LOUIS, etc.

25

J	I	H	A	D		C	S	P	A	N		S	S	T
A	T	A	R	I		A	L	E	U	T		T	W	O
W	A	T	E	R	T	R	O	U	G	H		A	I	R
		S	T	O	R	M			E	T	N	A		
S	N	L		G	O	O	D	E	N	O	U	G	H	
L	A	U	G	H	A	T		R	A	I	S	E	S	
I	S	L	E	Y		P	A	C	T					
T	H	U	M	B	I	N	G	T	H	R	O	U	G	H
			R	H	E	A		I	S	S	U	E		
	C	A	V	I	A	R		E	S	C	H	E	R	S
B	R	E	A	D	D	O	U	G	H		R	U	S	
R	E	N	T			D	R	U	I	D				
A	C	E		G	O	L	D	E	N	B	O	U	G	H
C	H	I		A	R	I	E	S		I	N	T	R	A
T	E	D		P	E	E	R	S		S	E	E	R	S

26

C	A	S	H		C	R	A	S	S		M	A	Z	E
A	N	T	E		Y	E	C	C	H		O	P	E	N
R	O	A	M		A	D	O	R	E		N	E	N	E
H	I	T	E	A	N	D	W	A	I	T	E			
O	N	E	N	D			P	L	A	Y	P	E	N	
P	T	S		D	A	S	H		A	L	B	U	M	S
			G	E	N	I	E	S		A	S	I	A	
	R	E	E	D	A	N	D	W	R	I	G	H	T	
C	A	R	T			O	D	I	U	M	S			
H	I	A	T	U	S		A	G	E	E		E	G	G
A	L	S	O	R	A	N			A	C	U	R	A	
	K	N	I	G	H	T	A	N	D	D	E	Y		
E	L	A	N		L	A	I	R	D		R	O	T	E
L	O	C	O		E	I	E	I	O		O	R	E	S
F	L	E	W		D	O	D	O	S		M	A	L	T

27

C	H	I	C		C	A	V	E		Y	I	E	L	D
H	I	D	E		A	R	I	D		E	R	R	O	R
E	V	E	N		M	A	N	E		S	A	L	S	A
F	E	A	T	H	E	R	O	N	E	S	N	E	S	T
	S	A	R	A		I	I	I						
A	A	H		R	A	T	T	L	E	R		P	T	A
T	R	E	S	S		A	S	I		S	O	O	N	
L	E	A	T	H	E	R	S	T	O	C	K	I	N	G
A	N	D	Y		V	A	T		L	I	N	E	R	
S	A	Y		C	A	Y	E	N	N	E		T	R	Y
	S	O	D		E	A	R	S						
H	E	A	T	H	E	R	L	O	C	K	L	E	A	R
A	G	R	E	E		E	A	C	H		U	R	S	A
H	A	L	E	R		A	R	O	O		M	I	E	N
A	D	O	R	E		P	A	N	S		P	E	A	K

28

E	X	P	A	T		J	O	V	E		P	T	A	S
M	E	E	S	E		A	H	E	M		L	A	M	E
I	N	A	W	E		L	A	R	A		E	X	E	C
L	A	K	E	S	H	O	R	E	C	A	B	I	N	
		S	H	A	P	E		I	R	E				
C	A	M	P	I	L	Y		B	A	T		B	M	T
I	C	I	E	R		E	A	T		F	A	I	R	
V	A	C	A	T	I	O	N	G	E	T	A	W	A	Y
I	S	A	K		M	T	V		H	I	L	T	S	
L	E	S		G	A	B		J	E	E	R	S	A	T
		D	U	G		F	O	R	A	Y				
S	E	A	S	I	D	E	C	O	T	T	A	G	E	
P	A	W	N		N	E	R	O		R	A	D	O	N
B	R	A	T		E	V	A	S		I	L	I	A	D
S	A	N	E		S	O	L	E		C	E	N	T	S

29

C	H	O	P		L	E	N	S		S	I	F	T	S
A	O	N	E		A	L	O	U		I	D	I	O	T
P	A	I	R		N	E	A	L		L	A	R	G	E
G	R	O	U	N	D	C	H	U	C	K		E	S	T
U	S	N		E	M	T		A	H	A	B			
N	E	S	T	E	A		I	N	A	R	U	S	H	
		S	T	R	A	P	S		T	I	G	E	R	
D	A	M	E		K	N	E	A	D		S	S	T	S
R	O	O	T	S		D	A	N	U	B	E			
S	L	O	S	H	E	S		C	E	S	S	N	A	
	N	E	A	R		A	K	A		A	I	R		
B	A	R		T	R	U	S	T	B	U	S	T	E	R
A	L	O	F	T		S	A	R	I		N	I	C	E
E	M	C	E	E		E	V	I	L		O	R	E	S
R	A	K	E	R		D	E	A	L		W	E	S	T

30

N	A	A	C	P		E	M	M	A		D	O	O	R
O	C	C	U	R		M	O	A	T		A	N	N	E
T	H	R	E	E	R	I	N	G	C	I	R	C	U	S
E	Y	E		P	O	G	O		H	O	N	E	S	T
		F	A	I	R		F	I	N					
J	E	R	R	Y	L	E	W	I	S		L	A	M	A
A	L	I	A	S		I	D	O		A	V	I	D	
N	O	D	S		F	E	L	O	N		B	E	A	M
E	P	E	E		A	D	M		N	O	R	M	A	
T	E	R	R		D	E	A	N	M	A	R	T	I	N
	P	E	N		E	A	T	S						
A	N	G	O	R	A		M	E	N	U		J	A	I
H	O	L	L	Y	W	O	O	D	O	R	B	U	S	T
O	P	E	D		A	L	O	E		A	O	R	T	A
Y	E	N	S		Y	A	R	D		L	O	Y	A	L

31

R	A	P	T		I	L	I	A	D		D	A	D	A
I	S	L	A		N	A	C	R	E		U	S	E	D
C	L	A	N		O	N	E	O	F	A	K	I	N	D
H	A	N	G	I	N	G	L	O	O	S	E			
I	N	T	O	W		M	R	T		I	D	S		
E	T	A		O	C	T	O		M	I	L	T	I	E
	T	E	N	D	E	R	S		A	S	A	N		
	F	I	T	T	I	N	G	E	N	D	I	N	G	
A	L	O	T		S	A	L	E	R	N	O			
M	O	N	E	T	S		N	A	D	A		B	I	O
Y	E	S		R	E	S			F	L	I	T	S	
	S	I	T	T	I	N	G	T	I	G	H	T		
B	A	B	Y	B	O	O	M	E	R		E	G	A	L
O	M	E	N		F	L	A	R	E		N	I	C	E
Z	I	N	C		F	E	N	D	S		S	E	A	R

32

B	I	B	B		P	I	A	F		O	F	O	L	D
O	N	E	A		U	G	L	I		R	E	N	E	E
M	E	L	O	N	B	A	L	L		Z	E	S	T	A
B	R	I	B	E	S		T	I	T	O		L	I	D
	T	E	A	M		S	O	A	K		E	A	T	S
	B	O	U	I	L	L	O	N	C	U	B	E		
A	D	D	S		M	A	D		R	O	G	E	T	
C	R	O		S	A	M		P	T	A		H	M	O
T	Y	P	O	S		A	A	A		S	T	E	N	
I	C	E	C	R	E	A	M	C	O	N	E			
V	E	N	T		S	C	A	T		E	E	L	S	
I	R	A		G	E	T	Z		R	E	S	O	L	E
S	E	N	S	E		S	O	L	I	D	F	O	O	D
T	A	C	I	T		U	N	T	O		I	S	P	Y
S	L	E	D	S		P	S	S	T		T	E	E	S

33

S	M	A	C	K		S	H	E	D		S	H	O	P
P	U	R	E	E		P	E	T	E		M	O	M	A
A	S	T	O	R		A	L	U	M		O	P	E	N
T	H	E	S	C	O	R	P	I	O	N	K	I	N	G
		H	E	E		T	O	Y						
O	R	C	H	I	D		C	A	I	N		J	F	K
R	E	L	E	E		H	A	L	O		T	E	L	E
T	H	E	A	F	R	I	C	A	N	Q	U	E	E	N
H	A	F	T		E	L	H	I		U	N	P	E	N
O	B	S		D	A	L	E		Y	E	A	S	T	Y
	S	E	C		H	I	E							
T	H	E	L	I	T	T	L	E	P	R	I	N	C	E
H	U	L	A		I	R	A	S		E	V	I	A	N
I	S	I	S		N	E	W	S		S	O	C	K	O
S	H	A	H		G	E	N	E		T	R	E	Y	S

34

E	M	A	I	L		R	O	C	C	O		T	A	B
A	O	R	T	A		I	N	L	A	W		E	L	I
C	R	E	A	M	E	D	C	O	R	N		N	I	L
H	E	A	L		T	E	E	T	H		S	D	A	K
	I	O	C		H	O	S	T	E	S	S			
C	R	A	C	K	E	D	P	E	P	P	E	R		
A	Y	N		S	T	A	R		F	I	F	T	H	
R	E	D	O		C	R	O	W	D		N	O	R	A
P	S	Y	C	H		B	E	E	R		O	U	I	
	W	H	I	P	P	E	D	B	U	T	T	E	R	
S	H	A	R	P	E	I		A	G	O				
E	I	R	E		A	L	I	S	T		O	H	M	E
M	P	H		C	H	I	P	P	E	D	B	E	E	F
I	P	O		S	E	N	S	E		C	A	R	A	T
S	O	L		I	N	G	O	D		I	D	O	L	S

35

T	H	A	W		S	L	E	W		A	B	O	M	B
A	U	R	A		T	U	N	A		R	E	L	E	E
U	S	E	R		A	C	I	D		G	L	I	N	T
T	H	A	T	S	R	I	D	I	C	U	L	O	U	S
			S	E	C	T			R	E	Y			
S	A	G		T	H	E	R	M	O	S		A	C	T
T	R	E	A	T		H	O	W		S	L	O	W	
A	R	E	Y	O	U	K	I	D	D	I	N	G	M	E
R	O	S	E		T	I	N		F	L	A	M	E	
E	W	E		D	I	N	E	T	T	E		E	A	T
			S	A	C			A	R	E	S			
D	O	N	T	M	A	K	E	M	E	L	A	U	G	H
A	L	O	O	P		E	V	A	N		T	R	E	E
S	E	R	V	E		M	E	L	D		I	G	O	R
H	O	M	E	R		P	R	E	Y		N	E	M	O

36

S	I	L	L		D	E	C	I		H	A	N	D	Y
A	R	I	A		E	L	A	N		E	I	E	I	O
F	E	A	R	L	E	S	S	F	O	S	D	I	C	K
E	N	N	E	A	D		H	R	H		A	L	E	E
R	E	A	D	S		C	L	A	I	M				
			O	H	A	R	E		O	A	T	E	R	S
S	E	W		V	I	S	A		I	N	D	I	A	
P	A	I	N	L	E	S	S	D	E	N	T	I	S	T
A	T	S	E	A		P	S	A	T		T	E	E	
T	S	E	T	S	E		O	R	D	E	R			
			S	P	A	C	E		R	A	S	T	A	
A	C	T	S		E	L	I		I	N	S	T	E	P
S	L	E	E	V	E	L	E	S	S	S	H	I	R	T
T	O	R	M	E		E	T	A	L		E	L	S	E
A	D	M	I	T		N	Y	S	E		S	E	E	R

37

T	I	E	S		S	I	Z	E		L	I	M	E	
A	R	C	O		K	N	O	T		I	N	O	N	
C	O	U	L	D	A	F	O	O	L	E	D	M	E	
O	N	A	D	A	T	E		N	A	D	I	A		
			B	E	A	R		P	T	S				
A	B	C	S		B	R	I	O		O	G	R	E	
T	O	O	T	O	O		S	N	O		U	A	W	
W	O	U	L	D	A	B	E	E	N	N	I	C	E	
A	N	N		S	R	O		M	O	U	S	E	R	
R	E	T	D		D	O	R	A		B	E	D	S	
		M	E	T		B	O	N	D					
	S	E	P	I	A		T	R	I	P	O	L	I	
S	H	O	U	L	D	A	G	U	E	S	S	E	D	
R	O	U	T		M	A	U	L		S	L	O	E	
I	T	T	Y		S	A	T	E		T	O	N	S	

38

H	E	L	D		A	L	E	G		F	U	R	S	
O	B	O	E		I	C	I	E	R		A	T	O	P
E	R	I	C		M	O	R	K	&	M	I	N	D	Y
D	O	S	E		S	R	A		P	U	R	E	E	S
		&	I	R	O	N		L	A	S				
V	I	C	T	O	R		M	I	S	T	A	K	E	N
A	L	L		O	R	S	O	N		S	L	A	V	E
L	O	A	D		Y	E	M	E	N		S	T	O	W
E	N	R	O	N		R	U	R	A	L		E	K	E
T	A	K	E	O	F	F	S		I	S	L	&	E	R
		R	L	S		N	A	D	I	A				
S	T	I	G	M	A		B	I	D		S	L	A	G
W	I	L	L	&	G	R	A	C	E		P	L	U	M
A	R	I	A		O	K	I	E	S		E	I	R	E
N	E	E	D		N	O	O	R		D	E	A	N	

39

A	R	E	N	A		S	L	E	D		M	E	M	O
T	A	P	I	R		C	A	N	I		A	D	A	M
O	N	I	C	E		A	S	T	A		L	I	M	A
P	I	C	K	O	F	T	H	E	L	I	T	T	E	R
			S	L	O			R	U	N				
L	A	O		A	R	T	S		P	L	A	S	M	A
E	L	M	S		G	A	I	T		A	G	A	I	N
F	L	I	C	K	O	F	T	H	E	W	R	I	S	T
T	I	T	A	N		T	E	A	L		A	L	T	O
Y	E	S	M	A	N		S	T	A	G		S	Y	N
			C	O	O			T	O	P				
T	H	I	C	K	O	F	T	H	E	F	I	G	H	T
A	I	D	A		S	T	O	A		I	N	N	E	R
O	V	E	R		E	E	G	S		S	T	A	R	E
S	E	A	T		S	N	A	P		H	A	T	E	S

40

S	T	I	R		T	O	M	B		S	O	N	J	A
C	A	R	E		O	V	A	L		A	D	I	O	S
O	P	A	L		A	I	D	E		N	A	P	E	S
F	I	N	E	A	N	D	D	A	N	D	Y			
F	R	I	E	N	D		R	O	I		S	R	A	
			A	F	R	O		H	E	P	T	A	D	
S	L	A	B		R	O	U	T		G	R	A	D	E
T	O	L	L	H	O	U	S	E	C	O	O	K	I	E
E	I	E	I	O		E	T	T	U		W	E	I	R
E	R	U	P	T	S		S	E	L	F				
P	E	T		W	E	B		D	O	T	T	I	E	
		F	A	R	E	T	H	E	E	W	E	L	L	
R	A	B	A	T		E	R	O	S		E	M	I	R
A	M	A	Z	E		N	A	P	A		E	P	E	E
N	A	D	E	R		E	P	I	C		T	I	D	Y

41

A	B	E	T		P	E	G	S		Z	E	L	I	G
P	E	D	I		E	D	I	T		E	V	I	T	A
S	L	I	D	E	R	U	L	E		P	I	L	O	T
E	L	F	I	N		C	A	T	C	H	L	I	N	E
S	A	Y	E	R	S		S	O	Y					
			D	I	T	C	H		T	R	E	B	L	E
E	T	A		C	U	R	I	O		F	L	A	W	
N	A	T	I	O	N	A	L	P	A	S	T	I	M	E
O	L	I	O		B	L	A	C	K		P	A	R	
S	E	T	U	P	S		S	L	E	E	P			
			E	U	R			S	T	R	E	A	M	
H	I	T	P	A	R	A	D	E		C	O	R	G	I
E	N	I	A	C		P	I	T	C	H	F	O	R	K
F	R	E	S	H		I	N	T	O		I	D	E	E
T	E	S	T	Y		D	E	A	N		T	E	E	S

42

A	C	H	I	P		P	O	S	H		A	F	A	R
T	E	E	T	H		R	I	P	E		C	A	R	O
E	R	A	T	O		I	L	I	A		E	L	M	O
A	E	R	O	B	I	C	S	C	L	A	S	S		
M	S	T		I	T	E		A	T	M		E	G	G
			P	A	I	L	S		H	O	W	N	O	W
D	A	D	A		S	I	T	E		N	E	A	L	E
E	X	E	R	C	I	S	E	R	E	G	I	M	E	N
L	O	A	T	H			T	E	R	N		R	E	M	S
O	N	L	Y	I	F		D	O	N	T	S			
S	S	T		L	I	C		R	U	E		B	O	A
			W	E	I	G	H	T	L	I	F	T	I	N	G
W	H	I	T		U	L	E	E		L	A	C	T	O
S	O	T	O		R	O	N	S		O	D	E	O	N
J	O	H	N		E	E	K	S		N	A	P	P	Y

43

S	T	U	C	C	O		C	O	L	D		S	P	A
C	A	L	L	O	N		L	U	A	U		T	A	X
U	P	T	O	S	C	R	A	T	C	H		E	L	I
F	I	R	S		E	A	R	L	Y		H	A	M	S
F	R	A	U	D		S	E	E		C	A	D		
			R	I	G	H	T	T	O	L	I	F	E	R
F	O	R	E	G	O	E	S		D	E	R	A	T	E
A	R	I		I	T	S		P	E	R		S	R	A
I	N	F	A	N	T		C	L	O	I	S	T	E	R
L	E	F	T	T	O	C	H	A	N	C	E			
			R	O	O		R	A	Y		S	A	B	L	E
S	P	A	M		P	E	N	A	L		L	A	I	T
E	L	F		D	O	W	N	T	O	E	A	R	T	H
R	E	F		A	L	E	E		O	R	N	E	R	Y
B	A	S		Y	E	L	L		P	E	T	R	E	L

44

S	H	E	S		R	A	S	P		B	L	A	Z	E
C	A	P	T		I	R	A	E		E	A	G	E	R
A	L	S	O		N	I	N	E		E	X	E	R	T
B	L	O	W	A	G	A	S	K	E	T		D	O	E
S	E	M	E	L	E			S	A	L	S			
			O	R	E	M		R	E	C	E	S	S	
A	S	T	R	O		T	A	R	T		O	D	I	E
F	L	Y	O	F	F	T	H	E	H	A	N	D	L	E
R	A	P	T		R	A	R	E		B	E	A	L	S
O	T	O	O	L	E		E	L	S	A				
			R	E	D	O			I	C	E	A	G	E
P	T	A		G	O	B	A	L	L	I	S	T	I	C
O	I	L	E	R		E	R	I	K		T	A	L	L
S	T	A	R	E		S	O	M	E		E	L	L	A
T	O	R	R	E		E	D	E	N		R	E	S	T

45

A	H	A	B		P	H	A	T		R	A	P	I	D
G	Y	R	O		L	E	C	H		E	L	E	N	A
A	D	I	A		A	M	M	O		L	E	A	F	Y
P	R	E	T	T	Y	P	E	N	N	Y		C	O	S
E	A	S	E	U	P		G	O	O	S	E			
			D	R	E	A	D		S	N	A	P	P	Y
A	R	P		I	N	V	A	D	E		M	I	L	O
L	E	A	R	N		O	N	E		R	E	P	A	Y
I	D	L	E		O	N	T	A	P	E		E	N	O
T	O	M	A	T	O		E	D	U	C	E			
			P	L	A	Z	A		L	A	N	C	E	S
L	E	I		P	E	N	C	I	L	P	O	I	N	T
O	X	L	I	P		G	A	S	P		U	L	E	E
S	P	O	K	E		U	G	L	I		G	I	M	P
T	O	T	E	D		S	E	E	N		H	A	Y	S

46

A	P	A	C	E		F	I	R	S	T		B	U	G
R	A	D	A	R		A	L	O	H	A		U	R	I
P	R	O	D	I	G	A	L	S	O	N		M	B	A
			R	C	A		U	S	E		S	P	A	N
R	E	P	E	A	L		M	I	S	S	P	E	N	T
O	P	U	S		I	V	E			A	R	R	A	S
S	I	S		A	L	E		E	T	H	I	C		
S	C	H	E	M	E	R		T	R	I	G	R	A	M
			K	A	B	O	B		T	A	B		O	L	E
A	R	I	S	E		H	U	M		A	P	E	S	
G	E	N	E	R	A	T	E		C	U	R	S	E	S
A	S	P	S		G	A	R		A	N	I			
V	O	L		J	A	B	B	E	R	W	O	C	K	Y
E	R	A		A	T	L	A	S		O	S	H	E	A
S	T	Y		R	E	E	L	S		N	E	I	G	H

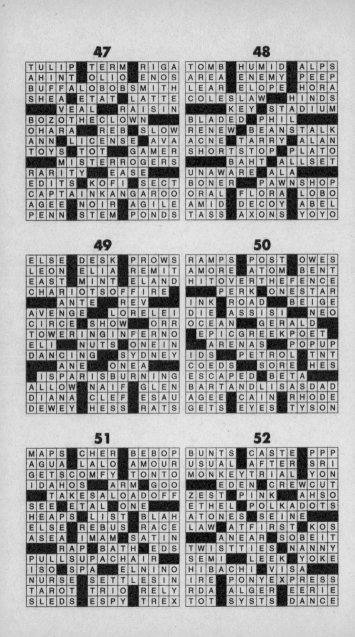

47

```
T U L I P   T E R M   R I G A
A H I N T   O L I O   E N O S
B U F F A L O B O B S M I T H
S H E A   V E A L   L A T T E
B O Z O T H E C L O W N   R A I S I N
O H A R A   R E B   S L O W
A N N   L I C E N S E   A V A
T O Y S   T O T   G A M E R
  M I S T E R R O G E R S
R A R I T Y   E A S E
E D I T S   K O F I   S E C T
C A P T A I N K A N G A R O O
A G E E   N O I R   A G I L E
P E N N   S T E M   P O N D S
```

48

```
T O M B   H U M I D   A L P S
A R E A   E N E M Y   P E E P
L E A R   E L O P E   H O R A
C O L E S L A W   H I N D S
    K E Y   S T A D I U M
B L A D E D   P H I L
R E N E W   B E A N S T A L K
A C N E   T A R R Y   A L A N
S H O R T S T O P   P L A T O
    B A H T   A L L S E T
U N A W A R E   A L A
B O N E R   P A W N S H O P
O R A L   F L O R A   L O B O
A M I D   D E C O Y   A B E L
T A S S   A X O N S   Y O Y O
```

49

```
E L S E   D E S K   P R O W S
L E O N   E L I A   R E M I T
E A S T   M I N T   E L A N D
C H A R I O T S O F F I R E
    A N T E   R E V
A V E N G E   L O R E L E I
C I R C E   S H O W   O R R
T O W E R I N G I N F E R N O
E L I   N U T S   O N E I N
D A N C I N G   S Y D N E Y
    A N E   O N E A
I S P A R I S B U R N I N G
A L L O W   N A I F   G L E N
D I A N A   C L E F   E S A U
D E W E Y   H E S S   R A T S
```

50

```
R A M P S   P O S T   O W E S
A M O R E   A T O M   B E N T
H I T O V E R T H E F E N C E
    P E R K   O N E S T A R
I N K   R O A D   B E I G E
D I E   A S S I S I   N E O
O C E A N   G E R A L D
E P I C G R E E K P O E T
A R E N A S   P O P U P
I D S   P E T R O L   T N T
C O E D S   S O R E   H E S
E S C A P E D   B E T A
B A R T A N D L I S A S D A D
A G E E   C A I N   R H O D E
G E T S   E Y E S   T Y S O N
```

51

```
M A P S   C H E R   B E B O P
A G U A   L A L O   A M O U R
G E T S C O M F Y   T O N T O
I D A H O S   A R M   G O O
    T A K E S A L O A D O F F
S E E   E T A L   O N E
H E A P S   L I S T   B L A H
E L S E   R E B U S   R A C E
A S E A   I M A M   S A T I N
    R A P   B A T H   E D S
P U L L S U P A C H A I R
I S O   S P A   E L N I N O
N U R S E   S E T T L E S I N
T A R O T   T R I O   R E L Y
S L E D S   E S P Y   T R E X
```

52

```
B U N T S   C A S T E   P P P
U S U A L   A F T E R   S R I
M O N K E Y T R I A L   Y O N
    E D E N   C R E W C U T
Z E S T   P I N K   A H S O
E T H E L   P O L K A D O T S
A T O N E S   S E I N E
L A W   A T F I R S T   K O S
  A N E A R   S O B E I T
T W I S T T I E S   N A N N Y
S E M I   L E E K   Y O K E
H I B A C H I   V I S A
I R E   P O N Y E X P R E S S
R D A   A L G E R   E E R I E
T O T   S Y S T S   D A N C E
```

53

S	T	A	B		N	A	S	A		K	A	P	P	A
A	I	D	A		A	L	L	S		A	C	O	R	N
G	L	O	W		V	E	A	L		T	I	L	E	D
A	L	L	D	A	Y	E	V	E	R	Y	D	A	Y	
		E	Y	E			S	E	E	D	S			
A	S	S		C	S	A		P	S	I		N	E	E	
S	E	C	S		A	R	M		E	D	M	O	N	D	
T	W	E	N	T	Y	F	O	U	R	S	E	V	E	N
R	U	N	L	O	W		E	N	V		L	A	M	A
O	P	T		P	H	I		E	E	R		S	Y	S
		S	T	E	N	O			E	S	C			
	A	R	O	U	N	D	T	H	E	C	L	O	C	K
G	R	O	A	N		I	T	E	S		A	T	O	N
A	L	I	V	E		R	E	A	P		N	I	C	E
S	O	L	E	S		A	R	T	Y		T	A	K	E

54

N	O	T		P	E	R	E	C		B	A	S	I	S
E	P	A		S	T	E	V	E		A	L	I	C	E
S	T	L		A	C	T	A	S		R	O	G	E	R
T	I	M	O	T	H	Y	D	A	L	T	O	N		
L	O	U	S			P	E	R	E		F	A	V	A
E	N	D	O	R	S	E		E	A	U		W	E	T
			L	E	E		O	A	R	S		A	X	E
		S	E	A	N	C	O	N	N	E	R	Y		
O	W	L		D	A	Y	7		E	R	E			
B	O	O		S	T	N		D	R	S	P	O	C	K
I	O	W	A		O	I	S	E		O	F	L	A	
	P	I	E	R	C	E	B	R	O	S	N	A	N	
M	O	O	R	E		I	T	R	I	P		O	R	S
U	R	K	E	L		S	T	I	L	T		T	E	A
S	E	E	R	S		M	O	S	E	S		E	T	S

55

A	L	B	A		I	N	D	I	A		A	J	A	R
N	A	R	C		L	I	E	N	S		R	A	G	E
K	N	I	C	K	K	N	A	C	K		S	C	U	D
H	A	N	O	I		E	D	I	E		E	K	E	S
S	I	E	S	T	A			S	W	A	N	K		
			T	H	R	I	C	E		M	I	N	E	S
L	A	B	S		G	O	O		D	O	C	I	L	E
O	U	R		D	O	U	B	L	E	K		F	A	T
O	R	I	G	I	N		R	E	B		M	E	L	S
P	A	C	E	R		S	A	N	I	T	Y			
		K	N	E	L	T			T	I	T	L	E	S
P	O	K	E		O	R	C	A		D	R	A	M	A
O	B	I	T		B	O	O	K	K	E	E	P	E	R
D	E	L	I		O	L	D	I	E		A	S	E	A
S	Y	N	C		S	L	A	N	G		T	E	R	N

56

S	T	E	T		F	L	A	K	E		P	E	T	A
P	A	R	R		L	E	T	I	N		E	L	O	N
U	C	L	A		A	C	T	E	D		R	A	F	T
D	O	E	S	N	T	H	A	V	E	A	C	L	U	E
			H	O	L	E			A	S	H			
C	H	A	T	T	Y		J	A	V	A		O	N	O
L	I	M	A	S		L	I	L	O		S	P	U	R
A	T	A	L	O	S	S	F	O	R	W	O	R	D	S
M	U	S	K		C	A	F	E		O	F	A	G	E
P	P	S		P	I	T	Y		M	O	T	H	E	R
			S	I	R			P	E	E	P			
B	A	C	K	T	O	S	Q	U	A	R	E	O	N	E
A	C	H	E		C	H	U	R	N		D	R	E	D
S	L	A	W		C	E	A	S	E		A	S	T	I
S	U	D	S		O	D	D	E	R		L	O	S	E

57

S	C	A	R		A	C	A	D		B	A	B	A	R
H	O	M	E		T	R	I	O		E	E	R	I	E
A	L	A	S		T	A	R	T		A	T	O	M	S
P	O	S	I	T	I	V	E	S	I	G	N			
E	N	S	N	A	R	E	D		C	L	A	S	P	S
			K	E	N		T	I	E		P	A	P	
E	R	A	S	E		D	E	E		D	E	B	I	
D	E	F	I	N	I	T	E	A	R	T	I	C	L	E
E	P	I	C		N	O	N		R	E	S	O	D	
N	O	R		A	C	E		L	E	A				
S	T	E	L	L	A		C	A	S	C	A	D	E	D
	A	B	S	O	L	U	T	E	Z	E	R	O		
A	R	O	M	A		R	A	R	A		T	E	R	N
L	O	R	E	N		B	R	E	T		E	R	O	O
S	T	O	R	Y		S	A	N	E		C	E	L	T

58

G	O	P		W	H	A	C	K		E	D	G	E	S
A	H	A		H	A	D	O	N		U	R	I	A	H
N	I	L		O	C	U	L	I		R	O	G	U	E
D	O	A	T	A	K	E	O	F	F	O	N			
H	A	T	E			R	E	O	P	E	N	E	D	
I	N	E	R	T	I	A			R	E	S	A	L	E
			R	U	S	S	I	A			R	L	S	
	F	L	I	G	H	T	O	F	F	A	N	C	Y	
I	I	I			I	N	T	O	T	O				
P	L	E	A	D	S			S	E	A	T	T	L	E
O	L	D	N	O	R	S	E			E	R	I	N	
		K	N	O	T	S	L	A	N	D	I	N	G	
K	O	A	L	A		A	T	O	N	E		A	T	E
I	N	L	E	T		G	E	T	T	O		G	E	L
N	O	L	T	E		E	S	S	E	N		E	L	S

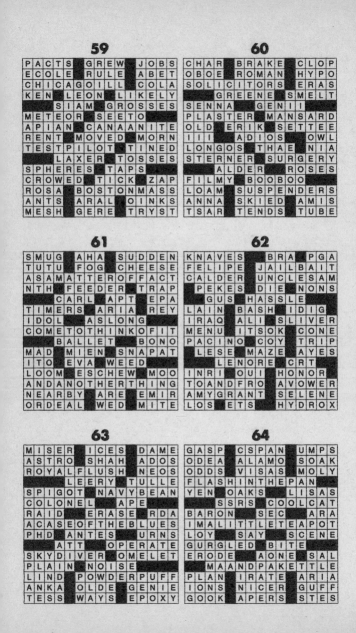

59

P	A	C	T	S		G	R	E	W		J	O	B	S
E	C	O	L	E		R	U	L	E		A	B	E	T
C	H	I	C	A	G	O	I	L	L		C	O	L	A
K	E	N		L	E	O	N		L	I	K	E	L	Y
			S	I	A	M		G	R	O	S	S	E	S
M	E	T	E	O	R		S	E	E	T	O			
A	P	I	A	N		C	A	N	A	A	N	I	T	E
R	E	N	T		M	O	V	E	D		M	O	R	N
T	E	S	T	P	I	L	O	T		T	I	N	E	D
			L	A	X	E	R		T	O	S	S	E	S
S	P	H	E	R	E	S		T	A	P	S			
C	R	O	W	E	D		T	I	C	K		Z	A	P
R	O	S	A		B	O	S	T	O	N	M	A	S	S
A	N	T	S		A	R	A	L		O	I	N	K	S
M	E	S	H		G	E	R	E		T	R	Y	S	T

60

C	H	A	R		B	R	A	K	E		C	L	O	P
O	B	O	E		R	O	M	A	N		H	Y	P	O
S	O	L	I	C	I	T	O	R	S		E	R	A	S
			G	R	E	E	N	E		S	M	E	L	T
S	E	N	N	A			G	E	N	I	I			
P	L	A	S	T	E	R		M	A	N	S	A	R	D
O	L	D		E	R	I	K		S	E	T	T	E	E
I	I	I		A	D	I	O	S				O	W	L
L	O	N	G	O	S		T	H	A	E		N	I	A
S	T	E	R	N	E	R		S	U	R	G	E	R	Y
			A	L	D	E	R		R	O	S	E	S	
F	I	L	M	Y		B	O	O	B	O	O			
L	O	A	M		S	U	S	P	E	N	D	E	R	S
A	N	N	A		S	K	I	E	D		A	M	I	S
T	S	A	R		T	E	N	D	S		T	U	B	E

61

S	M	U	G		A	H	A		S	U	D	D	E	N
T	U	T	U		F	O	G		C	H	E	E	S	E
A	S	A	M	A	T	T	E	R	O	F	F	A	C	T
N	T	H		F	E	E	D	E	R		T	R	A	P
			C	A	R	L		A	P	T		E	P	A
T	I	M	E	R	S		A	R	I	A		R	E	Y
I	D	O	L			A	S	L	O	N	G			
C	O	M	E	T	O	T	H	I	N	K	O	F	I	T
			B	A	L	L	E	T		B	O	N	O	
M	A	D		M	I	E	N		S	N	A	P	A	T
I	T	O		E	V	A		W	E	E	D			
L	O	O	M		E	S	C	H	E	W		M	O	O
A	N	D	A	N	O	T	H	E	R	T	H	I	N	G
N	E	A	R	B	Y		A	R	E		E	M	I	R
O	R	D	E	A	L		W	E	D		M	I	T	E

62

K	N	A	V	E	S		B	R	A		P	G	A	
F	E	L	I	P	E		J	A	I	L	B	A	I	T
C	A	L	D	E	R		U	N	C	L	E	S	A	M
P	E	K	E	S		D	I	E		N	O	N	S	
			G	U	S		H	A	S	S	L	E		
L	A	I	N		B	A	S	H		I	D	I	G	
I	R	A	Q		A	L	I		S	L	I	V	E	R
M	E	N	U		I	T	S	O	K			C	O	N	E
P	A	C	I	N	O		C	O	Y		T	R	I	P
L	E	S	E		M	A	Z	E		A	Y	E	S	
			L	E	N	O	R	E		C	R	T		
I	N	R	I		O	U	I		H	O	N	O	R	
T	O	A	N	D	F	R	O		A	V	O	W	E	R
A	M	Y	G	R	A	N	T		S	E	L	E	N	E
L	O	S		E	T	S		H	Y	D	R	O	X	

63

M	I	S	E	R		I	C	E	S		D	A	M	E
A	S	T	R	O		S	H	A	H		A	D	O	S
R	O	Y	A	L	F	L	U	S	H		N	E	O	S
			L	E	E	R	Y		T	U	L	L	E	
S	P	I	G	O	T		N	A	V	Y	B	E	A	N
C	O	L	O	N	E	L		A	P	E				
R	A	I	D		E	R	A	S	E		R	D	A	
A	C	A	S	E	O	F	T	H	E	B	L	U	E	S
P	H	D		A	N	T	E	S		U	R	N	S	
			A	T	T		O	P	E	R	A	T	E	
S	K	Y	D	I	V	E	R		O	M	E	L	E	T
P	L	A	I	N		N	O	I	S	E				
L	I	N	D		P	O	W	D	E	R	P	U	F	F
A	N	K	A		O	L	D	E		G	E	N	I	E
T	E	S	S		W	A	Y	S		E	P	O	X	Y

64

G	A	S	P		C	S	P	A	N		U	M	P	S
O	D	E	A		A	L	A	M	O		S	O	A	K
O	D	D	S		V	I	S	A	S		M	O	L	Y
F	L	A	S	H	I	N	T	H	E	P	A	N		
Y	E	N		O	A	K	S		L	I	S	A	S	
			S	S	R	S		C	O	O	L	C	A	T
B	A	R	O	N		S	E	C		A	R	A		
I	M	A	L	I	T	T	L	E	T	E	A	P	O	T
L	O	Y		S	A	Y		S	C	E	N	E		
G	U	R	G	L	E	D		B	I	T	E			
E	R	O	D	E		A	O	N	E		S	A	L	
			M	A	A	N	D	P	A	K	E	T	T	L	E
P	L	A	N		I	R	A	T	E		A	R	I	A
I	O	N	S		N	I	C	E	R		G	U	F	F
G	O	O	K		A	P	E	R	S		S	T	E	S

65

A	S	S	T		C	S	A			B	I	G	S	K	Y
L	A	I	R		O	W	N		A	N	Y	O	N	E	
I	N	G	A		W	A	G	O	N	T	R	A	I	N	
V	A	N	C	L	I	B	U	R	N		O	P	T	S	
E	A	S	T	O	N		S	E	E	M					
			I	N	A			G	R	A	N	A	R	Y	
S	W	E	A	T	E	R	S			J	O	S	I	E	
C	O	N	V	E	R	T	I	B	L	E	S	O	F	A	
A	V	O	I	R		P	R	E	S	E	N	T	S		
T	E	S	S	E	R	A		O	A	T					
			R	A	B	E		N	I	C	O	L	E		
S	P	A	S		S	E	D	A	N	C	H	A	I	R	
P	I	C	K	U	P	L	I	N	E		A	S	E	A	
I	N	C	I	S	E		C	D	S		F	I	N	S	
N	E	T	T	E	D		T	I	S			E	S	S	E

66

T	I	C	S		V	I	T	A		A	B	A	F	T
E	D	A	M		A	M	E	N		S	A	V	O	Y
R	E	P	E	L	L	E	N	T		S	T	A	R	S
I	M	P	E	I		A	P	I	E		T	I	T	O
			I	A	N	M	C	K	E	L	L	E	N	
H	O	T	A	I	R			H	E	R	E			
A	H	A	T		A	C	T	I		I	S	L	E	T
N	I	C	H	E	L	L	E	N	I	C	H	O	L	S
G	O	T	O	N		O	M	A	N			I	D	E	A
			M	O	O	S			A	P	P	E	A	R
V	O	W	E	L	L	E	N	G	T	H				
C	H	A	W		E	N	Y	A		O	R	T	H	O
H	A	S	I	D		E	L	L	E	N	S	H	O	W
I	R	A	T	E		S	O	B	S		T	O	O	L
P	A	T	H	S		S	N	A	P		U	S	P	S

67

G	O	T	T	A		P	R	O	W		S	Y	M	S
A	V	O	I	D		A	I	D	E		M	E	A	T
L	E	O	N	A	R	D	O	D	A	V	I	N	C	I
E	R	L		M	E	D		S	K	E	L	T	O	N
	C	S	A		E	L	I		L	E	A	N	T	
J	O	H	N	F	K	E	N	N	E	D	Y			
A	M	E	N	D			K	E	A		S	E	R	A
N	E	D		A	I	R	P	O	R	T		T	E	T
E	S	S	A		B	O	O		A	R	E	S	O	
			B	E	N	I	T	O	J	U	A	R	E	Z
L	O	T	S	A		S	T	P			T	N	T	
O	S	B	O	R	N	E		T	E	D		A	T	M
C	H	A	R	L	E	S	D	E	G	A	U	L	L	E
H	E	R	B		T	S	A	R		U	N	L	E	T
S	A	S	S		S	O	N	S		B	O	Y	D	S

68

M	A	M	B	A		Z	I	N	C		A	C	H	E
A	L	E	R	T		I	N	C	A		R	H	E	A
S	P	L	I	T	A	P	A	R	T		E	A	R	S
			S	H	E	S			N	E	A	R	B	Y
H	A	C	K	E	R		G	A	I	L		G	S	A
O	I	L		T	O	T	E	M	P	O	L	E		
A	M	I	G	O		O	T	I	S		E	A	R	P
R	E	M	A	P		W	A	D		M	A	H	A	L
D	E	B	S		M	A	W	S		A	R	E	N	A
			A	P	P	A	R	A	T	U	S			
A	P	B		A	N	D	Y		S	T	A	D	I	A
G	R	O	T	T	O			O	D	E	S			
R	O	A	R		W	A	L	K	A	R	O	U	N	D
E	U	R	O		A	M	O	R			E	N	T	E	R
E	D	D	Y		R	I	T	A		D	E	E	D	S

69

L	A	B	O	R		G	L	E	E		I	R	A	Q
A	L	E	V	E		R	U	B	Y		G	U	R	U
I	D	E	A	L		O	B	O	E		L	I	M	O
R	A	P	T	A	T	T	E	N	T	I	O	N		
			E	X	I	T			O	N	O			
M	E	T		N	O	G	O	O	D		B	B	C	
A	R	E	A	S			A	F	T	E	R	Y	O	U
R	A	P	P	E	D	O	N	T	H	E	D	O	O	R
S	T	I	R	R	I	N	G			D	A	N	T	E
H	O	D		E	R	A	S	E	R			E	S	S
			A	N	T			N	E	T	S			
		W	R	A	P	P	E	D	A	R	O	U	N	D
J	A	I	L		O	O	Z	E		A	R	R	A	Y
A	I	D	E		O	K	R	A		C	R	A	T	E
W	R	E	N		R	E	A	R		T	Y	L	E	R

70

U	P	P	E	R		L	A	P	S		B	I	D	E
S	A	L	V	O		O	M	I	T		O	D	O	R
U	S	E	A	B	E	E	P	E	R		O	O	Z	E
A	H	A		B	A	B	A		A	N	K	L	E	S
L	A	S	S	E	S			S	T	I	E	S		
			I	R	E	S		U	N	H	E	A	R	D
C	M	O	N		U	L	A	N			I	G	L	O	O
Z	I	N	G			P	A	G	E	S		M	E	M	O
A	S	K	E	R		T	O	R	T		E	X	A	M
R	E	P	R	I	S	E		S	O	W	N			
			P	I	E	R	S		P	A	T	A	K	I
P	H	R	A	S	E		A	V	I	V		M	U	D
R	O	O	T		S	E	N	A	T	E	A	I	D	E
A	B	E	T		A	P	E	S			A	U	T	O	S
Y	O	G	I		W	A	R	T		T	R	Y	S	T

71

A	B	A	T	E		S	L	U	R		T	A	G	S
R	A	D	A	R		T	O	F	U		A	B	E	L
E	L	E	N	A		A	N	O	N		R	E	N	O
S	I	N	G	S	O	N	G		S	E	P	T	E	T
			L	E	A	D		L	I	R	A			
R	O	P	E	R	S		P	I	N	G	P	O	N	G
I	C	Y		S	E	A	R	S		S	E	N	O	R
L	U	L	U		S	C	O	L	D		R	E	B	A
E	L	O	P	E		I	N	E	R	T		A	L	F
D	I	N	G	D	O	N	G		A	R	M	L	E	T
			R	A	N	G		V	I	I	I			
B	A	H	A	M	A		K	I	N	G	K	O	N	G
R	U	E	D		L	A	I	N		R	A	D	I	O
E	R	I	E		O	G	L	E		A	D	D	L	E
W	A	R	D		G	E	L	S		M	O	S	E	S

72

T	I	D	E		P	A	U	L		O	N	S	E	T
I	C	A	N		R	I	C	E		R	O	C	K	S
D	E	M	O		U	R	L	S		S	L	E	E	K
B	A	S	S	O	N	B	A	S	S	O	O	N		
I	I	G	O		N	E	A		I	N	V	A	I	N
T	E	N	S	E		G	O	N	E		E	R	N	O
			C	A	D		S	S	R		L	I	O	N
C	A	R	T	O	N	C	A	R	T	O	O	N		
M	A	T	A		T	R	A		A	R	S			
A	P	O	P		E	A	R	L		A	T	B	A	T
C	O	M	P	E	L		A	L	I		O	P	E	
		B	A	L	L	O	N	B	A	L	L	O	O	N
S	L	O	P	E		L	O	R	D		O	G	L	E
Y	E	M	E	N		G	O	A	L		L	I	L	T
D	E	B	R	A		A	N	T	E		L	E	O	S

73

E	W	E	R		S	A	S	S	Y		Z	E	S	T
B	A	M	A		O	U	T	D	O		E	L	L	E
A	C	I	D		B	R	A	I	N	D	R	A	I	N
Y	O	G	I	B	E	A	R		R	O	P	E	D	
			R	O	A	R	S		P	T	A		S	S	E
B	L	A	D	E	S		M	A	A	M		E	T	D
A	T	T	A	R		T	A	R	M	A	C			
T	R	E	Y		W	A	V	E	S		R	A	M	P
		S	H	A	P	E	D		M	I	S	E	R	
L	I	D		A	D	E	N		F	A	M	I	L	Y
A	L	E		Z	E	D		S	I	R	E	S		
P	L	A	C	E		I	C	E	C	R	E	A	M	
T	I	D	A	L	B	A	S	I	N		A	E	R	O
O	N	E	S		S	Y	N	O	D		T	I	N	A
P	I	N	K		A	E	O	N	S		E	T	O	N

74

S	T	E	S		B	O	L	T		A	L	T	A	R
T	A	L	C		O	K	I	E		L	O	R	R	E
R	U	D	E		W	R	E	N		S	C	U	F	F
O	P	E	N	C	L	A	S	S	R	O	O	M		
P	E	R	I	L			E	E	R		P	A	C	
			C	A	N	D	I	D	C	A	M	E	R	A
S	U	R		N	E	I	N		A	N	A	D	E	M
U	S	E	D		V	I	T	A	L		D	U	N	E
L	U	G	O	S	I		H	U	L	K		P	A	L
F	R	A	N	K	L	O	E	S	S	E	R			
A	P	R		I	L	S			M	O	O	L	A	
		D	I	R	E	C	T	D	E	P	O	S	I	T
F	E	I	N	T		A	H	O	Y		F	A	K	E
L	A	N	G	E		R	O	P	E		E	K	E	S
U	R	G	E	D		S	U	E	D		R	A	N	T

75

M	O	C	H	A		G	A	R	B	O		S	P	A
C	R	O	O	N		A	G	O	R	A		C	A	L
C	A	P	T	A	I	N	H	O	O	K		O	R	E
C	L	A	D		R	D	A	S		T	A	P	I	R
			O	H	O	H		P	R	I	E	S	T	
V	I	R	G	I	N	I	A	R	E	E	L			
A	B	A	S	E		L	O	N	E	S	O	M	E	
S	A	G		S	T	A	N	D			J	O	T	
T	R	U	S	T	I	E	R		O	P	A	R	T	
			A	S	S	E	M	B	L	Y	L	I	N	E
B	O	N	S	A	I			R	I	S	E			
I	C	I	E	R		E	V	I	L		D	A	L	I
G	A	G		D	I	V	I	N	I	N	G	R	O	D
O	L	E		O	R	A	N	G		R	E	E	V	E
T	A	R		M	A	N	E	S		A	S	S	E	S

76

A	B	C	D		L	I	M	B		F	A	I	L	S
L	I	A	R		I	D	O	L		I	N	D	U	S
S	A	T	E		E	L	L	A		E	J	E	C	T
	S	T	A	B	L	E	E	C	O	N	O	M	Y	
			M	O	O	S		K	U	D	U			
H	A	R	L	O	W		E	F	T	S		B	I	C
A	M	A	I	N		A	L	O	E		R	O	L	E
J	O	C	K	E	Y	S	F	O	R	P	O	W	E	R
J	U	K	E		I	S	I	T		A	B	I	D	E
I	R	S		A	K	I	N		A	G	R	E	E	S
			C	U	E	D		U	L	E	E			
	C	R	O	P	S	U	B	S	I	D	I	E	S	
F	L	O	R	A		O	U	R	S		N	Y	N	Y
T	O	M	E	I		U	N	D	O		E	R	I	E
S	P	E	A	R		S	T	A	N		R	E	P	S

77

B	A	L	L		D	O	D	O	S		B	L	A	H
O	R	E	O		E	N	O	L	A		L	O	C	O
S	E	N	D	I	N	T	H	E	C	L	O	W	N	S
C	A	D	E	N	Z	A	S			O	N	S	E	T
			H	E	P			I	Z	O	D			
P	A	S	T	E	L		E	M	I	N	E	N	C	E
A	C	T	O	R		F	R	A	N			A	H	A
T	H	R	E	E	R	I	N	G	C	I	R	C	U	S
C	O	O			E	R	I	E		B	A	R	R	E
H	O	M	E	B	A	S	E		R	E	P	E	L	S
			M	A	L	T		M	A	R				
C	R	E	E	K			S	E	M	I	T	O	N	E
B	A	R	N	U	M	A	N	D	B	A	I	L	E	Y
E	G	A	D		U	S	U	A	L		L	E	A	R
R	U	S	S		G	A	B	L	E		T	O	R	E

78

M	O	O	R		R	A	J	A	H		A	C	C	T
A	I	D	E		A	G	I	L	E		I	E	R	
P	L	O	D		Y	U	L	B	R	Y	N	N	E	R
S	Y	R	I	A		A	T	S	E	A		I	E	R
			A	L	A				T	R	I	C	K	Y
E	U	E	L	L	G	I	B	B	O	N	S			
M	F	R		A	C	E	R			S	A	M	B	A
M	O	O	D		R	A	D	A	R		Y	E	A	R
A	S	S	A	M		M	O	V	E			R	B	I
			Y	U	L	E	F	E	S	T	I	V	A	L
A	N	G	O	R	A				T	O	A			
B	O	O		A	D	D	L	E		O	G	L	E	S
Y	O	U	L	L	L	A	U	G	H		R	A	T	E
S	S	G	T		E	D	G	A	R		E	Z	R	A
S	E	E	D		D	E	E	D	S		E	Y	E	R

79

G	L	U	T		D	R	A	G		H	E	T	U	P
R	U	N	E		E	A	R	L		E	R	A	S	E
A	L	U	M		A	T	N	O		R	U	L	E	R
B	U	M	P	E	R	T	O	B	U	M	P	E	R	
			T	A	I	L			L	I	T			
A	R	R		R	E	E	L	E	C	T		E	N	D
C	O	A	S	T			A	D	E		A	L	A	I
R	U	S	H	H	O	U	R	T	R	A	F	F	I	C
E	S	P	Y		R	A	G			S	T	I	L	T
S	T	Y		R	A	R	E	B	I	T		N	S	A
			D	A	T			O	D	E	S			
	D	R	I	V	E	T	I	M	E	R	A	D	I	O
S	E	I	N	E		A	B	B	A		L	U	S	T
S	E	V	E	N		M	E	E	T		S	L	I	T
T	R	E	S	S		E	T	R	E		A	L	S	O

80

G	R	E	G		A	S	P	I	C		A	Q	U	A
R	E	A	R		F	A	U	N	A		B	U	R	R
O	L	G	A		A	L	T	A	R		L	A	N	K
S	I	L	V	E	R	T	O	N	G	U	E	D		
S	T	E	E	R			N	E	O	N		R	A	W
			L	E	A	K				T	I	A	R	A
C	B	S		L	E	A	D	F	O	O	T	E	D	
R	O	T	E		A	G	R	E	E			N	I	N	E
I	R	O	N	F	I	S	T	E	D			C	A	D
M	A	R	D	I				R	S	V	P			
E	X	E		E	V	I	L			E	R	A	S	E
		R	E	F	I	N	E	D	P	E	O	P	L	E
A	M	O	S		R	O	G	U	E		P	A	I	L
G	O	O	P		G	U	I	D	E		E	C	C	E
E	M	M	Y		O	T	T	E	R		L	E	E	R

81

S	P	A	M		A	C	M	E		S	C	H	M	O
T	O	G	A		B	A	I	L		A	R	E	A	R
A	L	E	C		O	R	M	E		L	A	M	P	S
P	E	N	E	L	O	P	E	C	R	U	Z			
L	A	D		I	K	E		T	O	T	E	B	A	G
E	X	A	C	T		T	W	I	C	E		A	L	A
			A	H	A		O	O	O		C	L	A	M
S	H	A	K	E	D	O	W	N	C	R	U	I	S	E
K	O	B	E		A	R	E		O	E	R			
A	P	E		E	G	A	D	S		L	E	A	R	Y
T	I	T	A	N	I	C		I	I	I		L	E	A
			G	R	O	U	N	D	S	C	R	E	W	S
M	A	R	G	O		L	O	N	E		A	X	I	S
A	V	A	I	L		A	V	E	R		M	E	R	E
J	E	W	E	L		R	A	Y	E		P	I	E	R

82

A	D	O	R	E		S	H	H		T	R	O	O	P
M	O	T	E	L		M	I	A		E	A	R	L	E
F	L	I	P	F	L	O	P	S	A	N	D	A	L	S
M	E	S	A		O	R	P	H	A	N		N	I	T
				S	C	R	E	E		H	I	N	G	E	S
R	A	P	T	O	R		S	A	S	S	Y			
E	U	R		W	I	D	T	H			S	E	D	G	E
F	R	E	E	B	E	E		A	S	H	T	R	A	Y
S	A	Y	S	O		M	E	T	O	O		E	E	R
			P	Y	L	O	N		M	E	D	D	L	E
S	T	R	O	B	E		C	E	A	S	E			
A	R	I		O	N	C	A	L	L		L	P	G	A
B	E	D	R	O	O	M	S	L	I	P	P	E	R	S
L	E	G	I	T		D	E	A		C	H	E	E	K
E	D	E	N	S		R	D	S		S	I	N	G	S

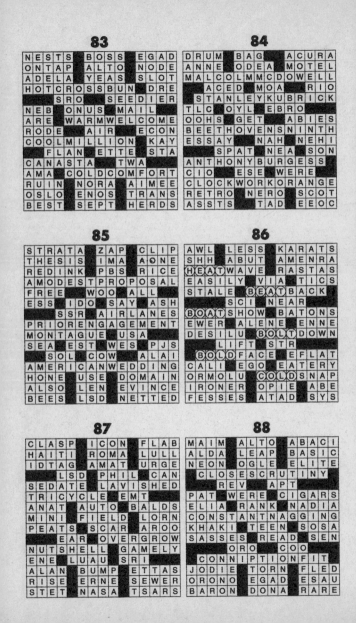

83

N	E	S	T	S		B	O	S	S		E	G	A	D
O	N	T	A	P		A	L	T	O		N	O	D	E
A	D	E	L	A		Y	E	A	S		S	L	O	T
H	O	T	C	R	O	S	S	B	U	N		D	R	E
			S	R	O			S	E	E	D	I	E	R
N	E	B		O	N	U	S		M	A	I	L		
A	R	E		W	A	R	M	W	E	L	C	O	M	E
R	O	D	E			A	I	R			E	C	O	N
C	O	O	L	M	I	L	L	I	O	N		K	A	Y
		F	L	A	N		E	T	T	E		S	T	A
C	A	N	A	S	T	A		T	W	A				
A	M	A		C	O	L	D	C	O	M	F	O	R	T
R	U	I	N		N	O	R	A		A	I	M	E	E
O	S	L	O		E	N	O	S		T	R	A	N	S
B	E	S	T		S	E	P	T		H	E	R	D	S

84

D	R	U	M		B	A	G		A	C	U	R	A	
A	N	N	E		O	D	E	A		M	O	T	E	L
M	A	L	C	O	L	M	M	C	D	O	W	E	L	L
	A	C	E	D		M	O	A			R	I	O	
S	T	A	N	L	E	Y	K	U	B	R	I	C	K	
T	L	C		O	Y	L		E	B	R	O			
O	O	H	S		G	E	T		A	B	I	E	S	
B	E	E	T	H	O	V	E	N	S	N	I	N	T	H
E	S	S	A	Y			N	A	H		N	E	H	I
			S	P	A	T		N	E	A		S	O	N
A	N	T	H	O	N	Y	B	U	R	G	E	S	S	
C	I	O			E	S	E			W	E	R	E	
C	L	O	C	K	W	O	R	K	O	R	A	N	G	E
R	E	T	R	O		N	E	R	O		S	C	O	T
A	S	S	T	S			T	A	D		E	E	O	C

85

S	T	R	A	T	A		Z	A	P		C	L	I	P
T	H	E	S	I	S		I	M	A		A	O	N	E
R	E	D	I	N	K		P	B	S		R	I	C	E
A	M	O	D	E	S	T	P	R	O	P	O	S	A	L
F	R	E	E			W	O	O		A	L	L		
E	S	S		I	D	O		S	A	Y		A	S	H
			S	S	R		A	I	R	L	A	N	E	S
P	R	I	O	R	E	N	G	A	G	E	M	E	N	T
M	O	N	T	A	G	U	E		U	S	A			
S	E	A		E	S	T		W	E	S		P	J	S
		S	O	L		C	O	W		A	L	A	I	
A	M	E	R	I	C	A	N	W	E	D	D	I	N	G
H	O	N	E		U	S	E		D	O	M	A	I	N
A	L	S	O		L	E	N		E	V	I	N	C	E
B	E	E	S		L	S	D		N	E	T	T	E	D

86

A	W	L		L	E	S	S		K	A	R	A	T	S
S	H	H		A	B	U	T		A	M	E	N	R	A
H	E	A	T	W	A	V	E		R	A	S	T	A	S
E	A	S	I	L	Y		V	I	A		T	I	C	S
S	T	A	L	E		B	E	A	T	B	A	C	K	
			S	C	I			N	E	A	R			
B	O	A	T	S	H	O	W		B	A	T	O	N	S
E	W	E	R		A	L	E	N	E		E	N	N	E
D	E	S	I	L	U		B	O	L	T	D	O	W	N
			L	I	F	T		S	T	R				
B	O	L	D	F	A	C	E		E	F	L	A	T	
C	A	L	I		E	G	O		E	A	T	E	R	Y
O	R	M	O	L	U		C	O	L	D	S	N	A	P
I	R	O	N	E	R		O	P	I	E		A	B	E
F	E	S	S	E	S		A	T	A	D		S	Y	S

87

C	L	A	S	P		I	C	O	N		F	L	A	B
H	A	I	T	I		R	O	M	A		L	U	L	L
I	D	T	A	G		A	M	A	T		U	R	G	E
		L	S	D		P	H	I	L		C	A	N	
S	E	D	A	T	E		L	A	V	I	S	H	E	D
T	R	I	C	Y	C	L	E			E	M	T		
A	N	A	T		A	U	T	O		B	A	L	D	S
M	I	N	I		F	I	E	L	D		L	O	R	N
P	E	A	T	S		S	C	A	R		A	R	O	O
			E	A	R		O	V	E	R	G	R	O	W
N	U	T	S	H	E	L	L		G	A	M	E	L	Y
E	N	E		L	U	A	U			S	R	I		
A	L	A	N		B	U	M	P		E	T	T	A	S
R	I	S	E		E	R	N	E		S	E	W	E	R
S	T	E	T		N	A	S	A		T	S	A	R	S

88

M	A	I	M		A	L	T	O		A	B	A	C	I
A	L	D	A		L	E	A	P		B	A	S	I	C
N	E	O	N		O	G	L	E		E	L	I	T	E
	C	L	O	S	E	S	C	R	U	T	I	N	Y	
			R	E	V			A	P	T				
P	A	T		W	E	R	E		C	I	G	A	R	S
E	L	I	A		R	A	N	K		N	A	D	I	A
C	O	N	S	T	A	N	T	N	A	G	G	I	N	G
K	H	A	K	I		T	E	E	N		S	O	S	A
S	A	S	S	E	S		R	E	A	D		S	E	N
			O	R	O			C	O	O				
C	O	N	N	I	P	T	I	O	N	F	I	T		
J	O	D	I	E		T	O	R	N		F	L	E	D
O	R	O	N	O		E	G	A	D		E	S	A	U
B	A	R	O	N		D	O	N	A		R	A	R	E

89
```
L A T H   U C L A   S T A I D
E C H O   M R E D   W A L D O
A L A S   B E A M   E N T E R
P U R P L E P R O S E   O A K
      E R E   N A P S
I P A N A   S H I V   M A S S
D I N E R O   I S O   E D N A
L A V E N D E R H I L L M O B
E N I D   E V E   R E T I R E
S O L E   S A S S   A S T E R
      D I S C   T A S
A H A   M A U V E D E C A D E
M A N I A   A E R O   H U R L
A L O N G   T I E R   E R A S
D O N N E   E L O N   W A G E
```

90
```
A R C H E R   S A L S   S H E
G A L O R E   I M A C   T A D
A D O N I S   L A V A T O R Y
T I S   E A V E   A M A N A S
H O E D   W I N G   A L E S
A S T E R   S T A I R C A S E
      N E O   L E S T   G E L
H O L Y C O W   A B I D E R S
A R I   E R R S   N S A
T A K E S T E P S   T Y P E S
T E A S   N O T O   O I L Y
T O N S I L   O D O R   N A S
A R E Y O U O K   H A C K I T
G I S   N A P E   E R M I N E
S O S   S U E D   R E D E E M
```

91
```
B O R E S   L A M A   C H A P
E L I T E   O W E D   R O S E
A G O R A   M O O D   O M I T
M A T E R I A L W I T N E S S
      E R N S   T H Y
P A R A D E   L I O N E S S
A M O S   S W O O N   A P E
S I G H T S E E I N G T R I P
T E E   H A T E S   A T R A
E S T E E M S   R A C H E L
      R I O   A M E N
O B S E R V A T I O N D E C K
T A L C   A L A N   A R L E N
T R O T   R O L E   L I S L E
O N E S   S E E D   S P A T E
```

92
```
A L T E R   B O A T   S R T A
P E E V E   A B L E   C O I L
E A S E L   L I E S   R A R E
    T R I C K S C H R O D E R
O T S   E P A   A L I S T
T R I P V A N W I N K L E
T I T L E   I N R E
O B E Y   V O D K A   A T M S
      C I A O   A R R A Y
T H A N K W I L L I A M S
S P O O N   G A S   P A T
T R U S S F E I N G O L D
R A P T   A C T I   R O O M Y
A T E E   C H E T   A V O I D
W E E D   T O M E   N E R D S
```

93
```
O D D S   S P O K E S   B A R
L I E U   E L A I N E   E M U
G E M M Y C A R T E R   F E B
A D O   E A T   G L O B E
W A N O L D R E A G A N
O L D E S T   A W A I T
V A U L T   D Y E R   H A L E
A C O L Y T E   L E V E L E R
L E S S   S L O T   A R D O R
      I R A T E   C L E A N S
J E S T E R A R T H U R
A X L E S   H U E   E R A
V I E   H A I R Y T R U M A N
A L P   I N C O M E   S I G N
N E T   P A Y E E S   A R E A
```

94
```
A C D C   L I N E   B A T T Y
A R E A   I T E M   A L O H A
H E N R Y F O R D   D I N E R
S E T T E E   D A N G   E N D
      E N V S   S O U P
W A L T E R C H R Y S L E R
V I D   A S T A   S I E G E
E L I S   T A I N T   S O Y A
I C E U P   N O U N   N P R
L O U I S C H E V R O L E T
      T Y P O   A N T I
L A D   C A T T   A C T S A S
E P O C H   B I G W H E E L S
A E I O U   E L I A   R E I N
F S T O P   D E N Y   S P A S
```

95

E	L	M	S		A	G	R	E	E		M	I	L	K
C	I	A	O		P	R	O	M	S		A	V	O	W
H	O	C	U	S	P	O	C	U	S		T	O	G	A
O	N	E		T	E	A	K		S	I	R	E	N	
			H	E	N	N	Y	P	E	N	N	Y		
D	E	M	A	N	D			A	D	O	S			
A	G	E	S		M	A	N	G	O		S	P	A	
D	O	T	H	E	H	O	K	E	Y	P	O	K	E	Y
E	S	E		B	A	N	A	L		N	Y	S	E	
			B	O	R	E		I	S	L	E	T	S	
		H	A	N	K	Y	P	A	N	K	Y			
S	T	O	R	Y		A	N	T	I		A	O	K	
P	A	G	E		H	O	D	G	E	P	O	D	G	E
A	R	A	L		M	A	R	I	N		V	A	L	E
M	A	N	Y		S	K	E	E	T		A	M	E	N

96

T	I	L		M	E	T	A	L		A	C	H	E	S
A	C	U		A	M	A	N	A		B	U	E	N	O
H	E	M		L	U	C	I	L	L	E	B	A	L	L
I	D	E	S	T			M	A	I	L	E	D		
T	I	N	K	E	R	B	E	L	L			S	O	N
I	N	S	I	D	E	R		A	T	H	E	A	R	T
					N	E	A			U	R	I	A	H
		T	W	O	D	O	L	L	A	R	B	I	L	L
T	H	I	N	E			I	S	E					
W	E	N	T	B	A	D		S	P	A	R	T	A	N
A	N	D			C	O	T	T	O	N	B	O	L	L
			P	O	C	O	N	O		A	I	S	L	E
C	H	I	C	A	G	O	B	U	L	L		S	P	A
C	O	P	T	S		R	A	T	I	O		E	R	S
S	T	E	A	K		S	T	E	I	G		D	O	T

97

E	U	R	O		E	M	I	T		A	L	I	A	S
S	T	A	N		P	O	R	E		B	A	D	G	E
C	A	K	E	W	A	L	K	S		S	W	E	E	T
	H	E	R	O		A	S	T	O		C	A	S	H
			U	R	L	S		E	T	A	L			
C	A	N	D	Y	S	T	R	I	P	E	R	S		
A	L	S			E	E	R		S	T	R	A	I	T
D	I	T	C	H		S	U	P		S	K	I	L	L
S	M	I	L	E	S		C	A	P		T	A	C	
		B	R	O	W	N	I	E	P	O	I	N	T	S
			I	S	O	N		A	L	T	O			
A	C	T	S		B	A	R	B		C	F	O	S	
T	O	O	T	H		P	I	E	C	H	A	R	T	S
V	I	D	E	O		E	G	A	D		I	S	E	E
S	N	O	R	E		T	A	R	S		R	O	M	A

98

O	L	A	V		E	R	A	S		A	C	H	E	D
J	A	P	E		X	O	U	T		B	O	O	T	Y
A	C	E	S		C	O	T	Y		D	U	R	A	N
Y	E	R	T	L	E	T	H	E	T	U	R	T	L	E
S	D	S		E	S	S	O		A	L	S	O		
			O	A	T	S		R	O	N		E	N	D	S
D	I	N	G	S		S	E	G	A		H	O	I	
D	R	S	E	U	S	S		O	O	B	L	E	C	K
A	M	A		P	L	O	T			S	T	A	S	H
Y	A	P	S		A	U	G		B	U	R	R		
			E	L	A	N		E	W	E	R		S	A	T
S	P	R	I	N	G	F	I	E	L	D	M	A	S	S
H	O	S	E	D		A	S	I	A		Y	W	C	A
A	R	O	S	E		Z	E	S	T		T	H	O	R
G	E	N	T	S		E	L	S	E		H	O	T	S

99

U	S	D	A		P	L	O	P		A	S	C	A	P
L	E	E	R		C	A	V	S		S	C	A	L	E
T	O	M	B	O	S	L	E	Y		P	O	K	E	S
R	U	M	O	R		A	R	C	H	I	T	E	C	T
A	L	E	R	T			H	A	R	T				
			H	A	L	F		W	E	B	C	A	M	
R	O	N	H	O	W	A	R	D		R	A	M	B	O
A	S	E	A		E	N	E	R	O		I	D	B	E
F	L	A	P	S		E	R	I	N	M	O	R	A	N
T	O	P	P	L	E		E	P	E	E				
			Y	O	U	R			C	A	N	A	L	
D	E	A	D	W	R	O	N	G		C	R	A	N	E
A	D	L	A	I		M	I	L	W	A	U	K	E	E
B	A	B	Y	S		P	L	E	A		B	E	N	D
S	M	A	S	H		S	E	E	D		A	D	D	S

100

S	T	E	A	M		T	N	O	T	E		B	A	R
C	R	A	V	E		R	O	W	E	D		A	M	O
H	E	R	E	S	J	O	H	N	N	Y		G	P	A
E	M	T		S	U	P				S	O	B	E	R
M	O	H	S		D	E	N	S			F	O	R	E
E	L	E	A			O	Z	O	N	E	L	A	Y	E	R
D	O	N	A	S			S	E	R	A		S	S	S
			B	I	G	C	H	E	E	S	E			
A	B	O		M	A	H	I			S	N	A	G	S
B	A	T	H	S	P	O	N	G	E		O	M	A	N
A	T	T	A		O	G	O	D			S	I	L	O
S	T	O	I	C			V	A	N			A	I	R
H	E	M		A	L	I	C	E	M	A	R	B	L	E
E	R	A		K	I	N	E	R		V	I	L	E	R
S	Y	N		E	P	S	O	N		Y	O	Y	O	S

101

L	O	W	S		W	A	S	P	S		A	M	P	S
O	A	H	U		A	L	L	I	N		D	O	L	E
I	T	O	L	D	Y	O	U	S	O		A	L	E	X
S	H	A	K	E	S	P	E	A	R	E	P	L	A	Y
			S	C	I			N	E	S	T			
A	S	H		A	D	A	M		S	A	L	S	A	
T	H	E	I	D	E	S	O	F		B	E	L	L	
W	O	R	S	E		O	V	I		B	L	O	O	P
A	V	O	N		F	I	F	T	E	E	N	T	H	
R	E	N	T	S		N	E	E	D		A	H	A	
			S	T	A	G		E	E	K				
F	A	M	O	U	S	L	A	S	T	W	O	R	D	S
I	B	A	R		S	O	O	T	H	S	A	Y	E	R
J	E	E	R		A	R	N	I	E		L	E	F	T
I	T	S	Y		D	Y	E	R	S		A	S	T	A

102

D	R	A	W	L		L	I	Z	A		E	G	G	O
R	O	M	E	O		A	D	A	M		S	O	I	L
A	S	P	I	C		P	A	N	E		S	A	M	E
P	I	E	R	O	F	T	H	E	R	E	A	L	M	
E	E	R			O	O	O			W	Y	L	I	E
D	R	E	A	M	U	P		A	S	E		O	C	T
			T	A	L		S	A	W		D	U	K	E
	Q	U	A	Y	T	O	T	H	E	C	I	T	Y	
F	U	N	D		I	V	Y		E	A	R			
D	I	S		S	P	A		A	T	L	E	A	S	T
A	B	E	T	S		A	D	O			S	T	U	
	B	E	R	T	H	O	F	A	N	A	T	I	O	N
A	L	M	A		I	H	O	P		B	E	T	O	N
R	E	L	Y		R	I	O	T		B	E	I	G	E
E	D	Y	S		T	O	T	S		A	N	S	E	L

103

L	I	L	I		E	W	E	R		D	W	A	R	F
E	D	E	N		V	I	C	E		O	N	C	U	E
G	O	N	E	W	I	T	H	T	H	E	W	I	N	D
O	L	D	P	A	L		O	R	E	S		D	T	S
			T	I	T	O		O	A	T	S			
B	A	M		T	W	A	S		T	I	M	B	E	R
A	L	O	E		I	S	E	E			M	O	O	L	A
S	I	N	G	I	N	I	N	T	H	E	R	A	I	N
E	V	E	R	T		S	O	H	O		E	T	T	A
D	E	T	E	S	T		R	O	T	H		S	E	T
			T	A	I	L		S	W	A	P			
A	O	L		D	E	E	M		A	G	E	N	D	A
T	H	E	P	E	R	F	E	C	T	S	T	O	R	M
T	I	A	R	A		T	A	P	E		T	R	E	E
Y	O	D	E	L		S	L	U	R		Y	A	W	N

104

J	U	L	E	P		P	L	A	N	B		G	S	A
A	R	O	A	R		R	O	S	S	I		O	M	S
B	E	W	R	I	T	E	B	A	C	K		N	U	S
			S	E	A	S	O	N		I	N	E	R	T
R	A	W		S	T	S		S	N	I	F	F	S	
O	D	E	T	T	A		D	O	M	I	N	I		
T	A	R	A	S		P	A	L	E		N	S	E	C
O	L	E	G		M	A	R	I	E		I	S	N	O
R	E	C	S		O	V	E	N		H	E	I	S	T
			L	A	S	S	E	R		H	A	S	O	U	T
V	I	O	L	A	S		P	E	R		N	E	A	
E	N	T	E	R		A	U	R	A	T	E			
I	S	H		O	U	T	T	O	L	A	U	N	C	H
N	E	E		N	A	M	E	S		C	R	E	P	E
S	T	D		G	R	O	P	E		K	O	O	L	S

105

M	A	C	S		H	O	U	R		H	A	Z	E	L
U	G	L	Y		E	S	S	E		A	V	E	R	Y
N	O	O	N		A	H	E	M		M	O	U	S	E
C	R	U	C	I	V	E	R	B	A	L	I	S	T	
H	A	D		T	E	A		R	U	E	D			
			B	E	N		M	A	R	T		J	A	B
A	X	I	O	M		B	O	N	A		C	O	L	A
C	R	O	S	S	W	O	R	D	E	D	I	T	O	R
H	A	W	N		H	O	S	T		I	N	S	E	T
E	Y	E		P	E	K	E		U	T	E			
			F	I	L	M		T	N	T		D	I	S
E	N	I	G	M	A	T	O	L	O	G	I	S	T	
G	L	E	N	S		K	A	T	E		R	O	L	E
U	B	O	A	T		E	X	E	S		I	D	E	A
M	A	N	L	Y		R	I	M	S		D	E	S	K

106

S	C	E	N	I	C		S	E	C		E	B	A	N
T	U	X	E	D	O		A	R	R		L	A	N	E
A	R	E	O	L	A		B	R	O		D	U	D	S
F	I	R		E	X	T	R	A	C	R	E	D	I	T
F	E	T	E		R	I	N	S	E	S				
			R	E	S	A	N	D		S	T	R	O	M
J	O	H	N	N	Y	C	A	S	H		O	P	A	
U	N	I	S	O	N		E	M	O	T	E	S		
S	T	E		C	L	A	I	M	C	H	E	C	K	
T	O	R	A	H		A	T	T	A	I	N			
			N	E	S	T	E	A			O	A	R	S
D	E	P	T	H	C	H	A	R	G	E		D	I	E
O	R	A	L		R	E	L		I	M	P	U	G	N
L	I	V	E		O	R	O		S	M	I	L	E	S
L	E	E	R		D	S	T		T	A	T	T	L	E

107

J	A	M	S		M	A	Y	O	R		S	E	L	F
O	B	O	E		A	R	E	W	E		T	R	I	O
T	E	N	C	O	M	M	A	N	D	M	E	N	T	S
S	T	O	O	L	I	E			D	A	V	I	E	S
			N	E	E	D	E	D		R	E	E	S	E
E	G	A	D	S			X	E	D	I	N			
C	L	U	E		P	A	P	U	A	N		M	B	A
H	U	N	D	R	E	D	A	C	R	E	W	O	O	D
O	T	T		U	S	E	N	E	T		H	A	Z	E
			G	L	O	P	S			H	I	T	O	N
F	A	I	R	E		T	E	A	M	U	P			
A	C	C	O	R	D			G	A	L	L	O	P	S
T	H	O	U	S	A	N	D	I	S	L	A	N	D	S
E	O	N	S		F	E	I	N	T		S	C	A	T
D	O	S	E		T	O	N	G	S		H	E	S	S

108

W	A	S	P		F	D	A			P	E	T	I	T
A	R	I	A		R	I	C	A		O	X	I	D	E
N	E	X	T		A	S	H	E		L	A	T	E	R
		T	H	E	C	H	E	R	R	Y	M	O	O	N
D	A	Y		N	A	Y		O	O	P	S			
I	N	S	E	T	S		U	S	P	S		S	R	O
S	T	E	V	E		A	N	T	E		A	W	A	Y
C	O	V	E	R	O	F	D	A	R	K	N	E	S	S
O	N	E	S		S	T	E	R		L	E	A	S	T
S	Y	N		A	L	E	R		H	U	S	T	L	E
			S	T	I	R		D	A	T		S	E	R
N	E	W	M	A	N	A	G	E	M	E	N	T		
O	C	H	E	R		L	U	L	L		E	A	T	S
S	T	O	L	I		L	A	V	E		M	I	R	A
H	O	S	T	S		M	E	T			O	N	I	T

109

P	A	S	T	E	L		T	B	A	R		A	L	T
E	L	O	I	S	E		I	A	G	O		L	E	A
C	O	U	N	T	R	Y	C	L	U	B		B	A	N
S	T	L		E	N	O		D	E	E	P	E	N	D
		M	O	S	E	Y	S			A	R	T	E	
M	C	A	N			R	O	C	K	B	O	T	T	O	M
P	U	T	T	S			H	O	Y	L	E			
H	E	E	H	A	W	S		P	E	E	R	S	A	T
			E	M	A	I	L			S	N	A	C	K
R	A	P	S	E	S	S	I	O	N		A	L	T	O
O	V	A	L			P	R	O	W	L	S			
L	I	L	Y	P	A	D		I	T	O		A	E	R
L	A	M		S	W	I	N	G	B	R	I	D	G	E
E	T	E		S	A	S	E		A	S	S	I	G	N
R	E	D		T	Y	K	E		D	E	S	P	O	T

110

A	B	E	T		L	A	U	D	S		M	E	A	T
L	U	L	U		O	N	S	E	T		E	R	G	O
G	R	A	N	D	P	A	N	J	A	N	D	R	U	M
A	G	L	A	R	E				A	R	O	U	S	E	S
			F	I	R	E	S			E	T	S		
C	L	I	P		D	U	D		C	A	G	E	D	
T	R	E	S			F	I	N	I	S	H		A	M	I
H	I	G	H	M	U	C	K	E	T	Y	M	U	C	K
A	B	A		E	N	T	I	T	Y		A	G	E	E
I	S	L	E	D		S	S	E		K	N	E	E	
			D	I	M		T	R	A	I	T			
E	T	H	I	C	A	L			S	W	I	V	E	L
T	H	E	B	I	G	E	N	C	H	I	L	A	D	A
C	E	L	L		I	N	U	R	E		L	I	E	N
H	Y	D	E		C	A	N	T	S		A	N	N	E

111

L	O	B	O		N	A	D	I	A		I	M	P	S
A	L	U	M		U	S	E	R	S		N	A	R	C
M	E	R	E		D	I	N	E	S		B	R	I	E
B	O	R	N	A	G	A	I	N		S	E	D	A	N
			S	K	I		M	E	A	L	T	I	M	E
B	T	U		I	N	C		S	O	W				
L	I	V	I	N	G	O	N	T	H	E	E	D	G	E
E	D	E	N			M	E	R			E	I	R	E
D	E	A	D	A	S	A	D	O	O	R	N	A	I	L
			I	W	O		N	Y	E		L	P	S	
R	E	V	E	R	S	E	S		S	P	A			
E	D	I	F	Y			T	H	A	T	S	L	I	F	E
U	G	L	I		O	H	A	R	E		A	L	E	X
S	E	L	L		L	E	V	E	R		M	I	L	E
E	D	A	M		D	R	E	S	S		O	A	T	S

112

B	U	R	P		V	O	C	E		B	E	B	O	P
A	V	E	R		I	B	E	T		A	L	O	N	E
R	E	N	O		B	E	A	U		R	I	N	S	O
B	A	T	T	E	R	Y	S	I	Z	E		D	E	N
			E	R	A	S	E		A	L	E	R	T	S
C	O	M	M	O	N			P	H	Y	L	A		
O	H	O		S	T	J	O	H	N		S	T	O	W
B	I	T	T	E		A	A	A		S	E	I	N	E
B	O	O	R		A	M	T	R	A	K		N	E	V
			R	I	F	T	S		T	A	N	G	L	E
D	A	G	G	E	R			S	P	A	T	E		
E	R	R		M	I	N	O	R	L	E	A	G	U	E
B	I	O	T	A		A	N	N	O		R	A	N	K
U	S	U	A	L		R	I	D	S		B	L	U	E
T	E	P	E	E		C	A	L	S		Y	A	M	S

113

F	A	R	O		A	R	R	O	W		O	P	U	S
O	L	A	F		U	H	H	U	H		M	E	T	A
W	A	I	F		G	O	O	S	E		S	T	U	B
L	I	L	Y	M	U	N	S	T	E	R		U	R	L
			E	A	S	E			D	I	A	N	N	E
D	E	P	A	R	T		B	I	L	O	X	I		
O	Z	A	R	K		J	I	B	E		E	A	T	S
U	R	N		S	L	A	K	E	R	S		P	O	T
P	A	S	T		A	P	E	X		H	A	I	T	I
		Y	A	W	N	E	R		D	O	D	G	E	R
H	E	Y	D	A	Y			B	E	A	D			
E	L	O		D	A	I	S	Y	C	L	O	V	E	R
M	I	K	E		R	H	I	N	O		N	O	P	E
A	Z	U	R		D	O	N	O	R		T	I	E	D
N	A	M	E		S	P	E	W	S		O	D	E	S

114

S	P	E	C		E	B	A	Y		C	O	M	B	O
H	I	L	L		D	E	L	I		O	N	I	O	N
A	Q	U	A		I	D	L	E		G	L	A	Z	E
N	U	D	I	S	T	C	O	L	O	N	Y			
D	E	E	R	E			H	Y	D	R	A		S	R	I
Y	T	D		D	I	E		S	E	C	T	I	O	N
			L	A	R	C	H					I	S	B	N
B	A	R	E	N	A	K	E	D	L	A	D	I	E	S
A	V	O	N			P	R	E	X	Y				
J	O	U	S	T	E	D		I	D	I		P	A	L
A	W	E		S	W	E	L	L		O	P	E	R	A
			T	H	E	F	U	L	L	M	O	N	T	Y
H	A	N	O	I		I	N	R	I		S	C	U	M
A	R	B	O	R		L	A	I	D		S	I	R	E
S	C	A	N	T		E	R	G	O		E	L	O	N

115

S	W	A	M		R	A	S	H		D	A	I	S	Y
O	H	N	O		E	S	T	A		O	L	D	I	E
N	E	A	T		E	S	A	U		A	G	E	N	T
G	E	T	T	O	F	I	R	S	T	B	A	S	E	
			O	N	E	S			O	L	E			
E	S	S		T	R	I	R	E	M	E		F	I	T
L	O	T	T	O			A	L	E		H	I	D	E
B	A	L	L	P	A	R	K	F	I	G	U	R	E	S
O	P	E	C		S	U	E		C	H	E	A	T	
W	Y	O		T	H	E	R	M	A	L		S	L	Y
			S	H	E			U	T	E	S			
O	U	T	I	N	L	E	F	T	F	I	E	L	D	
R	U	N	O	N		S	A	F	E		X	I	I	I
O	R	I	N	G		A	S	I	S		T	R	E	E
E	S	T	E	S		T	E	N	T		Y	E	N	S

116

I	B	E	R	I	A			J	A	I		S	T	A
D	A	N	I	N	G		C	U	T	S	H	O	R	T
O	N	E	D	G	E		A	L	L	E	Y	C	A	T
L	E	S	I	O	N		T	I	A		P	K	W	Y
			A	D	D		C	A	R	P	O	O	L	S
G	O	A	T		A	S	H		G	A	S			
A	C	C	E	S	S	C	O	D	E	S		F	A	B
L	H	A	S	A		A	F	R		T	A	L	I	A
S	O	D		F	O	R	T	U	N	A	T	E	L	Y
			F	E	R		H	M	O		L	E	S	S
C	A	M	I	S	O	L	E		N	S	A			
O	L	I	N		T	E	D		S	A	N	T	A	S
A	L	L	E	L	U	I	A		T	U	T	O	R	S
T	E	N	D	E	N	C	Y		O	N	A	P	A	R
S	S	E		I	D	A			P	A	N	E	L	S

117

A	P	T		C	H	I	L	I		G	O	R	E	N
D	A	Y		L	U	R	I	D		A	N	I	S	E
H	U	P	M	O	B	I	L	E		Z	A	P	P	A
O	L	E	I	N		S	Y	S	T	E	M			
C	A	S	S	I	S			A	B	A	S	E	D	
			O	N	E	L	U	M	P	O	R	T	W	O
M	A	D		G	R	E	T	A		S	C	R	E	W
A	L	I	E		B	A	T	O	N		H	A	R	E
S	P	A	Y	S		P	E	R	I	L		Y	S	L
T	H	R	E	E	S	T	R	I	K	E	S			
S	A	Y	S	N	O			E	V	E	N	E	D	
			L	O	W	E	R	S		I	R	A	Q	I
O	U	T	E	R		P	E	T	I	T	F	O	U	R
K	N	I	F	E		I	N	A	N	E		M	A	T
S	A	L	T	S		C	O	R	D	S		I	L	S

118

S	P	A	R	E		O	F	F	E	R		J	A	M
A	L	L	A	N		H	A	L	V	E		U	R	I
N	O	V	I	C	E	S	Q	U	A	D		N	I	L
S	W	A	N		M	U	S	E		T	O	K	E	N
			F	A	I	R			S	A	D	D	L	E
N	O	T	A	B	L	E	H	O	P	P	E	R		
U	V	U	L	A			A	C	R	E		A	I	R
D	A	N	L		P	A	R	T	Y		Y	W	C	A
E	L	I		T	E	M	P			C	O	E	U	R
			N	O	Y	E	S	O	F	C	O	U	R	S	E
A	R	G	Y	L	L			R	A	N	G			
R	I	F	L	E		O	B	I	S		O	O	N	A
G	T	O		N	O	M	A	D	H	A	T	T	E	R
O	E	R		O	R	A	N	G		S	M	O	R	E
T	S	K		L	A	R	G	E		S	E	E	D	S

119

```
J E T S   I M A   A R E T O O
U P R O O T E D   B A S I N S
T H U R G O O D   A Z T E C S
      B R O W N V B O A R D
S P R E E       E A R
H U I T   A N N E   E E L E D
O L D   A S E A   O D D I T Y
P L E S S Y V F E R G U S O N
P I R A T E   T R E E   T I A
E N S O R   E A R L   T E L S
      O P T       B I N E T
  O F E D U C A T I O N
P A R L O R   M A R S H A L L
A T E A M S   P R E S A G E S
C H E N E Y   S T S   T O D D
```

120

```
L A Y S   P H O N Y   A W A Y
O R E O   R A D I O   R I M S
G O A L   E L E G Y   E T A L
J U S T A S I T H O U G H T
A N T I C   T O T   H O M E R
M D S   T E E   C B S   A U K
      M I A   W A R   N Y R O
  U P R I G H T P I A N O S
A P E X   E O S   A W E
B L T   A R T   S R A   I F S
S I N A I   C E L   R A D I I
  F A I R T O M I D D L I N G
A T M S   I C I E R   A D I N
R E E L   L O T S A   N I T E
M D S E   T A S T Y   S T E T
```

121

```
D I R E   T R A M P   C A S A
I D O L   R E C U R   A V O N
R E D S K Y A T M O R N I N G
T S E   H I P S   A V A I L
      B A N S   F I N A N C E
S P R A N G   S O A K S
I R A N   K I N T E   T W O
D O G D A Y A F T E R N O O N
E W E   R E N T S   O G R E
      S N A G S   D R E A M S
T E M P E R A   H E A L
A L O E S   S O L I   A C E
B L U E S I N T H E N I G H T
L E N D   B E A U T   R E I N
E N D S   N O T M E   E D N A
```

122

```
N O D   A F T E R   P O P U P
A L E   D O N N E   E L E N A
R E T   D U T C H T R E A T Y
C O H E I R   L E E S   C I E
      R A N T S   A N O T H E R
W R O U G H T I R O N Y
E O N   S O S   R A R I N G
E V E R T   A S S   L O S E R
D E S I R E   U A R   V E E
      F U D G E F A C T O R Y
C O R T E G E   E C L A T
E R O   P A T S   E O C E N E
C O L L A R S T U D Y   D O E
I N L E T   O L L I E   I L L
L O A T H   N O E N D   N O S
```

123

```
M O L L   D E J A   P O S I T
E D I E   E R O S   A L I C E
S O S O   V E N I   N I L E S
A R T I F I C I A L T O O T H
      V A S T   I R S
L A C   T E S T I F Y   G T O
A R U B A   A R E   W R A P
P O P U L A R C A R D G A M E
E M I T   R F K   U N D E R
L A D   R E D S T A R   E R A
      T E N   A G E S
H I G H W A Y O V E R P A S S
A G O R A   A M E N   R U L E
T O N E R   P O R T   A R E A
S T E E D   S O N S   Y A W N
```

124

```
T A B U   K E E L S   A S C H
A V E S   A U D I E   R O L E
P A T E N T R I T E   T R U E
A S T R A Y   F E S T E R E D
S T E I N   C Y R   A M Y
      D A D A   R I S E R
H I S S   I M A M   A S I D E
A S H   T E E T E R S   T I E
S P I T E   L E N O   S E E K
H Y P E R   S E C T
  W A R   S P A   H I C K S
P E R M E A T E   C A L L I T
I T I S   B A C K U P L I T E
E T T U   A L A I N   E V E R
S E E P   B E N N Y   D E R N
```

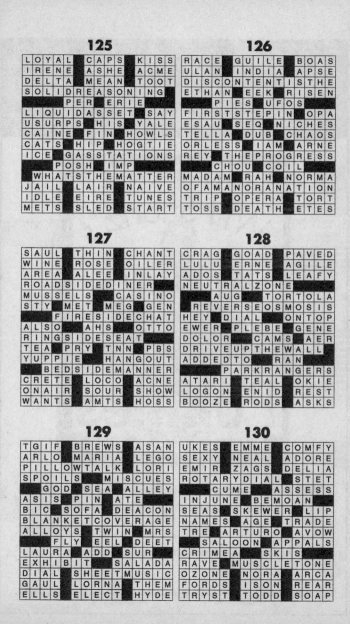

125

```
L O Y A L   C A P S   K I S S
I R E N E   A S H E   A C M E
D E L T A   M E A N   T O O T
S O L I D R E A S O N I N G
      P E R   E R I E
L I Q U I D A S S E T   S A Y
U S U R P S   H I S   Y A L E
C A I N E   F I N   H O W L S
C A T S   H I P   H O G T I E
I C E   G A S S T A T I O N S
      P O S H   I M P
  W H A T S T H E M A T T E R
J A I L   L A I R   N A I V E
I D L E   E I R E   T U N E S
M E T S   S L E D   S T A R T
```

126

```
R A C E   G U I L E   B O A S
U L A N   I N D I A   A P S E
D I S C O N T E N T I S T H E
E T H A N   E E K   R I S E N
      P I E S   U F O S
F I R S T S T E P I N   O P A
E S A U   S E Q   N I C H E S
T E L L A   D U B   C H A O S
O R L E S S   I A M   A R N E
R E Y   T H E P R O G R E S S
      C H O U   C O I L
M A D A M   R A H   N O R M A
O F A M A N O R A N A T I O N
T R I P   O P E R A   T O R T
T O S S   D E A T H   E T E S
```

127

```
S A U L   T H I N   C H A N T
W I N E   R O S E   O I L E R
A R E A   A L E E   I N L A Y
R O A D S I D E D I N E R
M U S S E L S   C A S I N O
S T Y   M E T   M E G   G E N
  F I R E S I D E C H A T
A L S O   A H S   O T T O
R I N G S I D E S E A T
T E A   P R Y   T N N   P B S
Y U P P I E   H A N G O U T
  B E D S I D E M A N N E R
C R E T E   L O C O   A C N E
O N A I R   S O U R   S H O W
W A N T S   A M T S   H O S S
```

128

```
C R A G   G O A D   P A V E D
L U L U   E R N E   A G I L E
A D O S   T A T S   L E A F Y
N E U T R A L Z O N E
    A U G   T O R T O L A
R E V E R S E O S M O S I S
H E Y   D I A L   O N T O P
E W E R   P L E B E   G E N E
D O L O R   C A M S   A E R
D R I V E U P T H E W A L L
A D D E D T O   R A N
  P A R K R A N G E R S
A T A R I   T E A L   O K I E
L O G O N   E N I D   R E S T
B O O Z E   R O D S   A S K S
```

129

```
T G I F   B R E W S   A S A N
A R L O   M A R I A   L E G O
P I L L O W T A L K   L O R I
S P O I L S   M I S C U E S
  G O D   S E A   A L L E Y
A S I S   P I N   A T E
B I C   S O F A   D E A C O N
B L A N K E T C O V E R A G E
A L L O Y S   T W I N   M R S
  F L Y   E E L   D E E T
L A U R A   A D D   S U R
E X H I B I T   S A L A D A
D I A L   S H E E T M U S I C
G A U L   L O R N A   T H E M
E L L S   E L E C T   H Y D E
```

130

```
U K E S   E M M E   C O M F Y
S E X Y   N E A L   A D O R E
E M I R   Z A G S   D E L I A
R O T A R Y D I A L   S T E T
    C U M E   A S S E S S
I N J U N E   B E M O A N
S E A S   S K E W E R   L I P
N A M E S   A G E   T R A D E
T R E   A R T U R O   A V O W
  S A L O O N   A P P A L S
C R I M E A   S K I S
R A V E   M U S C L E T O N E
O Z O N E   N O R A   A R C A
F O R D S   I S O N   R E A R
T R Y S T   T O D D   S O A P
```

The New York Times Crossword Puzzles

The #1 Name in Crosswords

 St. Martin's Griffin   Available at your local bookstore or online at nytimes.com/nytstore

NYT 01/06